Acclaim for Zachary Karabell's

The Last Campaign

"*The Last Campaign* is more than useful as history; it is an entertaining and elegantly wrought tale." — *Newsday*

"The story of 1948 is irresistible and Karabell tells it well. His book is full of illuminating details and anecdotes, and colorful characters and events." —*Boston Book Review*

"A lively, suspenseful, and informative account of the fateful 1948 presidential campaign. . . . Karabell reveals what happened behind the scenes, ever mindful of the election's significance for our own times." —Sean Wilentz, Princeton University

"Karabell is a talented historian and a gifted storyteller. It is impossible to read this engaging book and not share his nostalgia for the good old days when presidential candidates seemed more authentic, and political debate more meaningful." —*Chicago Tribune*

"Insightful and convincing." —*San Francisco Chronicle*

"An astute and rollicking account. . . . Anyone who thinks negative campaigning is a contemporary scourge will learn from Karabell's chronicle that, compared to the '48 hurly-burly, today's campaigns are high-minded." —*Booklist*

"*The Last Campaign* [is] a well-told chronicle of America's greatest political upset. Zachary Karabell writes with a graphic pungency and verve that sweeps us along right down to the climatic chapter in this legendary drama." —*The Washington Monthly*

Zachary Karabell

The Last Campaign

Zachary Karabell was educated at Columbia and Oxford, and at Harvard, where he received his Ph.D. in American History in 1996. He is the author of *What's College For? The Struggle to Define American Higher Education,* and *Architects of Intervention: The United States, the Third World, and the Cold War, 1946–1962.* He has taught at Harvard, the University of Massachusetts at Boston, and Dartmouth. His essays and reviews have appeared in the *Los Angeles Times, Salon, The Boston Globe, The Nation, The Washington Post, Foreign Policy, Smithsonian Magazine,* and *The Christian Science Monitor.*

The Last Campaign

The Last Campaign

HOW HARRY TRUMAN WON

THE 1948 ELECTION

ZACHARY KARABELL

VINTAGE BOOKS

A Division of Random House, Inc.

New York

FIRST VINTAGE BOOKS EDITION, APRIL 2001

All rights reserved under International and Pan-American
Copyright Conventions. Published in the United States by
Vintage Books, a division of Random House, Inc., New York,
and simultaneously in Canada by Random House of Canada
Limited, Toronto. Originally published in hardcover in the
United States by Alfred A. Knopf, a division of Random
House, New York, in 2000.

Vintage and colophon are registered trademarks of Random
House, Inc.

The Library of Congress has cataloged the Knopf edition as
follows:
Karabell, Zachary.
The last campaign : how Harry Truman won the 1948
election / by Zachary Karabell.
p.   cm.
Includes index.
1. Presidents—United States—Election—1948.
2. Truman, Harry S., 1884–1972.
3. Dewey, Thomas E. (Thomas Edmund), 1902–1971.
I. Title.
E815.K37   2000
324.973'0918—dc21   99-28567
CIP

Vintage ISBN: 0-375-70077-3

Author photograph © Elena Siebert
Book design by Robert C. Olsson

www.vintagebooks.com

Printed in the United States of America
10 9 8 7 6 5 4 3 2 1

Contents

Illustrations follow page 216

The Last Campaign

Introduction

IT WAS LATE in the afternoon, and there wasn't much more to say that hadn't already been said. Harry Truman could stay in his suite at the Muehlebach Hotel in Kansas City, glued to the returns and forced to listen to those radio people banter about what we could all look forward to during the Dewey administration. He could confront the downcast faces of his staff as they prepared to wait for the results that would show just how badly he had lost. But he didn't want to deal with the crowd of reporters and well-wishers who were gathered in the lobby. They had those fragile frantic smiles of people who knew that only false optimism was keeping them from tears. To them, he wasn't President Truman, he was Harry, one of them, and they couldn't bear what was about to happen. But as much as he wanted to be with them, he had something they didn't: faith. He believed—no, he knew—that the country would rally behind him. And when he saw in the faces of his advisers that not many of them shared his quiet, and what must have seemed to them foolish, confidence, he knew that he had to get out of there.

The Secret Service came and whisked him away to the Elms Hotel, across the Missouri River in Excelsior Springs. And there Harry settled in for the evening. That night there would be no poker playing with the boys from Missouri, no rough-and-tumble joking, no cigars and whiskey. Instead, Harry had a mineral bath and a rubdown, a light supper and a glass of buttermilk, and turned on the radio to hear the peculiar staccato voice of H.V. Kaltenborn tell the nation that, based on the early count, Truman was ahead but certain to lose once the results from Ohio and California were known. So Harry turned off the radio and went to bed without a drink. At least that's what all the papers reported, and what Charlie Ross, his loyal press secretary, stated.

Truman hadn't expected to be president in the first place. Most of his life had consisted of unforeseen developments. Early on, he thought he'd be a farmer, but though he'd worked hard on his land, he found that he didn't want to live that way forever. He thought that he'd be a haberdasher, but his store went bankrupt. He'd commanded men in battle in Europe, and done it well, but that wasn't a career. He never imagined that he'd be a county judge or a United States senator, but he was elected nonetheless, having been urged to campaign for the senate by his longtime patron, boss Tom Pendergast of Kansas City. Having won once, he won again, and in his second term, after a quiet career as a loyal Democratic backbencher who shone briefly as chairman of a committee investigating wartime profiteering by big business, he was selected by party bosses to be Franklin Roosevelt's running mate at the convention in 1944. And then, in the most surprising turn, Roosevelt died in April 1945, and Harry Truman became president.

Truman was one of those rare men who seemed content with himself and with his life. He enjoyed being a farmer; he liked being a senator; and he didn't much mind being president. He kept his hair neatly slicked back, dressed snappily in double-breasted suits, and wore thick glasses to compensate for his terrible eyesight. He adored his wife, and doted on his daughter, and if he sometimes felt that his job was too big for him, he managed to carry it off with at least as much authority and panache as most of his predecessors. After a tumultuous three years in the White House, Truman ran again, because there was no reason not to; and besides, he felt he was doing just about as good a job as any other Democrat could and a better job by far than any Republican might. And though the campaign had started on a low note, he assumed that it would all work out in the end, win or lose. The thing was, he didn't think the American people would vote him out of office. He felt that he'd done well, all things considered, and he was pretty sure that the voters would come to the same conclusion.

It turned out that Harry's faith was justified. Around 4 a.m., it happened: the returns indicated that he would win. By early morning, he was dressed and back at the Muehlebach in Charlie Ross's hotel room. "The news was good," he said, "and so I decided to come in to town." Stalwart campaign manager that he was, Ross blinked in astonishment at the sight of his cheerful boss, the once and future president of the United States, bouncing playfully around the room. By 10 a.m. on November 3, radio announcers throughout the country said words that none of them had thought they would utter: Truman won. Truman had beaten Thomas E. Dewey. The press and the pollsters would be dining on crow for weeks. Even his own staff were chagrined that they ever had doubts, but frankly, they just hadn't thought that victory was possible. There was no way that Truman could pull that particular rabbit out of that particular hat, no matter how much he smiled and gave 'em hell. But he did, and for Truman, the explanation was simple: "Labor did it." But the reasons went deeper than that, and for all of labor's support, he had lost Michigan and New York and New Jersey and Pennsylvania and nearly lost Ohio and Illinois. And what he had won, he'd won dirty. In elections as in street fights, rules were for losers. With the *Chicago Tribune* and Colonel Robert McCormick publishing the world's most incorrect headline—"Dewey Defeats Truman"—Truman was going to have some fun in the weeks ahead.

That night he told the crowds who gathered in Independence, Missouri, at the courthouse square that he was just a favorite son who had done well. He just wanted to be treated like any other Independence taxpayer, no special favors, no hoopla, just Harry Truman. For the next two days, as the train with his private car, the Ferdinand Magellan, made its way back to Washington, D.C., Truman took every opportunity to stop and greet people at stations along the way, an encore to the whistle-stops that had helped cement his victory. And wherever he went, he took a copy of the *Tribune* with him, and held it up with a grin as wide as the Kansas prairie, as if to say that the last laugh truly was his.[1]

FIFTEEN HUNDRED miles away in New York, Thomas Dewey was smiling as well. If you looked at him for just a moment, you couldn't have told whether he'd won or lost. It was the same slight smile that he'd worn for much of the campaign, and for much of his political career. It was a perfect smile, one that lacked only spontaneity and seemed to suit every occasion. There's Dewey at home for a quiet evening with the family, sitting on his couch in a suit and tie, playing with the old dog. There's Dewey on the farm in Pawling, New York, with the cattle in the background. There's Thomas Dewey, crimefighter extraordinaire, wunderkind governor of New York. It was Thomas Dewey, not really Tom. You'd never ask him to give 'em hell.

He was a good son who wrote regularly to his mother in Michigan, always addressing his letters "Dear Mater." For Dewey, life had been charmed. He knew—as the pollsters and the pundits knew and the radio commentators and the man on the street and everyone back in Owosso, Michigan, knew—that Thomas Dewey would beat Harry Truman on November 2, 1948. They knew that at the age of forty-six, he would become the youngest president since Teddy Roosevelt, and the first Republican in the White House since Herbert Hoover slunk away in Depression disgrace. He knew from early September that the race for the White House was all but over, that Truman should have had the good grace to concede rather than go on the warpath. During the final weeks of the campaign, Dewey withstood a ferocious Truman charge, and he was vilified by his opponents. But he refused to join Truman in the gutter. He wasn't going to risk alienating voters and, what's more, he wasn't going to sully himself with the crude campaign being run by his opponents. If ever there was a man comfortable on the high road, Thomas Dewey was that man.

In his midtown Manhattan campaign headquarters at the Roosevelt Hotel, Dewey awaited the morning of his anointment. He tried to play it coy; he voted with his wife at a nearby school on East Fifty-first Street and then waved at cameramen and reporters, saying humbly, "Well, I know of two votes we got anyway." He then took a victory walk back to the hotel, greeting well-wishers who assumed that they were gazing on the next occupant of the Oval Office. After a celebratory dinner at the Ninety-third Street home of longtime adviser Roger Straus, it was up to Suite 1527 to settle in for the evening and wait. Dewey wasn't anxious. He exuded confidence, just like his rival sitting in his mineral bath in Excelsior Springs, sipping his buttermilk. "I will be president," Dewey had said. "It is written in the stars." Of course, Dewey was surrounded by people who were as sure of the outcome as he was. Even the Secret Service chief had deserted Truman in Missouri to be with Dewey in New York. The mood was cheerful. Dewey's meal of roast duck and fried apples contrasted sharply with the cold sandwich that Truman was eating.

Dewey was just as confident, yet so totally wrong. Two men, two sets of advisers, two campaigns, one conventional wisdom. Dewey couldn't claim that the election was stolen; it was lost by a wide margin. Truman won by 2,135,747 votes, a final count of 24,105,812 to 21,970,065, with 303 electoral votes to Dewey's 189. How can you be so sure about something and yet be so wrong? Facing the press the morning after, Dewey seemed unaffected. His words reflected bewilderment: "I was just as surprised as you are. . . . It has been grand fun, boys and girls. I enjoyed it immensely."

But the previous night, in his armchair at the Roosevelt, Thomas Dewey sat calmly, hour after hour, listening to the radio, hoping that Kaltenborn was right, watching that strange new medium, television, with its fuzzy pictures and graphs and analysis organized by *Newsweek* magazine. The next morning, he may have been dying inside, but he was still able to look much as he had for each day of his public life, with that bland smile, the thin mustache, absolutely proper, absolutely impenetrable.[2]

AMERICANS DIDN'T know when they went to the polls in 1948 that they were at the end of something. After all, campaigns are about new beginnings. America didn't realize that something precious, something vital, was about to be lost, perhaps forever. In the midst of crises in Berlin and Eastern Europe, with the mounting fear over the awesome power released by the splitting of the atom, with relations between labor and business reaching a new low after the anti-strike Taft-Hartley Act, with returning GIs flocking to colleges and having babies, with the economy booming and prices rising, and with Truman widely disliked, Americans went about the election of 1948 with the usual combination of anticipation and dread, anger and adoration, fear and hope. They weren't particularly excited by the candidates fielded for their judgment, and barely 50 percent of those eligible to vote did so. There would always be other elections, with more dynamic candidates. The war was won, and the new one, the cold one, had not yet grabbed hold of popular consciousness. So why get excited? There were four major candidates, and a few minor ones as well. There always had been choices, they thought, and there always would be.

And on that count, the American people were wrong.

In 1948, Americans took for granted that they had a choice. Those on the far Left could vote without reservation for perhaps the most Leftist major candidate this century: former Roosevelt vice president and Truman commerce secretary Henry Wallace of the Progressive Party. Those on the far Right could gravitate toward the candidate of the States' Rights Party, Governor Strom Thurmond of South Carolina. The moderate conservatives, who believed in a less fettered free market and more fettered unions, had the youthful and pristine Governor Dewey as their standard-bearer. And the working-class, New Deal, immigrant, moderate Left had the man from Independence himself, Harry Truman. Added to the mix were a Prohibitionist candidate, Claude Watson, and the venerable anti-communist Socialist Norman Thomas.

For the last time in this century, an entire spectrum of ideologies was represented in the presidential election. And not simply represented, but debated and discussed in the mainstream media. Although the great majority of the final vote went to either Truman or Dewey, Wallace and Thurmond were an integral part of the campaign. The views of the four main candidates were aired on radio and dissected in print. Truman talked not only of Dewey and the "do-nothing" 80th Congress, but of the treacherous Dixiecrats and the protocommunist Progressives as well. Dewey's campaign strategy was to stand above the fray, but he still responded to accusations made by Truman and by the other candidates. It was a true campaign, and the last campaign.

IN 1952, something happened that changed forever the way American politics are conducted, something whose effects are still being felt, and whose influence is inescapable. Something that we still haven't fully come to grips with, and still haven't fully figured out the consequences of:

Television.

Did it destroy presidential politics? Is it true what the pundits and politicos and commentators say, that television eradicated debate, shrunk the political spectrum, and made it impossible for Americans to have a real choice? Surely, television as a medium has the potential to expand that spectrum, as it does in other countries. Not television, then, but network news, television as a business that relies on ratings and advertising, and the evening news as a show lasting twenty-two minutes and containing at most a few thousand words. Television news condenses everything, shrinks it, and simplifies it to fit the medium. No long speeches, no complex ideas survive the journey through the lens and into the living room. Year by year, presidential politics becomes more packaged, easier to understand, parceled into digestible bites of data that are prescreened, tested, and handed to us, the voters, with sexy graphics and bold-faced text. How different it all was in 1948, how incomprehensible by today's standards—an election with heated debate and substantive issues, candidates who disagreed passionately about the issues, a citizenry that took interest because elections mattered and were interesting.

At the dawn of the twenty-first century, we see a presidential politics dominated by two parties that split the center. Even with the end of the Cold War, with the passing of an external enemy that at times made people wary of highly partisan politics lest our adversaries witness our dirty laundry being aired in public, even with high prosperity, contemporary elections are marked by a narrow range of ideologies. It wasn't always that way. A country of hundreds of millions of literate and opinionated souls must have more than two hard-to-differentiate political positions. The 1948 election presented a smorgasbord of options, but subsequent elections have been slim pickings indeed. Nineteen forty-eight did some justice to the extraordinary multiplicity of views in American society; subsequent elections have seen these views crammed into a very tiny box.

It's easy to blame television for whatever we don't like about politics. It's even easier to hold television responsible for the infomercial quality of modern presidential campaigns. We all know that TV advertising is prohibitively expensive, and that airtime is the only reliable way for candidates to get their message—derived from focus groups and polls that have been test-marketed and honed and weeded to eliminate any offensive content—to the largest number of passive voters. We know that since 1948, politics has gone from high drama that hinged on lively, controversial conventions watched by nearly three-quarters of the population, to boring, packaged, and utterly predictable conventions that feature almost as much commentary by network talking heads as by party officials and candidates who themselves leave all substantive debate to back rooms, safely away from the glare of television klieg lights.

On television today, presidential races are entertainment, and not very good entertainment at that. In 1948, people predicted that a portion of television would go to "public service," such as free airtime for candidates. That didn't happen. Now, only money gets you on television, and it costs too much to take the risk of spontaneity or passion. Each second costs and counts. And if you don't grab your audience, it has 500 channels and the Internet and direct TV to turn to at whim. No, television has definitely not led to politics at its richest or fullest.

But was it so different on the eve of this brave new world of TV? Was 1948 a nobler time? Was there more to listen to, more content, more substance, more elevated public debate? Would we gladly take then for now? People look back with nostalgia, imagining a time when Americans felt more connected to national politics, more engaged. Many of us believe as we gaze back over the decades that it was better then, before television, before the Cold War solidified. We look on those years as a cozier time, a more intimate time, when we felt close to our presidential candidates and took what they said seriously. But is the nostalgia warranted? Those pictures of Truman on his train, surrounded by reporters with their sleeves rolled up, their ties hanging loose, the easy jocularity apparent to the naked eye and recorded forever by countless photographs—do these pictures depict a different ethos? Were print journalism and radio more able to capture the immediacy, the piquancy, the intimacy, and the complexity of politics? Has the medium changed the message? Does 1948 show us how far we have fallen or offer us any path back or forward?

Television did play a small role in politics in 1948. Cameras were at the conventions, and candidates gave a few televised speeches and interviews. But television was an infant in 1948. The year before, 162,181 sets were sold; in 1948, that figure tripled. Still, for most of the year, there wasn't much to watch, and most of the country couldn't watch it. Only on the East Coast could you be sure that there would be programs and reception, and then only in the major cities did AT&T's coaxial cable provide a fuzzy picture on those massive living-room consoles with their tiny seven-inch screens. The broadcast range of television was fifty miles, and in order to reach the widest constituency of viewers, the political parties chose Philadelphia as their convention site. From there the AT&T cables took images up and down the coast and into the living rooms of the select owners of the new boxes. Television was a fun gimmick in those years, with vast potential, but skeptics said it would never replace radio or become nearly as popular as the movies. The skeptics were right about television's technical limitations in 1948. The sound wasn't good and the picture was worse. Yet people were thrilled to get even mediocre pictures in their homes. Families could sit around the set, eat dinner, laugh, listen, and discuss politics.[3]

As a novelty, the 1948 conventions were an interesting TV show, but they were still a sideshow, watched by approximately 10 million people in a country of more than 125 million. The conventions went on as they had before, with a handful of fixed cameras stationed in the hall. With minimal commentary, rudimentary production, and a few choice interviews, TV didn't shape the way politics was conducted. The cameras were merely a mirror, recording routines and rituals that had developed before television and that went on with precious little regard for it. After 1948, the political process changed to meet the demands of television. But initially, it was TV that tried to mold itself to fit politics.

The 1948 election results were tracked on TV by the Radio Corporation of America's NBC and by the Columbia Broadcasting System (CBS). This election also marked *Newsweek*'s first-ever coverage of the returns. The Washington bureau chief, Ernest Lindley, was the maestro that evening, and he was surrounded by a bevy of carefully selected young women. Attractive and wholesome, these young ladies buzzed about the studio in stylish dresses, creating an aesthetic hum to hold the viewers' attention. Elections were serious business, however, and the women weren't allowed to smile or wave at the cameras to friends and family at home.

At the age of twenty-one, Theresa McGlinchey Zammiello, a

graduate of Catholic high school, was chosen to be one of the election girls. They all wore beautiful clothes, and almost everyone smoked, and she spent a goodly portion of her time fetching the five or ten cups of coffee a day for each person that fueled the whole enterprise. Her friends told her that yes, she had looked professional, but Theresa was just glad that she hadn't tripped over wires or accidentally collided with her buddy Elaine during the broadcast. At four in the morning they were done, and Elaine's boyfriend picked them up outside the studio. How odd that Harry Truman was still in it. Of course, at the time, Theresa was more amused by the pigeon that dive-bombed the windshield of Elaine's boyfriend's car. That seemed so funny. For them, after a tense night on national television trying so hard to act a part that was being scripted for the very first time, pigeon shit must have been a hilarious release. Then they stopped at an all-night diner for coffee and eggs, and in Theresa McGlinchey Zammiello's memory, everything they said was funny at that late hour. They giggled at poor Governor Dewey, and they laughed so hard they couldn't breathe when they pictured that angry man Strom Thurmond and that weird, compelling martyr Henry Wallace.[4]

We think campaigns are about the candidates, but we forget that behind each candidate are legions of volunteers, staffers, local politicos, speechwriters, advisers, moneymen, families, doctors, lawyers, caterers, florists, makeup artists, train conductors, truck drivers, college students, high-school students, parents' leagues, teacher associations, union reps, union bosses, foremen, showmen, actors, producers, club owners, restaurant owners, foreign leaders, farmers, cattlemen, ranchers, timber magnates, oil magnates, car dealers, radio salesmen, retirees, trustees. Every campaign is composed of layer upon layer of human experience, and only a very few of those layers come into direct contact with the candidates themselves. "The presidential campaign," said Truman's speechwriter George Elsey, "is like an iceberg. The public is aware of only a small part of it."[5] That is what makes a campaign, then and now, so vibrant and exciting. Campaigns juxtapose so many segments of society, so many layers of daily life, layers that usually go about their business oblivious or indifferent to each other but which, during a campaign, are suddenly and intimately thrust together for a common cause. The candidate is a peg on which thousands of people hang their agendas.

Campaigns are never simple. They are never neat, never tidy. And contrary to so many stories, they are never organized. Like war, they are messy. Like war, they essentialize life. All that is optional falls away, and what remains is a pure goal: winning. Everything is subsumed under that goal. And once in the rough and tumble of an actual campaign, the blueprints drawn up during careful strategy sessions don't always work in the inchoate chaotic world of voters, whistle-stops, speeches made and speeches missed, audiences happy and sad, rain and muggy weather, and people who don't really want to listen to the tidy oration that your staff wrote for you two days before.

Television has come to dominate public life more than radio ever did, and television has made it even easier to forget about the layers. Today, we portray a presidential election as a contest between two candidates (or more, during primary season) who square off against one another with the aid of a small circle of advisers. Television coverage of elections may be at its most distorting in what it doesn't convey and doesn't show. Watch television for decades, and you'd never know that you were only seeing the tip of that iceberg. You'd never even think about the county volunteers for the Democrats in Chicago wards, or the organizers of the Dixiecrats in segregated Mississippi, or the women who tried so hard to get New Englanders to vote for Henry Wallace. But they were there, as much a part of the campaign as the men in the pictures.

HENRY WALLACE was an Iowa son to the core. He always looked slightly unkempt; hair ruffled, suits hanging loosely and wrinkled, his face an amalgam of creases, jowls, and piercing eyes. The wealthiest candidate in 1948, he spent his early life obsessed not with politics, not with economics, not with family, but with corn—hybrid corn that would grow to knee-high by the Fourth of July and never wither. And having made a fortune on corn, Wallace turned to matters of the spirit, to Russian mystics and Tibetan scriptures, to Mongolian mysteries and gurus. From the food of life to the life of the soul, Wallace wanted to probe the meaning of it all.

During the New Deal, Franklin Roosevelt looked right and he looked left, and when he looked as far left as he possibly could, his eye fell on Wallace, son of a former secretary of agriculture and FDR's choice for his. The Agriculture Department in the 1930s was a vast fiefdom, and its secretary held one of the most powerful positions in government, so much so that Wallace was chosen as FDR's running mate in 1940. Southern conservatives objected, but no one crossed FDR in those days, unless he was trying to pack the Supreme Court. Wallace certainly wasn't a typical vice president of the United States, yet he so embodied the progressive spirit of Roosevelt's Democratic Party that his odd mysticism and his social awkwardness were not crippling liabilities, at least not at first. But as FDR aged, the party conservatives turned against Wallace, and he was dropped from Roosevelt's fourth-term ticket and shunted off to be secretary of commerce until he broke with Truman over policy toward the Soviet Union.

Wallace didn't believe in the Cold War. He didn't think that Americans had to compete with the Soviets. He didn't see why the United States and Russia couldn't just communicate and agree to disagree. He didn't see why Truman persisted in extending American commitments to far-off places near the Soviet Union, like Greece and Turkey. He didn't see why Stalin and Truman couldn't just sit down and talk.

That night in November 1948, Henry Wallace watched the disintegration of two years of opposition to Truman, to the Republicans in Congress, and to warmongers and conservatives; he watched it all collapse ignominiously, as the Progressive ticket went down to a defeat far more severe than anyone had predicted. The Progressive Party, which stood for American freedom, nonviolence, international trade, and the common man, got fewer votes than the racist Dixiecrats. That was not the outcome Wallace had in mind when he decided to run. He thought he was fighting the good fight. He had the conviction of Job, who knew that in spite of the abuse, he walked in the path of righteousness. He would lead, he said, a Gideon's army right up Capitol Hill, right into the White House. "The American dream is the dream of the prophets of old, the dream of each man living in peace under his own vine and fig tree; then all the nations of the world shall flow up to the mountains of the Lord and man shall learn more of the law," he told the delegates of the Progressive Party who assembled in Philadelphia in July

1948. "All of you who are within the sound of my voice tonight have been called to serve and to serve mightily, in fulfilling the dream of the prophets and the founders of the American system." He took his campaign and his message of freedom from the Cold War, from industrial capitalists, from moneymen on Wall Street, and from racial bigotry; he took that message even to the South and spoke as angry crowds barraged him with rotten fruit and foul words. But, like Jesus, he absorbed those blows and the hatred and the distrust and turned his other cheek to them. "We are in the midst of a fierce attack upon our freedom," he intoned. "It is no coincidence that this attack goes hand in hand with high prices, cuts in real wages, inadequate housing, and no security." Because, he warned futilely to a nation that wouldn't listen, the enemy was within. The enemy was the fear mongers, the elites of Washington and Wall Street, the barons of the South and the captains of the West who stoked the flames of the Cold War to draw attention away from the depredations they were waging against the American people. And it was time to stop, he said. It was time to reclaim the freedoms that Jefferson, Washington, and Lincoln had fought for. "All of you who are within the sound of my voice tonight have been called to serve," he said.

On election night at campaign headquarters in New York City, Wallace was prepared for a rough ride. He knew how much he was hated, but he also believed that behind the columnists who dismissed him as a nut, behind reporters like Westbrook Pegler who accused him of slavish devotion to an Eastern guru, behind Democrat operatives who spread the rumor that the Progressive Party was secretly taking orders from Moscow, behind the pollsters who warned that the Progressive Party was hemorrhaging support, behind all of those signs there was a vast untapped pool of votes, of sympathy, and of good will. He believed that, come election night, those supporters would flood polling booths and show the world the best side of America.

Arrayed on Wallace's side were editors and publishers and literati and laborers and housewives and former senators and farmers and singers and activists. They were the shock troops of Gideon's army and in later years they tried to explain how Wallace could have been vanquished so completely. They had tried to keep the flame alive, but that flame had all but expired by November 1948. Never again in the twentieth century would there be a serious party of the Left. Between the humiliation of Wallace at the polls and the viciousness of McCarthyism spurred by the Korean War, the progressive movement was crushed and then scattered. That night in New York, his wife broke down in tears and sobbed, "I told him so all the time. He should never have done it." Mrs. Wallace thought he should have trusted that there was sympathy for his message. Instead, he forced people to make a choice between their anxieties and their idealism. She believed, as did those literati and laborers and housewives and Wallace himself, that America chose its fears on November 2, 1948; only 1 million souls, only 2.37 percent of the total electorate, chose Wallace's idealism. Told of the danger of communism, warned about the risks that surrounded them, harangued about the instability of politics around the globe, most people succumbed to fear. It was a lot to ask of them—to vote their idealism, to pick Wallace. As it turned out, it was too much.[6]

GOVERNOR James Strom Thurmond of South Carolina was forty-six years old in 1948. As *Time* observed, Thurmond had been running for one thing or another most of his life. As a teenager, he ran for exercise around his father's farm in Edgefield, some fifty-four miles from the state capitol in Columbia. Then he enrolled at Clemson and joined the cross-country team. He neither smoked nor drank, and he exercised for nearly an hour a day. He was a fitness buff before his time, before there were health clubs and joggers. As governor, he liked to go to local beauty pageants and crown the winners. At one of these pageants he met Miss Jean Crouch, barely out of high school, and she agreed to be his wife. He exuded a certain robust charm, dressed well (with leather spats), and would even stand on his head to amuse her, as he did one afternoon for the photographers.

Thurmond was the governor of a state that was just over 50 percent white and just under 50 percent black, a state that had begun the Civil War with defiance at Fort Sumter, a state that celebrated John Calhoun as the best of all that was South Carolinian, a state that hadn't really reconciled itself either to industrialization or to the Depression, and certainly not to the murmurs of civil rights buzzing through the North. South Carolina intended to resist civil rights even if it meant fighting a second war. America was the land of freedom, and everyone in his right mind knew that civil rights were one step on the road to a police state. Until 1948, Thurmond hadn't really demonstrated much statesmanship. He'd been a capable county judge, and an easygoing governor, but when he heard about Truman's civil rights platform, he got angry, and then he got ambitious.

Though his physical competitiveness was matched by his political ambition, Thurmond always claimed that he didn't seek to lead the Dixiecrat bolt from the Democratic Party. He even said that he had planned to skip the rogue convention in Birmingham, Alabama, in July 1948, which convened after a group of southern delegates stormed out of the Democratic Convention in Philadelphia rather than accept a civil rights plank crafted by the mayor of Minneapolis, Hubert Humphrey. Thurmond had, he said, a prior engagement to inspect the South Carolina state guards, but to no one's surprise he was able to attend the Birmingham convention as well—the States' Rights Convention, as it was called. And though he wasn't the leader of the bolt, he managed to get the nomination all the same. In those days, he was known as a moderate.

"We have been betrayed, and the guilty shall not go unpunished," he thundered after the first days of the convention in Philadelphia. "States' Rights Americans are ready to stand, even at the expense of life itself, as Crockett, Bowie, and Houston stood in Texas, for individual liberty and freedom, and for the right of people to govern themselves." Truman and even Dewey were no different for Thurmond than Mussolini and Stalin. Any government that seeks to deprive its citizens of essential rights is fascist, communist, and whatever other terrible -ist one could think of. As for Wallace, he was a Communist, no question about it. So what was an honorable southern citizen to do when the Democratic Party threatened to mongrelize the white race, to sully the purity of white women, to stain the fabric of southern society? There comes a time when ignominy can't be suffered in silence, when reform and resistance can't be pursued from within. Like 1860 had been for others, 1948 was that time for Strom and the Dixiecrats.

That day in November, after months of backroads campaigning, traveling to little hamlets and farms by car and over dirt roads with little money and no pretense at a national base, Thurmond came home to Edgefield, South Carolina, to cast his vote. At 11:18 a.m., the governor strode up the steps of the Edgefield courthouse, flanked by his wife, Jean, and his mother and his sister. He wore a simple black suit, a white shirt, and a dark tie, his hair slicked back. Jean was voting in her first presidential election, but she had voted for Strom as governor in 1946. Asked how he felt, the governor said he had confidence that "a lot more people believe in personal liberties and constitutional government than any of the pollsters have yet predicted." From Edgefield, the governor returned to the state capital of Columbia to await the outcome. In the governor's mansion, Jean Thurmond found to her surprise that every room in the house had wires and teletype machines and microphones to monitor the returns. Even the back porch was hooked up.

In the end, the Dixiecrats won four states: Alabama, Mississippi, South Carolina, and Louisiana. Looking back years later, Thurmond had only one regret: "If we'd had television back then, we could have thrown the election into the House of Representatives." He knew that they'd never win, but he thought they could get enough votes to deny Truman an electoral college victory and force the election into the House for the first time since 1876. And there, someone other than Truman would be picked as a concession to Southern Democratic ire. But it didn't work out that way. Instead, the Dixiecrats lost the election, and the Democratic Party began to lose the South. The legacy of the Dixiecrat bolt is with us today: by the late 1990s, the South would vote almost entirely Republican in presidential elections.[7]

FOR EACH of these candidates, there was a vice presidential running mate, a campaign manager, speechwriters, strategists, advisers, friends, relatives, advance men, student volunteers, local VIPs, schedulers, party representatives, and businessmen. Thousands made these campaigns their lives for a year, dedicating themselves to the party and the candidates. And around each of these campaigns, young reporters were trying to make a name for themselves and veteran campaign correspondents were viewing everything through a lens coated with cynicism. There were the columnists, especially Walter Winchell, Drew Pearson, Westbrook Pegler, Walter Lippmann, and the Alsop brothers, who commanded respect and audiences. Then there were the pollsters, Gallup and Roper and Crossley, who suffered perhaps the greatest defeat of all when their scientific method turned out to be not so scientific and not so accurate. On November 3, the eminent Arthur Krock of the *New York Times* surveyed the wreckage of his own predictions. "The principal item on our menu will not be beefsteak, not terrapin, but crow."[8]

Of all the polls and all the newspapers and all the expert commentary, only one called the election correctly. In Kansas City, the Staley Milling Company conducted an informal survey in the weeks before the election. Farmers were asked to purchase their feed bags based on how they were planning to vote in the upcoming election. Dewey supporters were told to buy bags with an elephant, the symbol of the Republicans, while Truman backers bought bags with a donkey. On the eve of the election, Truman was ahead in the poll by 54 to 46 percent. The feed was called Pullet Atoms, so Truman won the Pullet Poll. The man who would be elected in no small measure by the farm vote won the only poll that was dominated by farmers. If only Elmo Roper and George Gallup and the rest had bothered to look to the heartland. Instead, on November 3 they prepared their suppers of crow while Thomas E. Dewey wore his thin smile on his way to nowhere, while Henry Wallace tried to gather the pieces of a shattered cause, while Strom Thurmond sulked and planned, and above all, while Harry Truman basked in the afterglow.

CHAPTER ONE

Prelude to the
Year That Was

THE WAR WAS OVER, but still it was everywhere. To live in 1948 was to live in the wake of global conflict and in the fallout of the Bomb. Nineteen forty-eight was a world defined by the war, shaped by the war, and still reacting to the war that had ended less than three years before. The men and women who voted in 1948 had last voted for president when more than ten million were in the armed services, when millions of women worked in the factories, when food was rationed, when sugar was a precious commodity, when every industry, every business, and every issue was linked to the battles raging in Italy, North Africa, France, Germany, Guam, Wake, Okinawa, and the Coral Sea. In 1948, the horrors of the Bataan Death March, when American GIs captured by the Japanese perished by the thousands, were still near the surface. People could still picture that grim but determined trio—Roosevelt, Churchill, and Stalin—conferring in Casablanca, Tehran, and Yalta. Americans thrilled to the memory of Paris liberated, and shuddered at the memory of concentration camps entered, and they could not shake the numbing unreality of corpses neatly piled row after row. They could still see innocent eighteen-year-old boys fighting and dying, raising the flag over Iwo Jima, ready to die on the shores of the island of Japan, if and when General Douglas MacArthur gave the order. Thanks to a mushroom cloud over New Mexico, followed quickly by Fat Man and Little Boy exploding over Hiroshima and Nagasaki, thanks to the wonder and horror of the atom split, that order was never given. But then Americans were left with a new danger, that of nuclear Armageddon.[1]

The years after the war were also defined by coming home to girlfriends and wives, by children born to women who didn't know if they would see their men again. The men came home, and they wanted only to have a house, and a job, and a family, to have a life uncluttered by tanks and guns and planes, and unclouded by death and mud. The women, who had found themselves out of the house and in the offices and factories, were quietly but firmly encouraged to return to domestic lives. They were told to be mothers and wives once again, and not Rosie the Riveter. Christian Dior, doyen of fashion, introduced the New Look for women, with long flowing skirts and a strong emphasis on nonpractical femininity. Hollywood films reintroduced the woman-as-wife as a stock character, and the soldiers put away their uniforms and went back to work, in jobs that women had shown they could do but that the men wanted back.

And these women and men did what most women and men do when they haven't seen one another for a long while. Alfred Eisenstadt's legendary photo, "V-J Day, Times Square, 1945," was a prelude. What came after wasn't shown, except when babies began popping out in maternity wards throughout the country. For to live in 1948 was to live amid constant marriage ceremonies and then amid little children, toddlers, and infants. Between 1945 and 1950, the marriage rate hit an all-time high and the birthrate increased by 25 percent for white women and by more than 30 percent for non-whites.[2]

After years of devoting their energies to producing jeeps and tanks, car manufacturers returned to cars and started selling millions of them. The car led to suburbs, unlike any that had existed before, unlike the train commutes and the trolley commutes of the past. Car suburbs sprang up everywhere. The federal government subsidized GIs' mortgages. Construction didn't just provide returning soldiers with homes; it was also good for the economy, and aided the growth of the subdivision. Newly married couples could move into their own homes, and millions of units were built in a postwar construction boom. And the most heralded of all of these was Levittown, New York.

Levittown, twenty-five miles from Manhattan on Long Island,

was the American dream reborn. To every family a home, and a yard, and a white picket fence, and a car in the garage, and new appliances: the refrigerator, and the electric iron, and the washing machine, and the toaster, and the electric mixer, and the peelers and carvers and cutters and steamers, the Hoover vacuum cleaners, the drip coffee machine, and the lawn mower, and, to cap it all off, the car. Levittown was the child of Abraham Levitt and his sons William and Alfred. The Levitts perfected the art of mass-producing cookie-cutter subdivisions, where families came and looked at model homes and purchased them. Each home had at least four rooms, one bath, a living room with a fireplace. Each home looked nice and cost pretty much what the next one cost, and some even came with an incentive, a built-in Bendix washing machine. And to Levittown, and to hundreds of other new bedroom communities, the returning GIs and their wives and children flocked.[3]

When the country demobilized in 1945, the politicians feared a repeat of 1919, when the end of war led to a steep recession. Instead, by 1946, the economy was racing ahead. After years of unfulfilled, pent-up desire, people finally had the money to buy things, and they did. Price controls in place from the war temporarily kept inflation in check, but prices still rose. As demand grew and supply dwindled, employers needed workers to produce what people wanted to buy. Labor unions recognized that they were in a strong position to bargain for better wages, but business leaders weren't so inclined to concede. Strikes were ubiquitous and bitter.

Most people wanted only to live a good, quiet, simple life. The late 1940s were the obverse of the war. Where there had been dark, people sought light; from dirt they fled to a vision of cleanness, however antiseptic; from noise and chaos, they yearned for order and calm. Cities were too reminiscent of the war: too crammed, like foxholes; too many lights, like flares; too many people, like battlefields. It had to be the suburbs, and space, and familiar roles, with women as wives and men as breadwinners. It had to be a society where the government was benign but not intrusive.

A thriving economy opened up possibilities for those returning soldiers and newlyweds, but there were also farmers and sharecroppers and elders who found that their world was in flux. Drawn by the bustling urban North, black sharecroppers of the South took advantage of the war's end and began to move to Detroit and Chicago, New York and Boston, Philadelphia and Baltimore. Starting in 1920 and gathering momentum after the war, their Great Trek, or Great Migration, changed the face of the nation, and the color of cities.[4]

That migration unsettled the urban life of the North and changed the outlook of the grandchildren of former slaves. American blacks had fought and died for their country during the war, and they had tasted, if only for an unreal moment, what it would be like to be equal in law and in attitude. To return to a world where they might be called "boy" and treated like children made even less sense than it ever had. As more than a million men, women, and children made their way north, official Washington started to attend to questions of race. In December 1946 Truman appointed a commission to study civil rights. And when that commission, sympathetic to civil rights, issued its report, its call for reform penetrated to the heart of southern society, and the white politicians of the Deep South blanched in horror at its implications.

In 1948, the New Deal coalition started to disintegrate. The unwieldy amalgamation of blacks, southern white conservatives, farmers, organized labor, and liberal northeastern elites, which had been held together by the charisma of Franklin Roosevelt and the glue of economic catastrophe, began to come apart. Civil rights was the catalyst. Truman tried to avoid a confrontation, but men like Governor Thurmond had other ideas. Deferential in their dealings with white power, black leaders at the National Association for the Advancement of Colored People (NAACP), which had grown to half a million strong, insisted that after the experience of the war, there could be no turning back. In the summer of 1946, they marched peaceably to the Lincoln Memorial to protest against the Ku Klux Klan and to remind Washington of one individual who had taken the risk to make sure that the United States would be purged of the scourge of slavery. Truman, pushed by his own conscience, by the liberal wing of the Democratic Party, and by the party's declining fortunes, responded, knowing that in solidifying one base he might well lose another. He responded to the demands of black leaders, black soldiers, and black families, that they no longer be barred from voting, that they no longer have to endure the bigotry of men like Senator Theodore Bilbo of Mississippi, or men like the president of the Alabama Bar Association, who declared, "No Negro is good enough and no Negro will ever be good enough to participate in making the law under which the white people in Alabama have to live."[5] Truman spoke of civil rights, and in response the leaders of the Deep South looked to remove him from the ticket in 1948.

Meanwhile, the farmers were dwindling in numbers, and they watched as large agribusiness and flight to the city eroded the populist base they once comprised. They listened to the radio from distant cities and heard the rumblings from the suburbs, and they realized that they no longer were the heart of America. They were still prominent and powerful in states like Kansas, Missouri, Nebraska, and Iowa, but they represented another era, not the present. The economic boom that followed the war passed them by, as farm prices fell. Struggling to survive, the farmers fought to be heard, as they had been heard by FDR and the New Deal, as they were to be for one final moment in 1948.

To live in 1948 was to live in the shadow of the New Deal. Not yet repudiated, the bold period of government activism was coming to a close. Though excoriated by conservatives as an era of government radicalism, the New Deal still enjoyed support. But people were tired of federal power, power that had been vastly expanded by the New Deal and then even more vastly expanded by the war. The alphabet programs—the WPA, CCC, AAA, and the rest—had served their purpose but, after a few years, people had had enough of agencies that told them where to work, how to work, and when to work. They were fed up with food rationing, and after being ordered to fight, being told what to produce and how much and what to buy and at what price, they wanted to relax.

Capitalizing on these feelings, the Republicans finally won back the Congress in 1946 (the theme was "Had Enough? Vote Republican"), but the best they could do was halt the New Deal and halt the expansion of federal power. They couldn't reverse it, even though they tried. They pressured Truman to end the price controls, which he did. Price controls gave the government more power than even the most liberal Democrats really desired. In the face of labor unrest, the Republicans passed the Taft-Hartley Act in 1947, which tried to restore the power of business over labor. If the New Deal had been the friend of organized labor, of the needs of the workers, the Taft-Hartley Act was a salve for employers and allowed them to sue unions for lost profits. Truman vetoed the bill, but it was over-ridden, as Senator Robert Taft, the ornery, crusty son of the former president, led the fight against the Democratic president.

Even so, the Republicans and conservative southern Democrats couldn't completely tear down what decades of depression and war had erected. They couldn't remove what FDR had put in place and what the threat of Nazi Germany had demanded. And in the face of the Soviet Union, they weren't about to weaken the power of the military. For the first time in its history, the United States was going to stay armed and dangerous in a time of peace. However much Americans wanted normalcy, however much they wanted that Ben-dix washer, the Chevy Convertible or Lincoln Continental with the tire on the back, the new RCA radio or television set, however much they wanted the two kids and the clean school and the upward mobility, they had to deal with the world outside. They had to face up to The Threat. Whether it was real or manufactured, whether it was ever truly a threat, for Americans in 1948, it was real, and it was visceral. They felt its presence, and it worried them. The Threat was communism, and people feared that communism would mean an end to subdivisions and radio and vacuum cleaners and God and Mom and apple pie and freedom.

Somewhere between the end of World War II and the election of 1948, the Cold War began. And it was a war, with sides and stakes and the looming threat of defeat. People were already concerned about physical annihilation, for though only the United States had successfully developed and deployed nuclear weapons, the very exis-tence of such weapons conjured up grim visions. People believed that defeat in the Cold War would mean the eradication of a way of life. They listened to the warnings of their leaders and to the mes-sages on the airwaves, and they digested the idea that the world was divided into two camps, one free and one the antithesis of freedom. "From Trieste in the Adriatic to Stettin in the Baltic, an Iron Curtain has descended across the continent [of Europe]," so said the former prime minister of Great Britain, Winston Churchill, as he stood with

Harry Truman in the gymnasium of Westminster College in Fulton, Missouri. The Cold War might have been over there somewhere, but its inauguration took place very much over here.

The war of words intensified. The paranoid yet oddly charming Soviet leader Joseph Stalin trumpeted plans to build up his nation's military strength. He said that conflict between East and West, between communism and capitalism, was inevitable and unavoidable. American leaders agreed. Truman spoke of the need to help all of those whose way of life was jeopardized by Stalin's creed. Announcing his intent to supply Greece and Turkey with hundreds of millions of dollars in aid, he raised the rhetorical stakes to new heights: "At the present moment in world history nearly every nation must choose between alternative ways of life. . . . One way of life is based upon the will of the majority and is distinguished by free institutions, representative government. . . . The second way of life is based upon the will of the minority forcibly imposed upon the majority." If the United States wanted to avoid the fate of minority dictatorship, Americans would have to undertake a new struggle.[6]

This was the language that Americans heard when they listened to Lowell Thomas or Edward R. Murrow on the radio, and it was the same language they read in the newspapers. Americans were told about Poland and the betrayal of Yalta, where Stalin promised free elections and then installed a puppet government. They learned about the Italian Communists, who were rumored to be taking orders from Moscow and who were a serious threat to win elections in 1948. They heard about dangers within the American government. They listened as Truman called for a loyalty test and then issued Executive Order 9835 instituting a loyalty oath for federal employees. They were told that communism was an insidious disease, a virus that could easily contaminate society and spread and, if unchecked, could kill and destroy, and turn even the remotest corner of the American heartland into a totalitarian nightmare.

It was a time when what was said publicly by elected officials and statesmen was respected. It was a time when senator and congressman and president and secretary were terms of great respect, when the words of these men—and they were nearly all men—were accorded a gravitas. If the president said that the world was divided between freedom and slavery, then it was a good bet that it was. If

Senator Taft or Senator Vandenberg said that yes, communism was a clear and present danger, then that was because they believed it. The gap between words and intent, between rhetoric and belief did not exist in the public mind the way it would in subsequent years. As Americans absorbed the rising crescendo of warnings, as they registered the seriousness in the voices of leaders both federal and local, they began to think that the dream of coming home could turn very dark very quickly.[7]

The average American wasn't inclined to give much thought to events in the world outside. Turmoil in Europe notwithstanding, many people didn't pay attention to the looming threat of communism, or to Stalin. Many people were optimistic about the future, and occupied with their daily lives. Yet, even though the country was in the midst of exciting, prosperous times, to live in 1948 was to know how perverse humans could be. To live in those years was to believe that the economy could collapse, that fields could dry out, that angry men with angry words could send the world to the brink. When Churchill spoke of an Iron Curtain, when Truman spoke of freedom and tyranny, when leaders murmured about enemies in our midst, it was all too credible. In 1948, millions read the words of Reinhold Niebuhr, the theologian who appeared on the cover of *Time* magazine. Niebuhr warned of the evil inherent in all of us and cautioned against false faith in the better nature of mankind. Men are selfish, he concluded, and they shouldn't be trusted. To be alive was to dwell on a planet full of sin, and only a fool would rely on the kindness of strangers. To have seen the horrors of Buchenwald, even if only in a brief flash on a newsreel before a Hepburn-Tracy film, to have known a friend, neighbor, or relative who had perished of starvation during the Bataan Death March, to have survived Omaha Beach or Okinawa, was to know that the monsters under the bed were real. It was to know that when Truman, or Churchill, or that young California congressman Richard Nixon, or the fiery South Dakota representative Karl Mundt warned of traitors in our midst who given a chance would bring our way of life to an end, they were warning of dangers that were all too real, and ready, at all times, to reemerge with a vengeance.

The fears may have been irrational, if by irrational we mean that the threat was less real than imagined. The fears may have been manufactured and stoked by opportunistic politicians, though these politicians themselves may have believed in the threat and may have been just as scared as that proverbial man on the street. Some of these fears may have, in the clear light of hindsight, been silly, stupid, boorish, misguided. The Soviet Union betrayed the spirit of Yalta and loomed at the border of Western Europe. That much was true. But whether it jeopardized the American way of life is much less clear, and communism was never a significant force in American politics or organized labor. Yet to live in these years was not to know that these concerns were anything less than a reasonable reaction to an unreasoning enemy, an enemy of ideology, an enemy whose agents looked just like us, sounded like us, lived among us, and yet wished us ill.

The year 1948 began with the end of democracy in Czechoslovakia, as the Soviet Union engineered a coup against the elected government, and in March the world watched as the Czech foreign minister "accidentally" fell out of a window while in detention in Prague. Jan Masaryk's defenestration was another sign, if one was needed, that the Cold War could easily turn hot, that confrontational words were the first step on a road that might end in confrontational actions. As the year progressed, and as the election evolved, Czechoslovakia loomed large, but not nearly as large as Berlin. After three years of postwar stalemate, the Soviet Union decided to force the issue. Divided between an American-French-British occupation zone and a Soviet zone, Berlin was surrounded by an East Germany under the sway of Stalin. In June 1948, Stalin said that the roads and the trains would be blocked, blocked from West Germany to East, and thus blocked from West Germany to West Berlin. Cut off from Western Europe, Berlin was now cut off from food and supplies, as Stalin intended. Now, he believed, the Americans would be forced to recognize the partition of Germany. They would have no choice but to evacuate Berlin and sign the treaty, making the division of Germany permanent.

But Truman had other ideas. Though he was not against the partition of Germany, he intended to maintain an American presence in Berlin. That decision was not made without debate within the administration, but Truman and Secretary of State George Marshall decided that however strategically untenable it was, the Western foothold in Berlin should be defended. The order was given to one of the American commanders in Europe, Lucius Clay, to begin an airlift of supplies. What started as an emergency relief measure ended up lasting more than a year. While the presidential election was being waged in the United States, American planes, with cooperation from Western European allies, flew in tons of food, fuel, medicine, and supplies every day to West Berlin. It was the most massive relief effort ever mounted. A year later, Stalin blinked and ended the blockade.[8]

By then Truman was facing a new set of challenges. Though conducted against the backdrop of the Cold War, the election of 1948 saw remarkably little debate between Dewey and Truman over it. Democrat and Republican agreed, as all who were responsible for American foreign policy agreed, that the Soviet Union was a threat that must be met. Furthermore, Truman was not vulnerable on foreign policy because he seemed to be managing the challenges. The Cold War was still in its early stages. The Soviets had not yet exploded their first nuclear weapon. The spy trials of the Rosenbergs and Alger Hiss had not yet begun, and the McCarthy investigations had not yet been conducted. The forces of Mao Tse-tung and the Chinese Communists had not yet defeated the Kuomintang and Chiang Kai-shek, and the invasion of South Korea by the North had not yet happened. Truman was not yet being assailed for mistakes and gaffes in foreign policy. That would change after the Soviets detonated their atomic bomb in 1949, after China was "lost" to communism, and after Korea was invaded. Though the Cold War was important, the bipartisan consensus combined with an absence of major crises other than Berlin made it difficult for Dewey to focus on Truman's conduct of foreign policy as a central issue of the campaign. The only person to puncture the consensus on foreign policy was the man on the Left, the first candidate and the most complicated, Henry Wallace.

Wallace was the last major presidential candidate this century to argue for both internationalism and pacifism. He understood that the emerging Cold War had inextricably linked domestic politics to foreign affairs, and he tried to graft domestic progressivism to American policy abroad. He became a passionate critic of Truman's conduct of foreign affairs, and, well into 1948, he seemed like a major and even fatal threat to the president's chances for reelection.

It had been a friendly, even adoring, audience at Madison Square Garden back on September 12, 1946. Wallace, then the secretary of commerce, made a speech during a rally organized by labor leaders to support the senate campaign of Herbert Lehman against a strong Republican challenger. Wallace had shown the speech to President Truman on the morning of September 10. Truman denied having done more than skim it. In the speech, Wallace enunciated his vision of international politics. He said that the Russians and the Americans could and should live and let live. He said that each country should respect the other's sphere of influence and that Russia deserved to feel secure in Eastern Europe, just as the United States deserved to feel secure in Latin America. He said that the United Nations should control atomic weapons, and thereby prevent future arms races. He said that the two countries could engage in peaceful competition. But what really made the speech distinctive was the idea of moral equivalency: the United States and the Soviet Union were both great powers, and in Wallace's view what the Soviets did in their sphere should be seen in the same light as what the Americans did in theirs. This view of the world was simply not acceptable to Truman or to his then secretary of state, James Byrnes.

The policy of the Truman administration was that American spheres were not equivalent to Soviet spheres because the Soviets were trying to expand theirs beyond the limits established at Yalta in early 1945. The official line in Washington was that atomic weapons were not to be shared, that peaceful competition was up to the Soviets, and that unless Stalin honored open elections in Poland and demilitarization in Germany and a whole host of other conditions, then there could be no peace. Byrnes, a man of no small ambition, a former senator from South Carolina and a former Supreme Court justice, could barely conceal his disdain for Truman but thought even less of Wallace. After hearing the speech, Byrnes, who was in the midst of negotiating with the Soviets, made it known to the president that either Wallace or he could serve in the cabinet, but not both of them. Either Byrnes would make foreign policy, or Wallace would. Truman, faced with a commerce secretary who seemed to be veering off dangerously in his own direction, who seemed to be burying his head in the sand of idealism, asked for Wallace's resignation.

"The foreign policy of this country is the most important question confronting us today," Truman announced as he presented Wallace's head to the press. "The people of the United States may disagree freely and publicly on any question, including that of foreign policy, but the Government of the United States must stand as a unit in its relations with the rest of the world." There was, Truman went on, a fundamental conflict between the views of Wallace and those of the president and the rest of the administration. He felt it best for Henry Wallace to make his own way in the world and, in the future, Truman warned, no one would speak for the foreign policy of his government unless it was first cleared with the secretary of state.

While Wallace would claim till his death that Truman had cleared the Madison Square Garden speech, the resignation meant that he was now free to champion his own brand of foreign policy. In the fall of 1946, he began to follow a new tangent, one that took him further from Truman than any could have predicted. Having questioned the need for conflict with the Soviet Union, Wallace began to question the motives of the Truman administration, of the Republicans, of the press, and of business leaders, and as he did so, he entered the choppy waters of radicalism.[9]

The Left in American politics was an exciting place to be in 1948. Factions within factions, a legacy of the 1930s, created kaleidoscopic eddies that only the most devoted practitioners could keep track of. The UDA, the CIO-PAC, the NC-PAC, the ICCASP, the PCA, the ADA—the story of the Left in the 1940s reads like the alphabet soup of the New Deal. The disputes between these groups were often bitter, always contentious, and rarely reconciled. Wallace went directly from his job as commerce secretary to the bully pulpit of the editorship of *The New Republic,* one of the major liberal weekly journals of opinion, which had been founded by Herbert Croly on the eve of World War I. From this post, he helped establish the Progressive Citizens of America (PCA), and out of that movement, Wallace began wandering down the path that would bring him once again into a direct confrontation with Truman. Over the course of 1947, Wallace realized that he neither liked nor agreed with his former boss. Wallace and the PCA pledged to fight for the heart of the New Deal, a heart that was being cut out by the Republican Congress that took over in January 1947. Of course, the Left being the Left, others split with Wallace the way that Wallace had split with Truman. The Americans for Democratic Action (ADA) was created by men and women who didn't like Wallace's equivocation on the issue of American communism. Led by luminaries like Eleanor Roosevelt and Leon Henderson, the ADA would do much of the dirty work for Truman. In 1948, it was the ADA that successfully assassinated Wallace's character, an assassination that he himself greatly facilitated.

As Wallace toured the country in 1947, people urged him to challenge Truman. The disenchanted and the disenfranchised and the liberal intelligentsia praised his integrity and questioned Truman's. They told Wallace that he was the rightful heir to the New Deal, that he was the true leader of Gideon's army, that only he could stand for the common man. And he felt that it was true. He began to talk about running for president, and maybe, just maybe, winning. At the least, he would show Truman that conceding to the Cold War was not just a sign of weak character but a betrayal of the New Deal. He watched in disgust as Truman called for universal military training to prepare America to fight communism. "Harry Truman is a son of a bitch," he told an associate, and he wanted the son of a bitch to lose.[10]

On December 29, 1947, Henry Wallace declared his candidacy for president. He announced his plans during a broadcast on the Mutual Broadcasting System radio network. He said that he would dedicate himself to world peace, that the Democratic Party had become the party of the Depression, that it had forgotten the common man, and left millions alone in the middle of a meaningless Cold War. And then his language grew more ominous: "We are not for Russia and we are not for Communism, but we recognize Hitlerite methods when we see them in our own land and we denounce the men who engage in such name-calling as enemies of the human race who would rather have World War III than put forth a genuine effort to bring about a peaceful settlement of differences." A challenge had been issued. If his adversaries would give him no quarter, he would give them none in return.[11]

Explaining his decision to run, Wallace evoked the legacy of third parties in America. "I am more than ever convinced that third parties have a significance far greater than is ever admitted in most of the press."[12] As he surveyed the past, he thought that he had found the key to the vibrancy of American democracy. It was the third parties, the ability of new movements to form, with new ideas that the established parties tried to exclude. It was, he recognized, the Republicans of the 1850s who secured America from slavery, the Greenbacks and People's Party who alerted the robber barons of the 1880s and 1890s that not everyone benefited from rapid industrialization, and the Progressives of 1912 and beyond who reminded America to have a social conscience. His "New Party" of 1948 would pull America back from the brink of an unnecessary, foolish war.

As Wallace began his crusade with the optimism of one who did not know what lay ahead, as Truman prepared to run his own seemingly hopeless campaign to be elected in his own right, and as Strom Thurmond and the rest of the southern conservatives fumed while civil rights moved to center stage, most Americans simply went about their lives, taking scant notice of these events. They were occupied with the new cars they wanted to buy, with subdivisions and babies and college degrees, and with their quiet lives on the other side of the war. All the same, many Americans felt a vague foreboding that the world outside was encroaching once again. It was an unsettling fear that the present was but a respite, that enemies in the form of Communists would soon call them away from those subdivisions, would soon pull them away from families and jobs, take them out of the radio fantasies they listened to each night, take them away from the summertime idyll of baseball, away from all that they had come back to and tried to build. But for the moment, there was no compelling reason to follow the minutiae of politics; most people didn't really care about the UDA and the ADA and the PCA and the southern conservatives and the Republican congress. They cared about what people have always cared about, their community and homes. They knew that they would soon vote, but they also suspected that the real decisions in politics would be made in "smoke-filled rooms" by party leaders who would determine in private who and what was best for the country.[13] And for most people, that was just fine.

CHAPTER TWO

Truman Plans Ahead

IT HAS BEEN said that the midterm elections of 1946 alarmed the Truman White House. The Republicans had taken both houses of Congress, and the Democrats were a minority party for the first time since the 1920s. Harry Truman couldn't so much as make a speech without being attacked by Republicans, and he couldn't advance his domestic agenda. The New Deal was everywhere under siege. In order to contest Soviet advances in Eastern Europe, Truman had to send his officials with their hats in hand to Senator Arthur Vandenberg, the Republican chairman of the Senate Foreign Relations Committee and the single most important guardian of U.S. foreign policy in 1947. Under Secretary of State Dean Acheson had to plead with Vandenberg to authorize aid to Greece and Turkey; Secretary of State George Marshall had to petition Vandenberg to allow a debate on a multibillion-dollar aid plan to Western Europe.

The cost of living was rising. The only thing Harry Truman could do for labor was veto the Taft-Hartley Act, thereby turning Senator Taft into an even greater adversary than he already was. By mid-1947 Truman was being attacked from the Right by Taft and his isolationist allies and excoriated on the Left by Henry Wallace in the pages of *The New Republic* and in speeches throughout the country. Even taking a baby step on civil rights and appointing a commission had led to calls for a revolt among southern Democrats. The Truman White House was much more than alarmed.

Yet the response was not panic but fervor. Truman was surrounded by an impressive number of ambitious, determined men, men who argued vehemently with each other over what course the president ought to follow but who were united by the desire to see him elected in 1948. Some wanted Truman to tack right in an effort to appease the conservative wing of the Democratic Party and accommodate the moderate tenor of the time. Others thought he should swing left in order to energize organized labor and outflank Henry Wallace. Still others counseled that he stay the course and try to appease as many of the opposing factions of the Democratic Party as he possibly could. As the election of 1948 approached, his advisers mapped out a strategy that turned out to be astonishingly prescient.

Clark Clifford and James Rowe couldn't have been any more accurate in their predictions unless they had been given a crystal ball. Clifford, a St. Louis lawyer and former naval officer who had come to the Truman White House in the office of special counsel, was a debonair man who enjoyed a stiff drink, a game of cards, and a political fight. He fell on the liberal side of the Democratic spectrum, but his was a hard-bitten liberalism that would use fair means and foul to advance itself. In midsummer 1947, Clifford received a memorandum from Rowe, an important adviser in the Roosevelt White House who had come to Washington in his early thirties after a childhood in Montana and taking a law degree at Harvard. Among other things, Rowe had been a key player during the debates leading up to the internment of the Japanese Americans in 1942. After the war, as a law partner in a firm headed by Washington power player Thomas "Tommy the Cork" Corcoran, Rowe was often sought out by fellow Democrats for his advice—but not by Truman, who distrusted Corcoran from Senate days a decade earlier. In the fall of 1947, Clifford, adapting Rowe's memo, put together a plan of action that he submitted to Truman under his name, knowing that Truman would disregard it if Rowe were identified as the author.[1]

Yes, the memo acknowledged, the Democratic Party was an ungainly amalgam of southern conservatives, western progressives, urban blacks, and big city labor. Yes, it would be hard to keep these incompatible factions together in 1948, hard to prevent the coalition hammered together by Franklin Roosevelt from splintering. Yes, the situation was bleak for Truman's election. But Clifford saw a clear bright line to victory, provided Truman do the following:

First, assume that Dewey would be the Republican nominee.

Then, assume that Wallace would run on a third-party ticket. Assume that the southern Democrats could kick and scream but that in the end they would have nowhere to go and would vote for Truman happily or unhappily. Then, work very hard to keep the West and organized labor excited and agitated. Work to make sure that they and the independent voters turned out to vote. Because if labor was alienated or the farmers of the West dissatisfied or the progressive voters of the cities offended or the black voters disillusioned with the state of civil rights, then Truman could start planning for his retirement. But if labor and the West voted heavily in Truman's favor, then the Democrats could win the election even if Dewey captured New York, Pennsylvania, Illinois, New Jersey, Ohio, and Massachusetts. For if Truman won the solid South and retained all the western states that FDR gained in 1944, he would have 216 of the needed 266 electoral votes. The other 50 votes could come from states like Missouri, Maryland, or Indiana.[2]

It was quite a memorandum, and it's no wonder politicians and historians have lauded its wisdom in the decades since. Indeed, it seems as if everyone who has written about the election of 1948 has genuflected toward this memorandum, copied it, summarized it, elaborated on it, and shown just how extraordinarily accurate it was. And it was accurate, with a few glaring exceptions. Clifford, following Rowe, dismissed the idea that the southern Democrats could or would bolt from the party even if Truman moved on civil rights. He thought that Dixie had no choice but to swallow its lumps and grudgingly support Truman. So he advised the president not to worry about alienating the South and instead focus on galvanizing the West and the progressives and independents and the farmers and labor. He recommended that Truman strive to keep black voters in the Democratic fold. Though Roosevelt had attracted them away from their traditional allegiance to the party of Abraham Lincoln, Clifford believed that they would tend toward Dewey unless Truman did something dramatic. Whatever that was, it was sure to anger Dixie, but so what?

On this score, the memo was wrong, and the South reacted far more vigorously than Clifford or Rowe anticipated. The rest they predicted almost perfectly. Yet it wasn't simply that they possessed unusual acuity, or that their instincts were remarkably sharp. The memo was so accurate because the election of 1948 was long over-due. The issues had been percolating for years, but they had never been fully aired. Whether it was the fall of France and the defense effort in 1940, or the war and Roosevelt's popularity in 1944, the reality was that there hadn't been a fully contested election in more than a decade. Everyone in politics was itching for a fight. Politicos had been complaining and plotting, and everyone knew what every-one else felt and where everyone else stood. American politics on the eve of 1948 was like a fight among siblings who had kept their dif-ferences in check as long as the father was alive. Finally, all the griev-ances and all the pent-up tensions were going to be released. What Clifford and Rowe did was to capture the fissures on paper.

Truman was faced with squaring a circle, and the odds were against a successful outcome. The New Deal coalition was breaking up, and even labor seemed disenchanted with the Democrats. A.F. Whitney, of the Brotherhood of Railway Trainmen, vowed to spend millions to see the president voted out of office,[3] and the ever-truculent John L. Lewis of the United Mine Workers seethed at the very mention of Truman's name. Dixie was ready to explode when Truman's civil rights commission made its report at the end of 1947, and the Wallaceites and progressives appeared to be gaining ground rapidly in the Northeast and California. Clifford and Rowe pro-vided a blueprint for Truman to solidify his base and Truman, smart man that he was, took most of the memo's advice.

The memo noted that the professional party machines were everywhere in decline. In truth, they had been in decline for many years, but with the passing of FDR, the Democratic Party was in shambles. Local leaders and bosses who for years had rounded up the votes had less influence than at any point since the rise of orga-nized modern parties in the nineteenth century. Urban machines like Tammany Hall in New York City, like the Pendergast people in Kansas City, or like Mayor James Curley in Boston still could muster some support, but gone were the days when the national party could simply coordinate with the local party organizations in order to pro-duce turnout and votes. While the local party organizations could do much to publicize Truman's candidacy, Clifford and Rowe weren't optimistic that these organizations could carry him to victory.

In order to compensate for the decline of political machines, the memo advised that the White House focus on building strong ties with organized labor. The great confederacies like the American Federation of Labor (AFL) and the Congress of Industrial Organizations (CIO) would rally to the Democrats only if Truman first made overtures to their leaders. Labor needed to be courted and wooed, said Clifford and Rowe, if the election was to be won.

The final recommendation was to isolate Henry Wallace. "Wallace should be put under attack whenever the moment is psychologically correct," the memo stated. But the attack should come from the Left, not from the White House. In order to destroy Wallace, Truman would have to step very carefully. The only way to neutralize Wallace was to have potential allies among the intelligentsia desert him. Then Truman could deflate Wallace's appeal by co-opting his positions. This meant that in order to win the election, Truman would have to move to the Left.

To the Left. How utterly incredible that sounds now. Truman would need to become more friendly to big labor, more strongly opposed to Wall Street and the moneymen in New York who comprised the Establishment of the Northeast. He would have to cater to the fear of farmers and workers and Populists and Progressives, fear that Wall Street and robber barons were out to profit at their expense, fear that their way of life, in towns and farms and communities throughout Iowa, Nebraska, upstate New York, rural Pennsylvania, and the prairies of Kansas and Oklahoma, would be destroyed if Dewey or Taft and Republican fat cats managed to take control of the White House. It was the same fear that helped Andrew Jackson fight against the United States Bank and centralized financing in the 1830s, the same fear that William Jennings Bryan preyed on in his 1896 "Cross of Gold" speech, and the same fear that Robert La Follette and the Wisconsin Progressives had addressed during the 1920s. Throughout the West, that fear had swung votes against Republicans for two decades, and unless Truman made aggressive moves, those votes could go to Henry Wallace in 1948.[4]

In vetoing the Taft-Hartley Act, Truman had already made strides in this direction, but as 1948 began, he moved more emphatically toward a populist-progressivism that stood in stark contrast to the Republican rejection of the New Deal. At the same time, however, Truman remained committed to internationalism, to American engagement with the problems of Europe and with the emerging conflict with the Soviet Union. Here, he attacked Wallace unequivocally. Where Wallace believed that the United States and the Soviet Union could chart a path of peaceful coexistence, Truman saw only Soviet aggression and believed only in a firm American response. Where Wallace thought that FDR would have found a way to placate Stalin, Truman felt that Wallace was living in a never-never land fantasy of the goodness of man. And when it came to Wallace and the Cold War, Truman was relentless in assailing the man who would have been president had FDR died a year earlier.

Embarking on the campaign, the Truman White House was blessed with unusual foresight. Advisers like Clifford provided the president with a forecast whose accuracy far outweighed its errors, and they pieced together a strategy that eventually guided Truman to a second term. At both the cabinet and subcabinet level, regular discussions were held to hash out campaign strategy. Every Monday or Wednesday night, a small group met at Washington's Wardman Park Hotel, as it had throughout 1947. That group not only discussed strategy in general but also helped establish a new unit in conjunction with the Democratic National Committee. Created in early 1948, the Research Division heralded a new era in presidential campaigns. Led by William Batt, a genial Philadelphia businessman and a prominent member of Americans for Democratic Action (ADA) who had run unsuccessfully for congress in 1946, the Research Division found offices in Dupont Circle and, with a $50,000 budget, hired Ph.D. candidates, former interns at Americans for Democratic Action, staffers from the American Veterans Committee, and a hodgepodge of others. The Research Division then began to compile reports on Henry Wallace and on Republican candidates Dewey, Vandenberg, and Taft. It assembled "Files of the Facts," which brought together economic statistics, farming data, employment data, inflation data, demographic data, polling results, anecdotes, views of the "man on the street," editorial opinions, radio excerpts, Washington gossip, and any rumors or speculations that could negatively affect Truman's campaign.

Eventually, the Research Division established close links with Truman's speech-writing team, then under Clifford's aegis, and in particular with special assistant George Elsey. The Research Division was complemented by an equally sophisticated press and publicity office organized by the Democratic National Committee. At the suggestion of DNC chairman Senator J. Howard McGrath, Jack Redding was appointed the director, and Samuel Brightman was made deputy director. Redding then recruited a number of people who had worked as radio reporters. In retrospect, what stands out is how unique the process was. Truman's advisers had created the first modern campaign team that systematically obtained, analyzed, and collated information on the total spectrum of issues and personalities. This meant that Truman could react to developments, produce a speech, or take a stand on an issue with the benefit of intensive prior research and information. The Dewey campaign, for all of Dewey's skill as a party leader, was not nearly as rigorous in its staff work. Though the activities and even the existence of the Research Division have escaped most people's notice, it would prove to be a vital component of Truman's victory.[5]

At the beginning of 1948, however, that victory seemed more like a fantasy than a viable possibility. Truman was perceived as a weak candidate compared to the Republican contenders, and there was talk he wouldn't even gain the support of his own party, let alone that of the electorate. Before Truman even got to the point where he could run for election, he had to establish his position within the Democratic Party, and as of January, the party seemed ready to jettison him in favor of someone, anyone, who might stand a better chance in the general election.

At the end of 1945, Harry Truman's approval rating stood at 87 percent. By the beginning of 1947, his party had lost control of Congress and his approval rating stood at less than 35 percent. People still thought he was honest and straightforward, but now they didn't have much faith in these characteristics. Though his approval ratings went back up in the middle of 1947, they plummeted again early in 1948. As political writer Richard Rovere commented, Truman had become "a symbol of weakness and incompetence." He had come far on a combination of sincerity, grit, directness, and humility. Though he owed his early career to the patronage of Pendergast and his Kansas City machine, and though Pendergast was ultimately convicted for various forms of fraud and corruption, Truman escaped with his reputation only mildly tarnished. Yet as the Cold

War intensified in response to the February 1948 communist coup d'etat in Czechoslovakia, and as the New Deal came under attack while the cost of living rose after the removal of wartime price controls, he became a lightning rod of criticism and derision.[6]

Within the Democratic Party, he was widely perceived as a fatal liability. In California, the state party machinery was split between bitterly opposed factions, one of which was led by James Roosevelt, son of FDR. Roosevelt made no secret of his ambition to prevent Truman from becoming the party's candidate, but others in California remained behind Truman, albeit uneasily. Roosevelt insisted that he was only thinking of the good of the party, but many believed he was thinking primarily of his own good. If he could throw Truman aside in favor of someone beholden to him and to the southern California machine, then he would become a national power broker. Roosevelt's discontent had implications for the Democrats in November. As the California party tore itself apart in internecine squabbles, Truman's viability came under scrutiny in places like New York and Illinois.[7]

Truman's unpopularity among California politicos was nothing compared to the vilification he was subjected to at the hands of southern Democrats. The trigger for southern animosity was the president's appointment of the Committee on Civil Rights, which issued its report in October 1947. Truman created the committee, headed by Charles E. Wilson, the president of General Electric, in December of 1946, a year marked by widespread violence and lynchings in the South, as well as by black defections from the Democrats to the Republicans in the midterm elections of 1946. Titled *To Secure These Rights*, the committee's report received extensive coverage, and its conclusions were stark, unsparing, and a bitter pill to southern Democrats.

The committee deliberately focused on what was worst about civil rights in America. Rather than dwell on areas where progress had been made, the report homed in on the crises. Not since the end of the Civil War had there been such a pressing need to revisit the whole issue of civil rights, and the committee made dozens of specific recommendations. Key among them were that the federal government pass an antilynching law, that the Justice Department open a civil rights section, and that poll taxes be outlawed. The language on lynching was especially unsparing. It noted that, while the number of lynchings in the South had actually declined from a high of sixty-four in 1921 to an average of about six a year in the 1940s, "a single lynching is one too many. . . . Lynching is the ultimate threat by which his inferior status is driven home to the Negro. As a terrorist device, it reinforces all the other disabilities placed upon him."[8]

Lynching wasn't simply murder. It was terror with a purpose. It was public destruction of an individual. It was a group of white men dragging a black man to a spot in the woods, tying him to a tree and hanging, whipping, punching, kicking, truncheoning, hacking, or burning him to death while the assembled crowd of men, women, and sometimes even children milled around and shouted hateful epithets. It was an act whose brutality stemmed from a cultural milieu of hate and power, and it was the single most graphic reminder of just how second-class southern blacks continued to be even after they had fought and died for their country in a war that had only ended a few years earlier.

Truman took the committee's report and distilled from it a civil rights program that he then unveiled in early February 1948. In keeping with the Clifford-Rowe memo, Truman moved aggressively on civil rights, at least in his rhetoric. He knew that the Republican Congress was unlikely to pass any of his domestic legislative initiatives in 1948, and that provided him with some cover as he promised the moon and the stars on civil rights. Knowing that there was little risk that his soaring rhetoric would be transformed into highly controversial and divisive legislation, Truman was able to deliver one of the most forceful and eloquent civil rights speeches that the American public had ever heard from its president.

He had outlined an approach to civil rights during his state-of-the-union address in January, but he went much further on February 2, 1948. "The founders of the United States," he declared, "proclaimed to the world the American belief that all men are created equal. . . . We shall not, however, finally achieve the ideals for which this nation was founded so long as any American suffers discrimination as a result of his race, or religion, or color, or the land of origin of his forefathers." There were still far too many examples of such discrimination, he said bluntly, and until "all our people have equal opportunities for jobs, for education, for health and for political expression," Americans should not and cannot be satisfied. Until the civil rights of all citizens were protected not just at the national but also at the state and local levels, the United States would fall short of its ideals and its potential.

To address these issues, Truman urged Congress to establish a variety of institutions and to enact a number of new laws. His recommendations essentially followed the lines laid out by the commission's report. He asked for the creation of a permanent civil rights commission under the auspices of Congress, for federal laws against lynching and the poll tax, for laws to prohibit discrimination on interstate trains and buses, and for a law setting up the Fair Employment Practices Commission (FEPC) to monitor job discrimination. He also called on Congress to settle the claims of Japanese Americans interned during the war and to grant statehood to Hawaii and Alaska and home rule to the District of Columbia.[9]

The *Washington Post*, the *New York Times*, and other major newspapers applauded the speech. Even the *Post*, however, questioned whether Congress should or could, under the Constitution, dictate to states the proper qualifications for voting, nor was the paper convinced that a federal law against lynching was a practical or workable solution. But if northern newspapers questioned the efficacy of some of Truman's proposals, south of the Mason-Dixon line the opinions were nearly unanimous and unequivocal in their outrage. Typical was Senator James Eastland of Mississippi, who railed that Truman's program constituted an attempt "to secure political favor from Red mongrels in the slums of the great cities of the East and Middle West." Truman's proposals, thundered Eastland, were nothing less than a repudiation of the great segregationists John C. Calhoun and Jefferson Davis, nothing less than a vindication of radical reconstruction and Thaddeus Stevens, of carpetbaggers, and of the second-class status of the South in American politics.[10]

The hostility toward Truman in the South far surpassed what Clifford and Rowe had predicted, and by February they must have wondered what other parts of their memo they had gotten wrong. Their calculation that the South had nowhere else to go was coming back to haunt them, as parts of the South appeared ready to abandon Truman and the Democratic Party. The southerners had had enough of northern businessmen, enough of Progressives, and enough talk of civil rights. Eastland evoked the spirit of Calhoun and Davis. Soon, men like Governor Strom Thurmond and Mississippi Governor Fielding L. Wright would follow in their footsteps and secede from the party.

Did Truman feel strongly about his civil rights message or was it all just politics? Did he give his speech simply because his advisers recommended that he make some bold gesture to regain the active support of northern blacks, people whose votes in Illinois, Ohio, California, and New York could be crucial come November? After all, he knew that the Republican-dominated Congress wouldn't pass any of his proposed bills, certainly not in an election year when any such legislation could help the president's cause in November. So how much did he care about the substance of what he was saying? How much of it was just cleverly phrased and well-timed rhetoric?

At the time, almost no one dismissed the message as "politics." Truman himself was hardly a paragon of racial tolerance. He had grown up in Missouri and was accustomed to seeing blacks treated as inferiors—socially, economically, and intellectually. But as president, he seems to have thought more seriously about the implications of a country divided by race. As president, he watched as black soldiers returning from the war were beaten in places like Mississippi. As president, he came to believe that the ideals that he truly held dear were being violated by the systematic denial of basic civil liberties to American blacks.

In the decades since 1948, Americans have come to distrust political rhetoric. They tend to believe that politicians say only what is politically viable, that idealism and politics don't mix and can't coexist. Truman spoke of civil rights with genuine passion, a passion that in no way diminished the political expediency of the message. And people took what he said seriously. That is, after all, why so many in the South felt so profoundly threatened. If it were just words, if it were just political jockeying, then the reaction of the Dixiecrats becomes impossible to explain. Dixie exploded because southerners took Truman's rhetoric as a fair reflection of his beliefs and of his plans.

February was the best of times and the worst of times for Harry Truman. It began with a bold statement of idealism that would not become reality until 1964 with the passage of the Civil Rights Act. It ended with large numbers of southerners on the verge of bolting from the Democratic Party. In the middle, Wallace gathered momentum when his candidate for Congress defeated a Democrat by a wide margin in a special election in the Bronx. Then, Truman attended the annual Jefferson-Jackson Day dinner, only to be greeted by an empty table at the front of the room. This annual affair was one of the most important Democratic Party events of an election year. The dinner offered attendees a chance to celebrate the two founders of the Democratic Party and an opportunity to raise funds for the election. Already, Truman and the party were taking a hit on civil rights. In the first two weeks of February, southerners canceled nearly half a million dollars in contributions to the national committee. Then came the snub.

The front table in the Mayflower Hotel ballroom had been purchased by Senator Olin Johnston of South Carolina. Johnston's wife, vice chairman of the event, angrily refused to attend the dinner, because, she said, she didn't want to take the risk of sitting next to a "Negro." The empty table was played up by the newspapers, even though 2,900 other people crammed into the Mayflower and paid $100 a head to listen to Truman. The press paid lavish attention to Mrs. Johnston's snub, and Henry Luce's *Time* magazine even sent a photographer to take pictures of the senator and his wife making dinner at home while the rest of the Washington Democratic Party elite spilled out of the Mayflower and into an overflow room at the Statler Hotel nearby.

The event generated more than a quarter of a million dollars for the Democratic campaign fund. The guests included Sam Rayburn, congresswoman Helen Gahagan Douglas of California, and the Bronx boss Edward J. Flynn. The guests dined on terrapin soup, breast of capon, and champagne, and at the Statler, as a sign of the times, they were served a special dessert called the "Bombe Atomic." They weren't all that moved by Truman's talk at the Mayflower, and his friend Les Biffle fell asleep at the head table. But, armed with a speech carefully crafted by Clark Clifford, Truman articulated a vision for the coming election, a vision that he characterized as "progressive liberalism." It was Jefferson, he said, who first organized the party of progressive liberalism, and it was Alexander Hamilton who first organized the party of "reactionary conservatism." Today, pro-claimed Truman, the Democrats were heirs to Jefferson, while the Republicans were heirs to Hamilton. He warned that his opponents were reactionaries and isolationists who would turn the United States away from the world and away from the ideals that lay at the heart of American society. He distorted history and maligned Hamilton, but there was no mistaking the battle lines he was drawing for the year ahead.[11]

In spite of the success of the evening—the ringing rhetoric, the money raised, and the vision presented—in spite of the careful planning of Clifford and Rowe and the Research Division and dozens of other advisers, Truman was nevertheless dogged by editorials questioning his leadership, by the empty table which symbolized the southerners rallying around the Confederate banner, and by rumblings within his own party that he would be pushed aside in favor of someone more electable. He had made a stand on principle and, at the time, it seemed as if that stand would become simply one more nail in the political coffin of Harry Truman, haberdasher become president, a job too big for the simple man from Missouri.

CHAPTER THREE

Dixie Reacts

ON JANUARY 20, 1948, Fielding L. Wright became governor of Mississippi. A scholarly, innocuous-looking man, Wright had practiced law in Rolling Fork, served as lieutenant-governor, speaker of the Mississippi House, and then as acting governor since 1946. Known as a reformer, he had been a champion of the first bill ever to use public funding to pave the roads in Mississippi. He had introduced a law raising the pay of public school teachers, and he loosened the enforcement of Prohibition. But on Jim Crow, he was anything but a reformer.

Wright was a man of the Mississippi Delta, a swampy land made up of numerous counties that were more than 70 percent black. It was also a land of old, conservative families that still lived on or near the Civil War plantations that had made their fortunes. For the whites in these counties, no white supremacy was supreme enough. Throughout Mississippi as a whole, the only thing that the conservative families of the delta and the poor whites of the hills could be sure to agree on was that Negroes were inferior. And while Wright may have come from a different part of the state from Theodore Bilbo, the corrupt, race-baiting senator, and was certainly less coarse in his manner, he was no less committed to the old southern racial hierarchy. And on January 20, he was angry at Harry Truman and the civil rights commission that Truman had appointed.

In his inaugural address, Wright claimed that Truman's proposals were designed to do nothing less than "to wreck the South and its institutions." He promised that as leader of Mississippi's Democrats, he would not stand idle and allow the South to be destroyed. "Vital principles and eternal truths transcend party lines, and the day is

now at hand when determined action must be taken." He had no
desire to leave the Democratic Party, he said, but he would not
remain if it continued on its current course. Wright had thrown
down a gauntlet, and Truman picked it up when he formalized the
civil rights program on February 2.[1]

A week after Wright's inauguration, "Big Jim" Folsom, the governor of Alabama, made a statewide radio address. A good ol' boy
who, by southern standards, was an unabashed liberal, Folsom liked
to campaign with hillbilly bands in the background and to engage in
marathon sessions of kissing women and children at political rallies.
He objected to any foreign policy that supported corrupt dictators
and tyrants, even if they were anticommunist. He could frequently
be heard denouncing monied interests on Wall Street, and he was
known as a strong defender of the rural poor. This defense did not
extend to the black rural poor, however, and he wanted no talk of
civil rights.

On January 20, Folsom announced that he was going to run for
president. "Right now," he told the white people of Alabama,
"you're living under a dark cloud. . . . Who's running our party in
Washington? The head of our party is a nice man. But he's not running our party any more. And he's not running our country. He's let
himself get hog-tied." Harry Truman, Folsom said, was being led by
some millionaires and Wall Street lawyers who were trying to steal
money from the farmers by using the Defense Department and the
State Department. "Monopolists, brass hats, Wall Street lawyers, tea
sippers. They're not real Democrats. . . . What have they got in common with the peace loving, God-fearing people of the Cotton Belt?"
Those men in Washington, Folsom charged, were spending billions
around the world for their own profit, and meanwhile prices were
going up at home. Folsom admitted that Truman was a nice man:
"He's been nice to me and I like him." But nice wasn't enough. Folsom could think of about twenty-five people who would do a better
job as the leader of the country and the party than Truman. And he
thought he was one of those people.[2]

This wasn't the first time that southern Democrats had strayed
from their northern brethren. In 1928, a Democratic grassroots
movement rejected the Democrat Alfred E. Smith because of his
Catholicism and his opposition to Prohibition, and threw the elec-

toral votes of Florida, Tennessee, North Carolina, Texas, and Virginia to the Republican nominee, Herbert Hoover. Throughout the New Deal, southern Democrats, not liking Roosevelt personally and dismayed at his radical expansion of federal power, made noises about quitting the party. In his second term, Roosevelt worked to see some of these Democrats defeated. In 1944, southern politicians tried, but failed, to wrest more control of the party machinery. The rebellion confronting the party after Truman's February 2 civil rights message had been a long time coming. The grievances were partly about race, and partly about money and power within the Democratic Party and the country as a whole. But not until an unpopular president went public with an unabashed civil rights agenda were these forces in the South able to coalesce. The turmoil may have been about more than race, but race gave southern politicians an issue that they could use not only to whip up animosity and rage, but to raise money as well.

The Deep South in 1948 was poor in a way that few Americans today can even imagine. Haunted faces, with despair etched deep, stare at us from another world in James Agee and Walker Evans's *Let Us Now Praise Famous Men*, a poetic pictorial of the South during the Depression. There were no paved roads, no electricity, no plumbing, no running water, no money, little food, less education, shanties, shacks, cotton, shreds of clothing, illiteracy. The South was slowly industrializing in the late 1940s, and cities like Birmingham resembled the steel metropolises of Pennsylvania and Ohio. Oil companies drilled in the tidelands region of the Gulf Coast and made millions for a select few in states like Louisiana and Mississippi. Large landholders maintained positions of power and prestige and clung to views that their great grandparents would have expressed at the end of the Civil War. Throughout the South, agrarian populism and traditional conservatism jockeyed for control of what was essentially a one-party system. Democrats ruled the South as they had since the end of Reconstruction in the late 1870s.[3]

This was the world that Fielding Wright, Jim Folsom, and Strom Thurmond occupied. This was the world that they believed was under assault, and that they intended to preserve.

At the beginning of February 1948, the southern governors assembled in Wakulla Springs, near Tallahassee, Florida, for their annual conference. Hearing Truman's message, the attendees held emergency sessions to plan a response. At first, most pundits and politicians outside the South dismissed the flap as just another tempest within the Democratic Party that would soon blow over. In his column in the *New York Times,* Arthur Krock was phlegmatic about the possibility of southern animosity actually leading to a split within the Democratic Party. Writing in *The Nation,* Robert Bendiner commented that "it has become a Southern custom since 1932 for the Claghorns to rise up early in an election year and serve notice, in the name of Robert E. Lee and white womanhood, that they are not to be taken for granted by the Democratic Party." Throughout the country, most informed observers believed, as Clifford and Rowe believed, that in the end, the southern Democrats simply had nowhere to go. But this was not just another flurry of resentment on the part of the South.

The governors were united in their hostility but could not agree on tactics or strategy. Led by Wright, some demanded an immediate revolt; others weren't as sure. After hours of debate, Strom Thurmond proposed that they all study the matter for forty days and then meet again. This "cooling-off" period drew the support of the caucus, and Thurmond cleverly invited the press to listen to the deliberations. There, in what John Popham of the *New York Times* called a "smoke filled room filled to capacity," the governors passed Thurmond's resolution. They also decided that he should lead a small delegation to meet with the chairman of the Democratic National Committee, Senator J. Howard McGrath, to see if Truman could be persuaded not to act on his proposals. In mid-February, Thurmond trekked to Washington during a cold spell and met with McGrath, but the chairman was noncommittal. He made no promises and gave no assurances. Thurmond left, disgusted and exasperated.[4]

The proposals that Thurmond's delegation asked Truman to reconsider were, by any reckoning at the time, radical. The 1944 Democratic platform included similar proposals, but they had not won Roosevelt's firm support, nor did he speak with the vehemence and passion that Truman summoned for his February speech. The legislative slate Truman recommended would have gone a long way toward ending segregation in the South, and segregation was the glue holding the traditional social order together. True, that social order had already started to erode. Supreme Court decisions throughout the 1940s had led to small but significant changes. Interstate buses were desegregated, as were some law schools. The court rulings were not enough to destroy Jim Crow, but they made people like Senator James Eastland nervous and angry. "The races live together in contentment," he assured an audience in February 1948. "Both races know and respect each other. The Negro receives a square deal. Both races recognize that the society of the South is built upon segregation."[5]

It was an old argument soon to lose its power, but in 1948 it still resonated. After McGrath rebuffed the governors, more than 4,000 people calling themselves "True White Jeffersonians" gathered in Jackson, Mississippi, at the behest of Governor Wright. They waved the Confederate flag and listened as Wright told them in sober tones that the South was at a crossroads. There could be no turning back, no compromise. The rally raised $61,500, and additional funds were pledged by W.W. Wright, the fifty-four-year-old president of Mississippi's largest grocery wholesaler.[6] Meanwhile, the nascent rebellion was pushing another man to the fore, a man who until February 1948 was known not for stringent opposition to civil rights but rather for moderation, even liberalism. Suddenly, the world seemed to offer new opportunities for Strom Thurmond. Until the early months of 1948, most people had assumed that Thurmond would run for the Senate in 1950. Most believed that he would continue advancing his not-so-ambitious agenda of law, order, and justice— southern style. No one imagined that by the summer of 1948 he would be running for president of the United States.

As a potential leader of the revolt in February, Fielding Wright, Jim Folsom, Ben Laney of Arkansas, James Eastland, or Governor Beauford Jester of Texas would have come to mind before Thurmond. There was hardly a dearth of Truman opponents in the South. The powerful bloc of southern Democratic senators, such as Richard B. Russell Jr. of Georgia, Allen Ellender of Louisiana, and John Stennis of Mississippi, all denounced the president. Even the moderate and well-respected Mississippi newspaper editor Hodding Carter spoke out against Truman, claiming that the president's shameless political opportunism would rend the South and damage the Democratic Party. He warned that the South wasn't ready for

such drastic change, and for proof he cited a gathering of the Ku
Klux Klan in Georgia to prevent a group of blacks from voting in a
state primary. "The Grand Dragon of the Klan, his face uncovered,
told his hooded colleagues that bloodshed would result from the
enactment of civil rights legislation." A picture of the Klan at
Wrightsville showed a stark scene: hundreds of hooded figures waving American flags form a circle around a burning cross twenty feet
high. Milling around the circle are women and children, smiling
and laughing as dusk falls, as if they were at a county fair or a circus. A few days later, when Ralph McGill, the editor of the *Atlanta
Constitution,* tried to speak at a debate, he was ridiculed and
booed because, though he was against civil rights legislation, he
was against it only on the grounds that Truman was politically
motivated.[7]

Senator Russell endorsed the action taken by the southern governors. In a private letter to Thurmond, Russell described Truman's
stance as "a vicious and unwarranted attack made by the President
of the United States on our Southern civilization." Russell was so
outraged, he said, that he couldn't think straight. Visions of desegre-
gation and miscegenation danced through his head. If passed, Truman's platform would "compel the intermingling of races in the
South." Russell accurately predicted that Republicans would be
forced to support the legislation or else risk losing the northern
"Negro and radical vote in the populous doubtful states." He bitterly observed that the great and noble tradition of southern democracy was about to be destroyed by "a bunch of Johnny-come-lately
pink-tinted radicals" who now controlled the national party. He
vowed to do everything in his power to oppose any efforts in Congress to "crucify the South." He further recommended that the governors use their power of selecting electors to the national
convention in July as a way to deny the presidential nomination to
Truman.

But Russell stopped short of advocating a bolt from the party.
Like many senators and congressmen, he was comfortable denouncing Truman and his program in the most vehement language possible. But as a major player in the Senate, with all the perks and power
that came with his position, he was not eager to leave the party. This
stance was telling. The split between the southern state politicians

and southern congressional representatives would prove lethal to the chances of the Dixiecrats in states like Georgia, Florida, and Arkansas. In early 1948, however, letters and telegrams poured into the offices of Governor Thurmond in Columbia, South Carolina, letters not just from Russell but from Governor Jester of Texas, who said that "the majority of Texas Democrats do not want Truman renominated for the Presidency"; from Senator Burnet Maybank of South Carolina, who stated that he would "violently oppose all of the bills proposed by the President on civil rights"; from Senator W. Lee O'Daniel of Texas, who believed that "communist Labor leader racketeers had taken over the Democratic Party with the sole intent of destroying the last free government on earth"; and from dozens of other southern representatives expressing their outrage.[8]

At the center of this storm were Strom Thurmond and Fielding Wright. Wright was far more adamant than Thurmond about a southern bolt from the Democratic Party, but Thurmond was more ambitious. Before February 1948, Thurmond probably did intend to run for Olin Johnston's senate seat in 1950. Before that date, he probably had no desire to ever run for president, but would have focused on local politics until his term expired. But this all changed in February 1948. In later years, no one would ever suggest that Thurmond had had a master plan, and no one would say he had been particularly committed to racial politics. But something happened in these months to transform Strom Thurmond, the county judge and genial governor, into the fiery leader of the most radical wing of the southern Democrats.

In early 1948, Thurmond was only the spokesman of the governors, and he had other priorities. Even after he had put forth his resolution at Wakulla Springs and after he had agreed to meet with McGrath, he still had time to go to a ball in Columbia. His wife, Jean, only twenty-three years old, wasn't overly fond of her husband's predilection for young beauties. She knew he had a roving eye, at the very least. After all, he had crowned her Miss South Carolina when she was still attending Winthrop College, and had hired her as his secretary; he proposed to her by sliding a letter across her desk. His appearances at beauty pageants were covered by the local press, and the voters clearly took some pleasure in images of their obviously virile governor. In a society that prized male vigor in politics, Strom Thurmond bragged about his physical conditioning and encouraged reporters to photograph him with an endless variety of young women.

So it was no surprise when, on Saturday, February 14, the governor attended the Valentine Ball at his alma mater, Clemson. There, he was delighted to crown Miss Marjorie Lucas, of Cayce, South Carolina, "Independent Sweetheart of 1948." Elected by members of the men's Independent club, Miss Lucas wore a black strapless gown with a big billowing white bow at her waist. To the sounds of Woody Woodward and his orchestra playing "I Get a Kick Out of You," Marjorie Lucas was led onto the dance floor by Governor Thurmond and the two danced while an admiring crowd looked on. They danced until midnight, and then the evening came to a close.[9]

Thurmond came from a family of politicians. His grandfather George Washington Thurmond fought in the Civil War, and his father, John, was a close ally of "Pitchfork" Ben Tillman, the governor and senator from South Carolina who threatened to stick a pitchfork into his enemies. John Thurmond took his boss's language and put it into action. One day, someone used "hot language," brandished a knife, and accused John Thurmond of being a Tillmanite. The elder Thurmond turned and shot the man. The jury refused to convict.

Strom's mother was a woman that people at the time liked to call "God-fearing." She was a stern presence and raised her three sons and three daughters in the First Baptist Church of Edgefield. A childhood in rural South Carolina in the early part of the century meant a life surrounded by tobacco plantations and a rigid hierarchy of races. Thurmond may not have based his political career on racial prejudice, at least not as explicitly as Senator Bilbo, but that didn't mean he was any less committed to the social order of the South. He was from the Piedmont part of South Carolina, an area of hills and mountains set off a bit from the lowlands that sloped down toward the Atlantic. The hills had proportionally fewer blacks than the low counties, and race-baiting didn't play quite as well. Thurmond's father may have been close to Pitchfork Ben, but Strom seemed a milder sort.

Thurmond was the only major candidate in 1948 who had served in the military during World War II. Even though his position as a county judge exempted him from military duty, he resigned his judgeship and was granted a commission in the Eighty-second Airborne Division. The Eighty-second was an instrumental part of the Allied landings during the D-Day invasion in June 1944, and Thurmond was injured while trying to land a glider on the cliffs. He received a Purple Heart and later went on to win many other medals for his fighting prowess while the First Army moved slowly across France, through the Low Countries, and into Germany.

On his return in 1946, he decided to run for governor, a race which had eleven candidates. Thurmond positioned himself as a liberal and a progressive. He promised that his administration would be for "the common man" and he called for "a progressive outlook, a progressive program and a progressive leadership." Like Fielding Wright in Mississippi, he vigorously promoted education and talked of expanding and modernizing public schools. Unlike Wright, he claimed that "Negro education" was no less important than the education of South Carolina's white citizens. "The low standing of South Carolina, educationally," he stated, "is due primarily to the high rate of illiteracy and lack of education among our Negroes." To raise the level of the state as a whole meant raising the educational level of blacks. He believed that poverty was the most pressing issue facing South Carolina. He believed that racial problems stemmed from economic problems. Address the causes of poverty, and race relations would improve. He didn't attempt to conceal these views when he ran for governor. Thurmond was as close to a New Dealer as anyone in the race. And he won.[10]

An administration for "the common man," long speeches about poverty, a champion of public financing for public works. At times, Thurmond sounded almost like Henry Wallace. Although people would later say that Wallace and the Progressives marked the far Left of American politics while Thurmond and the Dixiecrats marked the far Right, in certain important ways they were closer to each other politically than either were to Truman, Dewey, and the established parties. Though Truman stood for labor and the farmer, he rarely spoke explicitly about poverty, and neither did Dewey. Wallace and Thurmond may have appealed to very different constituencies, but they shared a sense that the American dream realized by victory in war still did not extend to everyone. They each spoke for the poor and the disenfranchised, though of course, Thurmond and the Dixiecrats pitted one set of the disenfranchised—poor southern whites—against another—poor southern blacks. It is so easy to glance back across the years and dismiss Thurmond and the Dixiecrats as racists. They were racists, but that is not all they were, nor was race the only aspect of life that they spoke to. Thurmond believed himself a liberal and a progressive, and southern conservatives who never bolted from the Democratic Party continued to see him that way. The use of these terms may strike us now as perplexing but, at that time, in that context, Thurmond fit those labels.

Throughout February and March, Thurmond's office in Columbia received a steady stream of mail. Almost all of it urged the governor to defend the honor of the South. Some suggested that Thurmond try to draft Senator Harry Byrd of Virginia as a States' Rights candidate whom a majority of southerners could support at the Democratic Convention in July. The letters poured in not just from South Carolina but from the Northeast as well. William Barber of New York urged Thurmond to expose the hypocrisy of Washington politicians who only stood for civil rights and antilynching laws in order to get votes. Lewis N. Clark of New York City wrote two long letters in late February and early March. He claimed to be the head of an informal group of secessionist Democrats in the Northeast who numbered more than 200. Clark had watched as "one American liberty after another" was dismantled first by FDR and now by Truman, who was setting up a "Sovietland" in its stead. Of course, intoned Clark, the real enemy was a cabal of "Jewish lawyers" in New York, Chicago, and Philadelphia who "have rushed to the rescue of the Negro." This "handful of wealthy Jews with their hirelings is running this country today," Clark continued. It was up to Thurmond to halt these developments, he said. The contest was nothing less than a battle between Jews and Communists on the one hand, and true Americans on the other. In addition to the letters, William Donnachie of Philadelphia sent the governor highlights from the film *The Birth of a Nation*, D.W. Griffith's 1915 Hollywood epic about the rise of the Ku Klux Klan and one of the most egregiously racist films that Hollywood ever produced.

Letter after letter railed that the Democratic Party was selling out to ethnic and black votes in the North. The writers warned of a conspiracy led by Jews and assisted by blacks, and they predicted disaster for the South. From Little Rock, Arkansas, L.R. Bunson conveyed his distress at reading the papers and watching as "the D- niggers is trying to force themselves into the schools with white children. . . . I cannot tolerate," Bunson fulminated, "a D- nigger mixing up with the white people. . . . Please try and do everything in your power to keep the nigger in his place. . . . Stick to your guns and keep a rigid Jim Crow law in force and save the white race in the South." In response, Thurmond wrote to these petitioners that, in his opinion, "the people of South Carolina have had enough of President Truman," and he thanked the writers for their support.[11]

The rhetoric wasn't pretty, and the racism was disturbing. At the same time, Wright and Thurmond and the thousands who were prepared to abandon the Democratic Party and work for a new cause were participating fully, eagerly, enthusiastically in the political life of the nation. They felt that their cherished beliefs were threatened. They worried that if they allowed Truman to continue, they would soon have no voice in national government and would thereby lose the ability to participate in the national debate. Instead of retreating sullenly and withholding their votes, they took action.

Today, we may not like what the Dixiecrats believed and what they stood for. But at any given time in a healthy multiracial democracy, one group of people hates, dislikes, and distrusts what another group says, thinks, or advocates. In 1948, the cacophony of voices was part of the process. The debates were visible. In later elections, debate would be pushed from the center of presidential elections to the margins. The process since 1948 has become more civil, more sanitary. In 1948, there were alternatives, even though some in retrospect appear far more palatable than others.

The forty-day cooling-off period came to an end in mid-March. As promised, the committee met in Washington, D.C., to decide how to proceed. These seven representatives of southern democracy—six governors as well as Senator Byrd, who acted as a proxy for the governor of Virginia—issued a report stating that they would "fight to the last ditch" against the nomination or election of Harry Truman as president. They warned that the civil rights legislation "would constitute a total departure from the fundamental principles upon which the government of the United States was founded. It would be a major alteration in the division of governmental powers and sovereignty between the States and the Federal Government established in the Constitution of the United States." Sprinkled throughout the report were warnings that under Truman's aegis, the federal government would create a federal police agency "like the ill-famed Gestapo" that would have the right to barge into any business and enforce regulations. The committee advised the southern state conventions to instruct their delegates to the national convention not to vote for Truman or anyone else committed to civil rights. The report concluded with an exhortation that southern states take concerted action to use the electoral college to prevent any pro–civil rights Democrat from winning the general election.[12]

Though the decision to bolt from the party had not yet been made in March, Thurmond and Wright and the rest of the committee were moving rapidly in that direction. Ringing rhetoric aside, they did not at any point during 1948 believe that they had a chance of winning the general election. They hoped only to capture as many of the South's electoral votes as they possibly could. If they won enough votes, they could deny any candidate from obtaining a majority in the electoral college. Then, under the Constitution, the election would be decided by the House of Representatives, as it had been in 1801 when Thomas Jefferson was chosen over Aaron Burr, as it had in 1825 when John Quincy Adams won as a result of a bitterly divisive bargain with Henry Clay, as it had in 1877 when Congress, despite the popular vote in favor of Samuel Tilden, threw the election to Rutherford B. Hayes. In the House, the decision would be made state by state, and each state's delegation would have one vote. If, as the Dixiecrats hoped, the 1948 election ended up in the House, the southern states would determine who would be president, and they would choose someone like Harry Byrd, possibly acceptable to the North but who would never think of disrupting the social order of the South.

If this report was troubling for Truman, the fact that only seven people attended the Washington meeting was ominous for the Dixiecrats. Even at Wakulla Springs, some of the governors had spoken against an outright departure from the party. James McCord of Tennessee had made it clear that he would not support what the committee was now urging. He believed that in the end, party loyalty was the predominant virtue, no matter how outrageous the president's proposals were. Senator Claude Pepper of Florida distanced himself from what Wright and Thurmond were doing and blasted them for attempting to take Truman off the ballot. He said that their actions were "striking at the roots of democracy." For Pepper, criticizing Truman and taking steps within the party machinery to reject his proposals were acceptable, but threatening to disrupt the Democratic Party wasn't. Risking a Republican victory in November was political suicide. As it turned out, Pepper had staked out a position that many southern Democrats would emulate.[13]

As of mid-March, however, Thurmond and Wright were building momentum. In Jackson, a States' Rights movement had coalesced, with headquarters at the Heidelberg Hotel. Wright called for a national meeting of states' righters in Jackson on May 10. He said he was launching a "grass roots" movement, but added that he was not willing to run for president. He would focus on organizing the May meeting and on rallying support first throughout Mississippi and then throughout the neighboring states. The purpose of the May meeting would be to restate the principles of southern democracy and to determine the best course of action. The goal was to defeat, utterly and permanently, federal civil rights legislation. And if Truman could be humiliated, all the better, because the fight wasn't just political—it was also personal. Truman was a son of the South—from Missouri, but a southerner nonetheless. "If we do nothing but beat Truman, I'll be satisfied," declared E.G. Truly of Fayette, Mississippi. "We are going to have the pleasure of beating a Southern renegade. Any man whose grandfather was a member of the Confederate Army and who would recommend such laws as Truman has is a renegade Southerner. I'd rather have an enemy than a renegade as president."[14] For Truly and millions of others, betrayal of the South was one of the worst sins imaginable, one for which there could be no forgiveness.

It was, therefore, bad timing when Truman officially declared on March 8, 1948, that he would be a candidate for president. The announcement was made by Senator McGrath in the White House lobby. "The president has authorized me to say," McGrath said, reading from a statement, "that if nominated by the Democratic National Convention, he will accept and run." Commenting on the announcement, Edward T. Folliard of the *Washington Post* noted the peculiar timing of the announcement, coming as did in the midst of southern outrage over civil rights and in the wake of the stunning victory of Henry Wallace's party in a special congressional election in the Bronx. During the press conference, McGrath studiously avoided mentioning Wallace's name, but that didn't stop the *Post* reporter from mentioning it repeatedly. Wallace was very much on Truman's mind, and, for a time, it seemed that Dixie was less of a threat to Truman than the liberals and progressives who were deserting the president and flocking to the man from Iowa, Henry Agard Wallace.[15]

CHAPTER FOUR

Wallace Gets Going

THE DAY AFTER he announced his candidacy in December 1947, Henry Wallace stood on the stage of the Milwaukee Auditorium in front of an audience of 3,600 people who had paid between fifty cents and two dollars to attend. The evening was expertly staged. The sculptor Jo Davidson, who was a leading figure in the Progressive Party, conceived of a Wallace speech as a multimedia spectacle. There would be stirring songs by Paul Robeson, the famous black singer with the mellifluous baritone voice and a reputation as a communist "fellow traveler." There would be the usual introductory speeches, often raucous, while the crowd milled about and settled down. Then the room would go dark, a spotlight would shine on a distant door, and Wallace—"the chosen man," as Davidson put it— would appear and drums would start pounding, rising to a crescendo until Wallace ascended to the stage and began to speak.[1]

For the next six months, Wallace would appear on many such stages, often with Robeson or other singers such as Pete Seeger and Woody Guthrie. These events were never free, though neither were they expensive to attend. For every event attended by 5,000 people, Wallace could raise five or six thousand dollars, and given the financial demands of campaigning for president, he needed to speak as often as he could simply to raise the minimum amount of money he needed to be a credible candidate.

Wallace was a serious speaker, but not a stirring one. With his wavy, messy gray hair, and bushy eyebrows, the fifty-nine-year-old former vice president spoke like a preacher or a prophet. He thundered against the "bipartisan" foreign policy championed by Truman and the Republican Congress. He criticized the multibillion-dollar aid to Europe that Secretary of State Marshall had proposed during a Harvard University commencement address the previous June. He called for international control of nuclear weapons and a sharing of nuclear secrets with the Soviet Union. Most of all, he denounced Washington politicians for generating a climate of fear in the world. It didn't have to be that way, he assured his audience. We didn't need to live in a world defined by fear and marked by weapons of mass destruction. We didn't need to live in a world of loyalty oaths and suspicion, a world ruled by Wall Street and governed by senators and congressmen and presidents who cared not one whit for the common man.

One of the most acute portraits of Henry Wallace was drawn by his one-time friend Max Lerner. Lerner, the editorial page editor of the liberal New York daily newspaper *PM*, refused to support Wallace's third-party movement, but like many editors in early 1948, he viewed Wallace as a bonafide contender. He believed Wallace could attract somewhere between five and ten million votes and that he could easily prevent Truman from winning. For Lerner, Wallace was defined by three things. First, he was a Populist insurgent. Like William Jennings Bryan in the 1890s and Robert La Follette in the 1920s, Wallace was a man of the agrarian Midwest, a man of the farms who saw American values in terms of the small landowner and not in terms of Wall Street and big business. Even though Wallace had made a fortune developing and selling hybrid corn, he remained a Populist in temperament and demeanor. Second, Wallace was a man of science. He saw the world as a rational place subject to rational answers. For every problem, there was a solution, whether it be how to grow crops in sparse soil or how to live with Stalin and the Soviet Union. In Wallace's cosmology, conflict occurred only when man failed to find the solution; it was never and would never be inevitable. Finally, Lerner observed, Wallace was "deeply Christian." He believed he was called to lead a noble crusade in the path of righteousness. He believed he was leading a Gideon's army. He believed he was a latter-day Isaiah, destined to stand against injustice, destined to suffer perhaps, but always with God at his side. Of course, remarked Freda Kirchwey of *The Nation*, though Wallace compared himself to Gideon and other prophets, he still had no chance of winning. He could spoil Truman's chances, but he could not lead his Gideon's army to victory.[2]

In the first months of his campaign, Wallace received extensive coverage in newspapers and in the press. He garnered as much attention as Truman and more than Thomas Dewey or Robert Taft or Harold Stassen or Strom Thurmond. His columns appeared weekly in *The New Republic*. He was heard frequently on the radio, particularly on the Mutual Broadcasting Network and the National Broadcasting Company. For a third-party candidate, Wallace dominated discussions among what are now sometimes called the "opinion elites." But he never quite grasped the ruthlessness of American politics. He believed in saying what he believed, again and again, bluntly, whether or not that was politically palatable to the electorate and to the elites. Even more significant, Wallace was perceived as so dangerous to the Democrats' chances in November that aggressive steps were taken to dismantle his candidacy. Few presidential aspirants have received as much publicity so early in the election cycle and few have received as much negative publicity as Henry Wallace did through the spring of 1948. Not only did the Democratic Party and the national committee led by J. Howard McGrath mobilize against Wallace, but many of his former allies turned on him with a vehemence and passion that only ex-friends can have for each other.

Until his break with Truman in the fall of 1946 and for some months thereafter, Wallace was one of the leaders of New Deal liberalism, and, with the exception of Harold Ickes, he was the most prominent former New Dealer to part ways with Truman. In the traditional liberal circles of the Northeast literati and in the smoky meeting halls of the American Federation of Labor, he was a hero. Throughout 1947, when Progressives and Liberals looked to the future and their prospects politically, Henry Wallace's name was never far from anyone's lips. Of course, among writers, journalists, and labor leaders, Wallace did have enemies and adversaries. Since the 1930s, when New York Leftists had torn each other to intellectual shreds over who was a Trotskyite, a Schachtmanite, and a Stalinist, Americans on the Left had made a blood sport of demolishing each other. One of the most vociferous Wallace detractors was the critic Dwight Macdonald, who felt compelled to publish a book in early 1948 that lambasted Wallace for being, among other things, a mystic, "an amateur of esoteric doctrines," a chameleon who changed his positions out of political expediency rather than ideology, a cutthroat politician whose ambition knew no bounds, a hysteric, a moralist, a Stalinoid, a "chronic reneger," and, not least of all, a man who was viciously competitive at tennis. Like everything Macdonald put his pen to, the book was brilliant literature, even though the author clearly took more delight in skewering Wallace than in presenting him fairly.[3]

Macdonald's ire went deeper than personal animosity. Wallace exposed the major fault line of the postwar American Left. In 1948, he was a lone voice favoring accommodation with the Soviet Union, and alone among the major figures of New Deal liberalism he refused to condemn communism as the principal danger to the American way of life. Wallace's stance led to a split on the Left in 1947, with the result that, by 1948, Wallace was hated by many people whom he had once considered friends and allies. Throughout 1947, the people and groups once united on the Left formed two bitterly antagonistic camps, with the Progressive Citizens of America (PCA) and Wallace on one side, and the Americans for Democratic Action (ADA) on the other. And when Wallace announced his candidacy, the ADA took it upon itself to destroy him.

The leaders of the ADA had little love for Harry Truman, and later in the spring they mounted an effort within the Democratic Party to replace Truman with either U.S. Army Chief of Staff Dwight D. Eisenhower or Supreme Court Justice William O. Douglas. But in a true marriage of convenience, the ADA and the Truman White House developed a symbiotic relationship when it came to Henry Wallace. As Clark Clifford and James Rowe had set out in their memo, the Truman campaign needed to both neutralize Wallace and solidify support on the Left. For its part, the ADA needed to neutralize Wallace in order to secure its claims to liberal leadership.

The ADA was influential because of its power among the opinion makers, who were based largely in New York City. With the possible exception of Hollywood, New York in the 1940s was the cultural center of the United States. Most writers, artists, radio announcers, and national journalists lived there, though some of the major syndicated columnists like Joseph and Stewart Alsop, Walter Lippmann, and James Reston resided in Washington, D.C. The New York circle was small, and almost certainly numbered under a thousand. Yet this group of people shaped the national culture and affected national politics. The culture was an elite culture, defined by a cluster of white men and the occasional white woman. They socialized with one another, argued with one another, and interacted with the political and financial luminaries of Wall Street and Capitol Hill. The ADA may have had a relatively small membership, but its influence on this group gave it immense cultural and political power. The fact that it had a substantial budget and chapters in key cities outside the Northeast made the organization that much more formidable.

Many of the people in the ADA had been fellow travelers in the 1930s. They had flirted with communism, but by the early 1940s, most had changed their views about the Soviet Union. Similarly, some of the journalists who reported on Wallace during the campaign had moved from the far Left in the 1930s to the anticommunist Left in the 1940s. James Wechsler of the *New York Post* covered the Wallace campaign for ten months. He had been a member of the Communist Youth League in the 1930s, but by 1948 he was one of the many liberal voices standing against Wallace. He observed that Wallace "was almost a caricature of an innocent, murmuring the sentences which left-wing ghosts had usually written for him and denying that ghosts existed, parroting the old communist clichés as if they were rare insights he had just acquired on his way to a press conference." Wallace did say things that resembled communist propaganda. He did speak of "the lords of American monopoly," and he did talk about the Marshall Plan and the Truman Doctrine as if they were screens used by industrialists to profiteer in war-ravaged Europe. Of course, in time, Truman would also denounce "monopolists," and Populists had been criticizing Wall Street for generations. But that perspective was lost on most journalists. Like many of those covering the Wallace campaign, Wechsler was anything but objective or nonpartisan. Few journalists were unbiased about Wallace, and most were overtly hostile. Unlike Truman, or Dewey, or Thurmond, or any other figure during the election, Wallace was seen by them as an apostate, and they pursued him with the vigor of inquisitors.[4]

By 1948, Wallace was hemmorrhaging supporters. Not just Eleanor Roosevelt, but ADA leaders James Loeb and Leon Henderson, labor bosses Walter Reuther and Philip Murray, intellectuals such as Arthur Schlesinger Jr., and associates such as Harold Ickes, Bartley Crum, and former PCA board member Frank Kingdon all broke with Wallace, claiming that the forces behind the third-party movement were anathema. Those forces, sometimes named explicitly, sometimes not, were really one force: communism.

At no point did Wallace distance himself from American Communists. For that reason above all, he was vilified. He was called a communist dupe, a tool of Stalin, and a traitor. The ADA characterized the Progressive Citizens of America as "an unholy alliance of Communists and reactionaries." Despite these attacks, Wallace welcomed the support of any group that chose to offer it. The American Communist Party decided in 1947 to support Wallace and the PCA, and rather than denouncing that decision, Wallace embraced it. "The most frequent charge made against the American Communists is that they advocate the violent overthrow of the Government of the United States," he told a group of 2,000 supporters in Columbus, Ohio, in February 1948. "I have not seen evidence to substantiate the charge. . . . Any Communist who supports the independent ticket will be supporting our program, not the Communist program. I am not a Communist, or Socialist, or Marxist of any description, but I find nothing criminal in the advocacy of different economic and social ideas." Noble ideals, perhaps, but not ones that the elites in New York and Washington were buying. On the contrary, the very fact that Wallace could make such statements was interpreted by the ADA and much of the Left as proof that Wallace wasn't just a fool, but that he was in thrall to dark forces that were secretly pulling the strings of the PCA.[5]

Though many Americans at the time were convinced that the movement was secretly controlled by Communists, that is too simplistic. It is true that the Communist Party endorsed Wallace and campaigned actively on his behalf. By 1948, the American Communist Party led by William Z. Foster seemed to be receptive to whatever strategy Moscow dictated, and though Stalin had no illusions about the prospects for a communist government in the United States, he probably hoped that Wallace's third party would be a step in that direction. Some American Communists were dedicated to the

Soviet Union, but others were simply American radicals. There was confusion at the time, and there has been confusion since, about the difference between these two types of people. Both were present in the Wallace camp, but the more influential communist-sympathizers in the Progressive tent were not members of the Communist Party as of 1948 and they were not interested in doing Moscow's bidding.

As the year wore on and Wallace lost support, men such as Lee Pressman and John Abt assumed a more central role in the third party. Pressman, who had been counsel for the CIO until Philip Murray told him to either renounce Wallace or leave, was widely rumored to be a Communist, as was Abt, who like Pressman was formerly a union lawyer. Long after 1948, Pressman revealed that he had been a one-time member of the Communist Party, and he was instrumental in formulating the Progressive Party platform. In addition to Pressman and Abt (whose earlier Communist Party membership also became clear in later years), prominent members of Wallace's inner circle such as Paul Robeson and speechwriter Lewis Frank were also thought to be "fellow travelers." The influence of these men may have led the Progressives to take an even more accommodating stance toward Stalin, but unlike the Communist Party, they believed in Wallace's program, not in Stalin's.[6]

As for Wallace himself, he was nothing more and nothing less than a genuine American Populist Progressive, whose lineage stretched back to the agrarian Populism of the 1890s. Most of his supporters could claim a similar heritage, as could many other Progressive Party luminaries, such as former Governor Elmer Benson of Minnesota and Wallace's campaign manager, C.B. Baldwin. Though Wallace tolerated and later on even welcomed the support of Communists, the only person Henry Wallace answered to was Henry Wallace.

But given the political climate of 1948, the very presence of Communists in the Progressive Party gave the movement's opponents ample ammunition.

The ADA denounced Wallace, the press corps followed suit, the Democratic National Committee hired prominent ADA members like William Batt to work with the White House in defaming him, and the White House used ADA research papers in order to target the candidates. Reports prepared by ADA staffers made their way to

Clark Clifford and presidential speechwriters and to McGrath and his staff. One such report noted that while the ADA "unreservedly condemned" Wallace for his supposed collusion with communism, Wallace was such an active campaigner that it was difficult to keep track of, much less effectively rebut, what he was saying. By the end of March, the ADA estimated, Wallace had made more than twenty-five major speeches and personally addressed more than 75,000 people in addition to giving radio talks that reached hundreds of thousands of others. The ADA observed that "Wallace will have conducted the equivalent of nearly two full presidential campaigns by the time the major parties and the third party hold their conventions." Though that may have been hyperbole, Wallace did hit the campaign trail early and often, thereby putting pressure on the ADA and the White House to respond.[7]

By February, not only was the ADA galvanized against Wallace, but organized labor was responding as well. Again, the Clifford and Rowe memo had charted a course that called on Truman to solidify links to labor, and Wallace made that rapprochement easier. Phil Murray, the steelworkers' union leader who had vowed in 1946 to defeat Truman, now chose the president as a lesser evil. The American Federation of Labor (AFL) denounced Wallace as a "front, spokesman, and apologist for the Communist Party," and on behalf of the federation's 7,200,000 members, the AFL leadership voted to reject Wallace's third-party candidacy. The CIO also rejected Wallace. Organized labor and the intelligentsia represented the traditional bulwarks of left-liberalism, and without these two groups, Wallace and the PCA were in a precarious position.[8]

At the time, however, Wallace interpreted the attention he was getting as a sign that his movement was building momentum. He had avid followers and a skilled campaign manager in C.B. "Beanie" Baldwin. Baldwin, forty-six years old, was a slightly jowly, distinguished-looking Virginian who had joined Wallace's Agriculture Department in 1933. He soon became allied not just with Wallace, but also with Rexford Tugwell, the influential Columbia economist, FDR adviser, and Wallace's undersecretary of agriculture. Having been active in Roosevelt's 1944 reelection, Baldwin fell out of favor when Truman became president because of his adamant refusal to accept the confrontational policy toward the Soviet Union.

Some people saw Baldwin as a left-wing ideologue; others criticized him as a political operator who shifted ideology to suit his patrons. But within the Progressive Party, he was strongly respected, and he had Wallace's absolute trust.[9]

Baldwin and Wallace were encouraged by rumors of polls that showed the Progressives with between 10 and 15 percent of the vote come November. As the volume of newspaper articles and radio commentary mounted, Wallace may have thought that his adversaries' attention meant that he was actually becoming a threat. In mid-February, something happened that seemed to confirm that Wallace was more than a protest candidate, that he was in fact the harbinger of a new force in American politics, one that might not just defeat Truman but which might actually be for postwar politics what the Republican Party had been in the 1850s: a radical new presence on the American political landscape.

On Tuesday, February 17, a special election was held in the Twenty-fourth Congressional District in the Bronx, New York, an area packed with tenement houses and inhabited by tens of thousands of poor, working-class families. The district was controlled politically by Democratic boss Ed Flynn. Flynn chose as his candidate for the by-election Karl Propper, a middle-aged lawyer whom almost all informed local observers assumed would easily beat his opponent, Leo Isaacson of the American Labor Party. Isaacson's record consisted of years as a labor lawyer, one term in the New York State Assembly, and the dubious distinction of being considered a front man for the left-wing American Labor Party, a local party in New York that had once been part of the Fiorello La Guardia coalition. Given that the district was 35 percent Jewish, 18 percent black, with the rest made up of Irish, Italians, and Spanish-speakers, there was absolutely no chance that the Republican nominee would be a factor.

Isaacson intended to win. Henry Wallace and the PCA hoped to send a message that the third party was viable. The ALP was already supporting the Progressives, so it was simple to combine resources and work for Isaacson's election. Wallace appeared at rallies on behalf of the charismatic young labor lawyer, along with Paul Robeson and the one ALP congressman from New York, Vito Marcantonio. While Propper and Boss Flynn relied on the traditional patronage mechanisms of the political machine, Isaacson's people went door to door, handing out leaflets in English, Yiddish, and Spanish. They drove trucks around the Bronx with loudspeakers squawking messages denouncing Truman for his pallid support of Israeli independence and for the Democratic leadership's lukewarm defense of rent-control laws.

To the astonishment and dismay of the Democratic Party, Isaacson won in a landslide. He obtained 22,697 votes to Propper's 12,578 in a district where the ALP had only 16,000 registered voters. The result stunned Flynn and Mayor William O'Dwyer, and set off alarms in the White House and throughout the ADA. The election was regarded as a resounding triumph for Henry Wallace, who was pictured, arms raised in victory, with Isaacson by his side. "Beanie" Baldwin gleefully declared the outcome "a clear-cut people's repudiation of the subservient do-nothing policy of a President and an administration which have blithely handed the American Government over to Wall Street and the military."

Truman officials tried to get a handle on the situation. The FBI sent a report to the White House describing Isaacson as at best a proto-Communist and at worst "a card carrying member of the Party." The *New York Times* used the upset as a pretext to run a long article laying out Wallace's prospects in November. The piece surveyed Wallace's chances in fourteen states ranging from New York and New Jersey to Illinois, Minnesota, Indiana, and California. In both New York and California, Wallace was thought to command significant strength. In places such as Indiana and Missouri, Wallace was neither well known nor particularly popular. But the article projected that he could win as much as 20 percent of the Democratic vote in California and more than enough in New York to deny the state to the Democrats. After Isaacson's upset, no one was sure how far Wallace and the Progressives could go.[10]

Over the next four weeks, the war of words between Truman and Wallace intensified. Wallace accused the president of leading the United States toward war with Russia, and he continued to denounce the Marshall Plan. He critiqued Truman's proposal to institute Universal Military Training and called instead for universal peace. The National Wallace for President Committee placed ads in the *New York Times* stating that "since last Tuesday's smashing

Congressional election triumph by Leo Isaacson every war-maker in Washington—every monopoly minded financier in Wall Street—hates Henry Wallace even more." And then Wallace made a gaffe. Asked about his reactions to the communist coup in Czechoslovakia, Wallace declared that the affair was regrettable but that the real cause was the Truman Doctrine and American foreign policy. Instead of speaking against Soviet machinations, Wallace took the opportunity to assail Truman and Congress. That affirmed the conviction of his opponents that he was becoming a mouthpiece for communist propaganda.[11]

Truman returned Wallace's fire, as did the ADA. The ADA was deeply split over whether to endorse Truman, but at its annual convention in Philadelphia in February, the group "unreservedly condemned" Wallace and the Progressives and stated that the third-party movement would serve only to elect an isolationist and reactionary Congress and a Republican president. During an address in New York City to the Friendly Sons of St. Patrick, Truman lamented the loss of Eastern Europe to the Soviet Union and then launched into an assault on Wallace. "We must be aware of those who are devoting themselves to sowing the seeds of disunity among our people," he intoned. "We must not fall victim to the insidious propaganda that peace can be obtained solely by wanting peace. . . . I do not want and I will not accept the political support of Henry Wallace and his Communists. If joining them or permitting them to join me is the price of victory, I recommend defeat. These are days of high prices for everything, but any price for Wallace and his Communists is too much for me to pay. I'm not buying."[12]

Wallace was furious. He demanded that the four major radio networks give him time to respond to Truman's "personal and political attack on me and the millions of Americans who support our program for peace." He was granted time by the Mutual Broadcasting Company, and CBS promised to cover Wallace's April 10 address at the Chicago Stadium. Wallace then accused Truman of instituting a "reign of terror" against the Progressives, and he cited incidents where college professors had been dismissed from their jobs for announcing their allegiance to the PCA. He also complained bitterly about the paucity of airtime and the biased coverage that his campaign was receiving in the news.[13]

In 1948, radio was the most important medium in America. Tens of millions listened each night to the variety of shows offered by the networks, gathered around in living rooms and dining rooms and bars. They listened to *Amos 'n' Andy,* to *The Jack Benny Show, The Edgar Bergen Show,* to *The Lone Ranger* and *The Green Hornet* and to Milton Berle and the Answer Man, and they listened to uplifting sermons by Monsignor Fulton Sheen, and to news by Eric Sevareid and by the dean of radio journalists, Edward R. Murrow, and they listened to commentary by Lowell Thomas and especially to gossip sent out to Mister and Missus North America by Walter Winchell.

During an election year, the public listened not only to the candidates as they spoke, but also to "political spots" (which were thirty-second ads touting one man or another), and to interviews and conversations. The broadcasting companies felt that it was their duty to bring the political process to the people, and the Federal Communications Commission (FCC), another legacy of the New Deal, mandated that once a station allowed one candidate to air his views, it had to afford "equal opportunity" to all other viable candidates. That meant not just offering equal time, but offering it during the same period of the day so that the same number of people would be exposed to the different positions, voices, and agendas. But in order for a candidate to get himself heard, he couldn't rely on the FCC. In order for a party to win in November, someone had to pay for time, and that time was expensive.

In 1948, both CBS and NBC had more than 160 stations nationwide; the American Broadcasting Corporation controlled nearly 200. If a candidate wanted to purchase fifteen minutes of radio time for a national broadcast, it would cost $10,938 on NBC, $11,500 on CBS, and $6,200 on ABC. The cost could be negotiated, and the networks gave discounts if candidates committed to multiple weeks and multiple time blocks. In order to air fifteen minutes a week for a month on NBC, for example, a candidate would have to spend in the neighborhood of $35,000. Purchasing local or state radio time cost considerably less, but a month of state radio could easily run upwards of $5,000. To put those figures in perspective, an average male worker in 1948 earned between $2,500 and $4,000 a year. Sixty minutes of national radio time, therefore, was the equivalent of the combined annual salaries of eight average Americans.

For Wallace and the PCA to get their message out, they needed to reach a wide audience. Little of the national or local press coverage was favorable, so in order to counteract the negative messages that people were receiving, the Wallace campaign had to raise money to circulate pamphlets, to make buttons, to record and distribute phonograph albums of Wallace speeches, to mail out letters to Progressive Party supporters or potential supporters, to pay for a skeleton staff at branch offices throughout the country that would then supervise the legions of volunteers and students and housewives and unemployed workers, and to try somehow to purchase as much radio time at the best hours and in the best markets that the budget would allow.

The PCA may have had more than 100,000 dues-paying members, but that didn't begin to cover expenses for a national campaign. Wallace received large contributions from Anita McCormick Blaine of Chicago, the eighty-two-year-old daughter of International Harvester magnate Cyrus McCormick and one-time daughter-in-law of Senator James Blaine. The widow donated more than half a million dollars in the latter part of 1948 alone. Wallace also obtained support from Elinor Gimbel, heir to the department store fortune and organizer of the Women-for-Wallace group, and from a variety of other, smaller backers, including artists and writers such as Lillian Hellman and Norman Mailer. Even so, it was far more difficult for Wallace to raise money than it was for the major party candidates. At the Jefferson-Jackson Day speech, the Democrats managed to raise a quarter of a million dollars. At the rates the Progressives charged to attend an event, Wallace needed to make thirty or forty speeches just to match what Truman could raise in one evening.

In the age of television, the lament is that entering national politics is so costly that only the rich or those in bed with the rich can run for office. But in 1948, radio advertising was dearly expensive. In a long and bitter piece written for the *New York Times Magazine,* a former member of the Oregon legislature named Richard Neuberger discussed the financial burdens of a campaign in 1948. Called "It Costs Too Much to Run for Office," the essay observed that the amount of money it took to get elected had risen precipitously since the invention of radio. Not only did it cost $50,000 or $60,000 to run for Senate in a rural state like Oregon, but for a presidential candidate the figure was almost certainly more than $13,000,000. Though the Hatch Act prohibited individuals from giving more than $5,000 to a campaign and set a limit of $3,000,000 for spending by a committee such as the Democratic National Committee or the National Wallace for President Committee, state and independent organizations were able to circumvent most restrictions.

"Now it used to be that a man with a few dollars, a sturdy throat and principles held firmly could stump a sprawling state effectively," Neuberger commented. But by 1948, those days were gone. Neuberger quoted a former governor of Oregon, who ran for office in 1910. "I was elected with $3,000," the governor reminisced. "But today $3,000 would just about buy you half an hour on a state-wide radio hook-up. Folks once came from miles around by horse and by buckboard to attend a political rally. Now they wait for you to go into their homes by radio and newspaper advertising or direct mail. That takes a lot of money. It makes a candidate reliant on outside financing, unless he happens to be very rich."[14]

Decades later, the same criticism would be made, the only difference that "television" would be substituted for "radio." Some politicians and journalists look back at 1948 with nostalgia for a time of purer politics, nobler vision, more honest candidates less in thrall to special interests and fat cats. But American politics have almost always been characterized by money and influence, and 1948 was no exception. The cost of radio time alone made it extraordinarily hard for any candidate to run outside of the party system. The Democratic and Republican Parties controlled huge lists of donors, some formal and some informal; the national committees distributed money to their candidates, and that money gave the two parties an almost insurmountable edge over third-party candidates like Henry Wallace or Strom Thurmond. The fact that Wallace and Thurmond were ultimately crushed is less surprising than the fact that they were so visible, so present, and so much a part of the election for so much of the year. Television altered the way candidates were seen, literally and figuratively, but the medium did not make it qualitatively harder to run for office. The financial imperatives were as troubling to people observing elections in 1948 as they are to people observing elections now. What makes 1948 so exceptional is that even with those constraints, even with the insurmountable disadvantages that third-party movement like the Dixiecrats and the Progressives faced, there were still alternatives presented early in the campaign and there were still options available at the end.

As OF March 1948, Harry Truman was being opposed from within his own party, from the left and from the right and from the center. He didn't just seem vulnerable. He appeared to be on the verge of political death. The Republicans could sense the victory that had eluded them since Herbert Hoover's win in 1928. But while Truman's plight looked almost certain to be the Republicans' gain, his weakness undermined the strength of the man who had been anointed his most likely challenger. Thomas Dewey was the consensus favorite to win the Republican nomination so long as it seemed that Truman would pose a challenge. Dewey had done well against a very popular Franklin Roosevelt in 1944, and he was perceived as a good candidate. More important, he was seen as electable. But once it appeared that Truman was fatally compromised, the need for a candidate like Dewey diminished. Other presidential hopefuls within the Republican Party could now argue that since any Republican could defeat Truman and the Democrats, then the field should be thrown open. Dewey may have had the early momentum, but going into the spring of 1948, he was no longer a shoo-in for the nomination. The golden boy of the Republicans was about to face a challenge that he wasn't expecting, that he didn't want, and that he almost didn't surmount.

CHAPTER FIVE

Dewey and His Rivals

IN JANUARY 1948, Governor Thomas E. Dewey of New York announced his candidacy for president of the United States. He was the third major Republican contender to enter the race officially. Already, Senator Robert Taft of Ohio was actively campaigning, and former governor Harold Stassen of Minnesota had been out on the hustings for more than a year. Dewey's announcement capped months of speculation and assumption in the press; it also formalized what the governor and his staff had been doing for the past six months. As Dewey wrote his mother on January 20, "Dear Mater, I hope you liked the announcement last week concerning the presidential nomination. It seems we had to comment on the Oregon primaries and this was an appropriate way to do it and to get what appeared to be an inevitable statement behind us."[1]

He did not know just how pivotal the Oregon primary scheduled for May would be. As of January, he was the presumptive front-runner, and he hoped that by the time May rolled around, Oregon would be no contest. He did not know that he would be challenged by a candidate even younger than he, even more vigorous, and even more modern.

Dewey grew up in Owosso, Michigan, population 8,000, the only child of a newspaper editor and his wife. He went to the University of Michigan right after World War I and then decided not to become a professional singer as he had once planned and instead enrolled at Columbia Law School. He married Frances Eileen Hutt and became a successful New York attorney in a prominent firm, which led to his election as District Attorney. He won accolades for prosecuting the major mob bosses of the 1930s, for putting "Lucky"

Luciano in prison for running a prostitution ring, and for jailing the former head of the New York Stock Exchange on the charge of grand larceny. He ran for president in 1940 only to lose the nomination to Wendell Willkie. In 1942 he won the governorship of New York in a state that hadn't seen many Republican governors since Theodore Roosevelt. He ran for president in 1944 only to lose to Franklin Roosevelt in the general election. Now, because he gained more votes in defeat than many had thought possible, because he was reelected in New York in 1946 by a huge margin of more than half a million votes, he was running again.

Dewey also spent long hours trying to become a competent farmer on his 486-acre spread in Pawling, New York. He had campaign photos taken of his family at home, designed to show him in a more relaxed environment. The results were decidedly mixed. He was pictured wearing a three-piece suit. Next to him sat his two teenage sons in suits, and though they appeared to be playing with the dog and reading about baseball, the whole scene looked as staged as it was. Political operatives like Buffalo's Edwin Jaeckle and Republican National Committeeman Herbert Brownell Jr. loved to have Dewey chairing a meeting. Apparently, he was a skilled manager who encouraged serious discussion. Even so, the public Dewey was a man whom people respected but didn't necessarily like. He was the little man on top of the wedding cake, quipped Alice Roosevelt Longworth. Thomas Dewey, it was rumored, was a man you had to get to know really well to dislike fully.[2]

Thomas Dewey was all of this, and like any man, he was more. His children have their own memories of him, his friends others, and his wife and parents had their stories. The problem is, few of these stories made their way into the public realm. For a national politician, Dewey's private life was kept remarkably private. Americans saw him pictured at Yankee games with his children, but no one could say for sure whether he actually enjoyed baseball. People knew that Truman loved Independence, Missouri, but few people knew what made Dewey tick. He may have been a charming suitor as a young man. He may have been a kind, warm family man. He may have been a skilled party leader, and he may have assembled a talented group of advisers to manage the statehouse in Albany and to run his national campaign. But what stands out about Thomas

Dewey is none of these things. For a man who governed what was then the most populous state in the union, for a man who was nominated for president not once but twice by his party, for a man whom journalists interviewed hundreds of times and whose friends and acquaintances spoke of on the record hundreds more, Dewey remained extraordinarily opaque.

If there was a dimensional Thomas Dewey underneath the image, it was lost at the time and it is lost to history. He appeared to be an acceptable, an electable, and a competent candidate. But not then and not now did he seem totally real. That is the conundrum of Dewey, and it is one that explains both his success and his failure. Truman, Wallace, and Thurmond were more or less what they appeared to be. Dewey could be many things to many people, but in the end, it isn't entirely clear what he was to himself.

No doubt he was ambitious. He wanted to be president, and he believed that he would be. But Truman's misfortunes made it seem that any Republican could win, so it mattered less if that Republican were Dewey. In the first months of 1948, therefore, both Stassen and Taft gained momentum, while Dewey began to stall.

If anyone wanted to be president more than Dewey, it was Robert Taft. Son of former president and Chief Justice of the Supreme Court William Howard Taft, Robert Taft epitomized the conservative core of the Republican Party in the 1940s, so much so that he was known as "Mr. Republican." Indeed, it was said that if you were to create a composite of all of the Republicans, you would come up with Taft. On most major issues, he stood apart from Dewey. Isolationist where Dewey was internationalist, against the Marshall Plan, against the international economic order created at Bretton Woods in 1945, against much of what the United Nations proposed to do, Taft was also hostile to organized labor, opposed to the minimum wage, and uncomfortable with federal restrictions on the work week. He championed a legislative agenda designed to help all Americans obtain homes and health care without expanding the scope of the federal government. He was known for his razor-sharp intellect, but people found him cold and dour as a campaigner. Austere, with wireless glasses and a receding hairline, Taft was a power broker within the Republican Party, but at a cocktail party or an interview, people preferred talking to his charming wife, Martha.[3]

Taft was strong within the Republican Party, but Harold Stassen posed the greatest challenge to Dewey. Until 1948, few presidential candidates had waged an aggressive door-to-door campaign, but Stassen changed that. Because his position in the national Republican Party was tenuous, he made his personal charm and charisma into assets by taking himself and his message directly to the people. He was known as the "Boy Governor," because, at age thirty-one in 1938, he wasn't just the youngest chief executive ever to serve in the statehouse in St. Paul, Minnesota, he was also the youngest ever elected governor in any state. A big, bulky man who exuded a hardy Norwegian strength from every ounce of his six-foot, three-inch frame, Stassen guzzled coffee but didn't smoke, drank in moderation, served in the Pacific under Admiral "Bull" Halsey, and was a significant presence at the United Nations founding conference in San Francisco in 1945. He had been campaigning for president since 1946.

Running for president two years before the general election just wasn't done in the 1940s or at any time previously. Ambitious men may have wanted to be president, but it wasn't considered good form to show it and declare it, and it certainly wasn't good politics. Stassen ran too young, too early, and too hard. The press delighted in adding up the number of miles he covered in short spans of time. In February 1948, according to *Life* magazine, he traversed 6,000 miles throughout the South and West. On those campaign trips—trips that he made by plane, train, bus, and car—he shook hands vigorously, asked people what they thought, made short speeches. He raised money from thousands of small donors, and he attracted funds from big corporate sponsors, including the Pillsbury family. He gathered college students who formed "Paul Revere" brigades that went door-to-door for him. He wrote articles detailing his agenda. Up-and-coming young Minnesotans like Warren E. Burger, who would later serve as chief justice, helped run his campaign.

Stassen was an unabashed internationalist. He believed in a world society and he believed that it was America's destiny to lead it. He believed in the Marshall Plan. He also favored strong unions, tax credits for small businesses, and government housing programs. On communism he was unyielding, and his inviting smile could turn to a scowl. He hated Communists, hated Stalin, and thought that any

American who so much as winked in the direction of Marx didn't deserve to participate in the public life of the country.[4]

If Taft and Stassen weren't challenging enough, Dewey had to contend with a month of uncertainty until Dwight Eisenhower announced that he wouldn't accept the Republican nomination. Instead, the general decided to take up a new career, as president of Columbia University. But another war hero loomed in the distance, literally. Douglas MacArthur, who hadn't set foot on the United States mainland in more than a decade, let it be known from his headquarters in Tokyo that he wouldn't be averse if someone decided to put his name forward as a Republican nominee. And then there were the dark horses.

Primaries in 1948 were a way to test the electoral waters and get one's name known, but the nomination was won or lost at the national convention. One of the most significant changes provoked by television was the shift away from party bosses and nominating conventions and toward a primary system. After the violence of the Democratic National Convention in Chicago in 1968, the parties instituted radical changes. Leaders believed that television images of rioting in Lincoln Park while the delegates met caused incalculable damage to the Democrats. Before television, a raucous convention, even an angry, divisive convention, was only witnessed firsthand by the people in the hall. With television, that conflict was projected into every living room. To avoid that, the parties stripped their conventions of most of their nominating functions. No longer would candidates be picked by the state delegates and their chairpersons. Instead, candidates would win delegates in primaries and these delegates would then be bound to vote for that candidate at the convention. Today, conventions don't nominate; they coronate.

But in 1948 only a small portion of the delegates were picked by the primaries. Most of those who would choose the next candidate would be selected by the party leaders of each particular state, not by popular vote. The primaries were a way to gauge one's strength in the rough-and-tumble of direct democracy, but a candidate couldn't gain the nomination just from primaries. However, he could lose it. In prior years, some candidates hadn't entered any of the primaries, either because they were so firmly in control of the national party that most state leaders would appoint delegates who would vote

favorably or because the only chance they had was as a dark horse at
the convention. Early in 1948, Dewey was ahead, but not by nearly
enough to skip the primaries. He needed the exposure, and he needed
to convince wavering state leaders that he should be the Republican
standard-bearer come November.

That strategy carried its own risks. The Republicans, like the
Democrats, were scheduled to assemble in Philadelphia in early summer. If no clear front-runner emerged by then, it would be a wide-
open race among the state delegates and the party leaders. Already
in the early months, Republicans speculated that none of the three
main contenders would emerge from the primaries unblemished.
That would open the door to others, such as Arthur Vandenberg, the
Michigan senator who led the Republican majority in Congress on
foreign policy, or the popular Governor Earl Warren of California,
or Speaker of the House Joseph Martin of Massachusetts.

What seems so simple in retrospect was anything but in early
1948. Contrary to the Clifford-Rowe memo, Taft appeared very
much alive in early 1948. In February, the *New York Times* was
already predicting a Dewey-Taft stalemate that would result in Vandenberg's selection in Philadelphia. Back in 1946, Arthur Krock
forecast that Republican gains in Congress might reveal fault lines in
the party that had been hidden so long as the Democrats were the
majority. In the early months of 1948, those fault lines were visible
to all. Journalists and pundits assumed that Truman was dead and
that the Republican field was wide-open. And in Albany, Dewey and
his men needed to arrive at a strategy that would position the governor for victory in Philadelphia. The place to start was nearby: in
New Hampshire.[5]

After reforms in the nominating procedure in the 1970s, the
New Hampshire primary became a vastly consequential affair. Candidates with marginal chances could make a splash on the national
stage by doing well in New Hampshire, and leading contenders could
severely tarnish their chances. But in 1948, when primaries were still
only a secondary factor leading to the nomination, New Hampshire
was what one would expect New Hampshire to be: a small state
with a few delegates. Dewey wanted to use the primary in early
March to make a statement that he was the man to beat. Given that
Dewey was governor of a nearby state, it was particularly important

that he make a strong showing in New Hampshire. A win in the Granite State would lead the Massachusetts, Maine, and Connecticut delegations to favor Dewey while a poor showing might cause maverick New England Republican leaders to start reconsidering their pro-Dewey inclinations. Dewey wouldn't be a first choice for Massachusetts because the state Republicans would initially vote for a favorite-son candidate such as Joseph Martin. At the nominating convention, states often voted for their favorite sons in the first round as a show of loyalty and support. That nominee almost never won on the initial ballot, so the second and third choices actually mattered more than the first.

As the contest heated up, Dewey remained sanguine about his chances. He convened a small dinner of his inner circle at the Ten Eyck Hotel in Albany in early February. He asked Ed Jaeckle of Buffalo to be a central part of the campaign, and Jaeckle, to his later regret, agreed. He was taken with Dewey, though he had his problems with other members of the team. He thought the governor was a good political operator, but he noticed even in February that the campaign staff that included Herbert Brownell, Elliot Bell, Paul Lockwood, and John Foster Dulles on foreign policy tended to be guided by poll numbers. "Dewey was absolutely convinced," Jaeckle recalled, "that he would win because of the polls. He was a great believer in these polls, these private polls." The polls said that he was ahead, albeit tenuously, and Dewey planned to campaign like a man with a lead, like a man with something to lose.[6]

Dewey's faith in polls was unshaken by the outcome in the Bronx congressional election in February. In late February, he received a letter from Bruce Barton, who, as president of the advertising agency Batten, Barton, Durstine and Osborn, was one of several people who helped shape the candidate's public image. Barton wrote that after the surprising Isaacson victory, the campaign could "afford to throw away the Gallup polls and forget all the racial and economic groups to whom platforms try to make their appeals." Instead, the governor could now focus on one great issue, one great message that what was good for the United States was good for the world. Dewey warmly thanked Barton for the advice, but cautioned, "Don't sell Gallup down the river. He forecast the Bronx election precisely. . . . This election is not in the bag and we have a tremendous problem ahead of us to make sure that it is." Until the night of the election, Dewey believed that the polls accurately reflected voter sentiments. But though he was cool and at times complacent, he also knew that polls notwithstanding, many things could go wrong on the campaign trail.

Important though New Hampshire was, Dewey never got closer to the state than Boston. He won the primary on March 9 and earned six at-large delegates; Stassen got two. But Stassen and his volunteers took the grassroots approach while Dewey followed the path of the managed campaign: ordered, neat, professional, modern. He met with Governor Dale and got the New Hampshire Republican party behind him. He used local radio stations and paid for multiple "platters," several-minute spots featuring Dewey speaking on one issue or another. The campaign distributed booklets that told the Dewey story and paid for advertisements in local papers. Staff members circulated brochures about Dewey's stance on inflation (he was against it). They commissioned Cornell professor of agriculture and Dewey family friend Thomas Babcock to write a personal letter about Dewey the Pawling farmer that was then printed and distributed to New Hampshire farmers. The cost: just under $9,000. It was streamlined, it was expensive, and it worked.[7]

From the start, Dewey perfected the art of the managed campaign. In his view, the stakes were so high that he would leave as little as he could to chance and fate. That meant minimizing risk and avoiding sharp edges. During a campaign, people are both drawn to and repelled by strong passions. The same speech that might galvanize one group because of its conviction may alienate another. Candidates like Stassen, Wallace, and Thurmond needed all the passion, all the grassroots support, and all the luck they could obtain, manufacture, buy, or generate. Dewey understood the risks of appearing on the stump and saying the wrong thing even more than he recognized the advantages of saying the right thing. Relative to his Republican adversaries, this strategy served him superbly.

He relied on two things to place him in position to win in Philadelphia: good relations with state party leaders and a smooth publicity operation. For publicity, he turned to several New York advertising firms, including Albert Frank-Guenther Law. As outlined by the chairman of the firm, the purpose of the publicity campaign was to impress the governor "upon the public consciousness as a living personality—a man instead of a name, and a man whom people will approve." Rather than trying to make Dewey into something he was not in order to appeal to different groups, Albert Frank-Guenther Law suggested presenting him as he was. Of course, that didn't mean that the public relations campaign couldn't offset certain negative impressions that Dewey was a "cold-blooded prosecutor," but the point was to highlight preexisting strengths, not manufacture new ones. Two audiences would be targeted: "the general public which reads newspapers and magazines, listens to the radio, and forms preferences among candidates largely on the basis of the knowledge thus acquired . . . and the political group which includes the convention delegates or is influential in selecting them." The first group pressured the second, so it was especially important to craft a favorable public image, which the agency set out to do. It selected urban newspapers, farm papers, college papers, business papers, and foreign language papers and ran ads. It targeted magazines, both general interest and trade-related, and worked with editors to craft features on Dewey that would reflect the man that the campaign wanted to reflect. It organized direct mailings of leaflets and pamphlets, commissioned private research companies to conduct surveys and polls to test the results of its efforts, and coordinated the buying of airtime on national and local radio.[8]

The men around Dewey were thorough. They began planning in the fall of 1947, and they met and talked and refined their plans for months. By February, they were anticipating not just New Hampshire but the primaries in Wisconsin (April 6), Nebraska (April 13), Ohio (May 4), and Oregon (May 21). For the Wisconsin primary, the Dewey team predicted that MacArthur, who had briefly lived in Milwaukee as a teenager, would be a major factor and would probably win. Ohio was Taft country and, unless Taft won resoundingly in his home state, his chances would be significantly diminished. Stassen needed to do well in Wisconsin and Nebraska, both near Minnesota, to have any chance at building momentum. And so in February Dewey's people started mailing out booklets to the Wisconsin delegates. They prepared radio platters crafted specifically for Wisconsin about dairy issues and farm issues and German issues. They created hundreds of posters, postcards, and buttons. Another piece by Babcock was run. Their budget was $23,854.[9]

Dewey may have created the quintessential well-oiled machine, but after New Hampshire, more people voiced doubts. Truman's fortunes were sinking to new lows, and the pundits began to question whether the Republicans would need Dewey. Taft's liability had always been that he wasn't perceived as a good "vote getter," but if the Democrats were so weak, then Taft's strengths as a respected party leader could emerge more prominently. The MacArthur bandwagon seemed to be picking up some steam and, though Stassen evoked memories of the much-maligned Wendell Willkie, his aggressive, unorthodox style was beginning to win converts even in the press. According to projections by the *New York Times* in late March, the Grand Old Party was going to win in November. It seemed certain the GOP would carry at least twenty-two states with 281 electoral votes and that Henry Wallace would make it impossible for Truman to carry Illinois, Pennsylvania, New York, and New Jersey against any Republican contender.

Dewey took heed of the warning signs and applied himself to winning Wisconsin. Publicly, he and his managers stated that they fully expected MacArthur to win and that they only hoped to make a respectable showing. Privately, they hoped that Dewey would win resoundingly. He went on the road—but not door-to-door like Stassen—and gave scheduled talks to farm groups in Eau Claire and veterans in Milwaukee. He made radio addresses and briefly stopped in Appleton. But Dewey stayed in Wisconsin for only two days, while Stassen campaigned for weeks. Stassen also benefited from the support of the state Republican party. What's more, not only was Dewey flailing relative to Stassen, but MacArthur, who as an active army officer couldn't even campaign and who in any event was 7,000 miles away in Japan, was expected to win. As Dewey wrote his mother on April 4, "You must expect MacArthur to win triumphantly in Wisconsin. That is bad but it is not fatal. We think we will do better in Nebraska. . . . I hope you liked the speech Thursday night. I will do my best to make the next two acceptable but they will not be on national air."[10]

To almost everyone's surprise, Stassen carried Wisconsin and won Nebraska a week later. Dewey had campaigned more energetically in Nebraska than he ever had in his life, more in fact than he ever believed possible. He made eighteen speeches in three days. He told his mother that his campaign had "made a lot of progress. If I had not gone out I would have run very poorly I think. Maybe I will anyway. . . ." At one stop in Lincoln, he addressed a college crowd on a blustery day at the university. One woman present at the speech remembered that he was an hour late and didn't even apologize. "We all thought he was looking down his nose at us," she recalled decades later. Apparently, other Nebraska voters agreed and 79,000 of them voted for Stassen to 63,000 for Dewey. Twelve days later, a Gallup poll showed Stassen ahead of Dewey in popular opinion, with Taft hanging on—barely. Stassen closed out a magnificent month by besting Dewey in a write-in primary in Pennsylvania.[11]

For all of his preparation, for all of the test-marketing and the private polls, for all of the advance coronation by the press, Dewey now faced the prospect that the nomination would slip away. Taft had once seemed destined for the presidency, and yet that wasn't the way his career was unfolding. Dewey had seemed ready to coast into Philadelphia, but he hit a large roadblock in the shape of Harold Stassen. The Ohio primary loomed as a do-or-die test for Taft but, for Dewey, the upcoming contest in Oregon assumed a sudden urgency. Dewey was going to have to run the campaign of his life, and the real election hadn't even begun. If Stassen beat him in Oregon, then all that careful planning would be for nothing. So Dewey ventured to the other end of the country in early May. His staff set up headquarters at the Multnomah Hotel in Portland and prepared to fight Stassen the way Stassen had been fighting them. And in Washington, the struggling Harry Truman—mired in the internecine squabbles that threatened to tear his party apart, faced with plummeting approval ratings, and greeted each day in the press and on the radio with yet another premature obituary—might have felt a brief gust of spring air carrying the faint scent of hope.

CHAPTER SIX

The Cruelest Month

DEWEY'S TROUBLES might have been a comfort to Truman, but if there was a low point for him that year, it was almost certainly April. It's one thing when enemies assail you, when adversaries attack you, and when fair-weather friends desert you. But in April, the core of Truman's support—from organized labor to the state Democratic leaders to the ADA—seriously considered jettisoning a sitting president and looking for a candidate who could at least not embarrass himself come November.

The first alternative choice of the ADA was Dwight Eisenhower. Though the ADA continued to hammer away at the "Communist" Wallace, the membership was thoroughly disgusted with Truman. Hubert Humphrey, the young, energetic, and opportunistic mayor of Minneapolis, who temporarily served as the ADA's acting chairman, wrote to James Loeb in March of 1948 expressing his dissatisfaction with the president. "The subject everyone is talking about: How can we peacefully and effectively get rid of the present incumbent. There is no enthusiasm for Truman out here. Our right wing CIO and AFL boys are holding tough against the Third Party, but they keep asking me 'Who are we for?' the tacit assumption being that we certainly aren't for Truman." Humphrey conceded that Eisenhower would certainly be a winning candidate, but he thought that an even better option would be Supreme Court Justice William O. Douglas.[1]

Humphrey was hardly alone in his feelings. The entire Roosevelt clan lined up against Truman. James in California, Eleanor in New York, and sons Franklin Jr. and Elliot, all prominent in liberal Democratic politics, issued statements saying that the party ought to turn to Eisenhower. The two leading liberal journals, *The Nation* and

The New Republic, chimed in that Truman was no longer viable, and the cover of *The New Republic* on April 5 stated bluntly, "Truman Should Quit." Though it had once been edited by Henry Wallace, *The New Republic* did not suggest that Wallace would be a better alternative than Truman, only that Truman should not be the next president. In the words of editor Michael Straight, "The president of the United States is today the leader of world democracy. Truman has neither the vision nor the strength that leadership demands."[2]

By early April, the movement against Truman seemed to be growing so strong that many thought it was only a matter of weeks before he would be forced to bow out. The *New York Times* reported that Truman would not win the nomination at the convention in July. There was talk that Phil Murray of the CIO was negotiating with the leaders of the ADA to get Eisenhower to step in. The Democratic boss of Chicago, Jacob Arvey, declared for Eisenhower, claiming that Ike would be "the kind of liberal with whom we could win, both nationally and locally." Mayor William O'Dwyer of New York City and Ed Flynn of the Bronx expressed similar sentiments. Southern senators who were opposed to the Thurmond-Wright bolt urged Truman to recuse himself. Claude Pepper of Florida, one of the only southerners to support the president on civil rights, refused to say whether he was for or against Truman in the coming election.[3]

After 1948, when the South turned increasingly Republican and liberals were increasingly marginalized in national elections, it became clear that the forces aligning against Truman were only the beginning of a major political realignment. But at the time, *The Nation* observed that "Mr. Truman's present weakness, as a candidate and a president, is not the result of the rebellion but rather the cause of it."[4] At the time, then, the problem was seen as Truman, and Truman alone. The Dixiecrat rebellion, the Wallace movement, the ADA's angst—all were taken not as demonstrations of turmoil within the Democratic Party but rather as signs of Truman's ineptitude. If Truman were strong, people seemed to be saying, the natural churning that accompanies any election would be taking place either behind closed doors or would be limited to angry words. But because of Truman, the Democratic coalition was about to unravel.

Of course, it wasn't so simple, and developments in the years after showed just how fragile the Democratic Party and the New Deal coalition were in 1948. But that spring, neither Truman nor others in the party could say with certainty that the Dixiecrats and Wallace and the rumblings about Eisenhower were anything but a reflection of an ineffective president who had lost not only his popular mandate but the enthusiasm of his own party. In the words of the executive director of the California Democratic State Committee, Harold McGrath, "The dissident part of the '48 group . . . came from people who viewed things pragmatically, that Mr. Truman's cause was hopeless and therefore, something else must be found; and they, for want of a better front man, all coalesced in the delusion that General Eisenhower could be drafted to serve."[5]

Eisenhower had already informed the Republicans that he was not interested in running and that he was not even amenable to having others enter his name as a candidate. As commander of U.S. and Allied forces in Europe, he had avoided partisan statements, and his political views were amorphous. But from what little could be discerned, it seemed that he was uncomfortable with the big government that the New Deal represented, even if he was firmly behind Truman's initiatives on foreign policy. Why any Democrat in the spring of 1948 thought that Eisenhower would run as a Democrat is as hard to fathom now as it was then, and Eisenhower himself could think of only one explanation: the Democrats, Ike told some friends while golfing at Augusta in late spring, "were desperately searching around for someone to save their skins." And he had absolutely no intention of being that someone.[6]

Added to Truman's woes was a bruising debate over what to do about the conflict raging in Palestine. The British were due to withdraw their troops from the region in May, and they had already diminished their presence. In the meantime, Palestinian Arabs and the neighboring Arab states were trying to prevent Jewish settlers from securing the portion of Palestine that had been assigned to them by the United Nations in the fall of 1947. State Department officials urged Truman not to recognize the new Jewish state of Israel that would come into existence on May 14. But Truman was also being pressured by Jewish groups in New York and Illinois to take the opposite stance. Secretary of State Marshall objected that recognizing Israel would harm U.S. relations with the oil-producing

Arab states, but Jewish groups warned that if Truman didn't grant Israel official recognition, they would take their votes elsewhere come November. Throughout the spring Truman waffled and political bosses like Ed Flynn and Jacob Arvey calculated that standing by Truman would only cost them their jobs.[7]

But why was Truman so unpopular? Was he in the habit of making major gaffes? Was the economy stagnant? Was he inept? Why did so few people have confidence in his abilities as president?

In part, Truman suffered from being president during a tumultuous period. Prosperity had led to social and demographic upheavals and labor conflicts at the same time that the United States was assuming an unprecedented role in international affairs. Truman also took the blame for the Democrats' sagging fortunes. The loss of the 80th Congress to the Republicans in the midterm elections of 1946 shook the Democratic party. For the first time since before the New Deal, the Democrats didn't control the legislative branch, and they couldn't determine what legislation would pass. Truman had always been seen as a poor substitute for Roosevelt, and the loss of Congress confirmed the doubts of skeptics who had never had much faith in the one-time Missouri pol. For their part, the Republicans were angry and vindictive. They had been in the minority so long that they didn't know what to do with the power and didn't want to do anything that might help the Democrats. Republicans like Robert Taft opposed the internationalist bent of Truman's foreign policy, and much of the Republican 80th Congress was focused on curtailing Social Security and preventing its growth. The tense climate in Washington became even tenser in 1947, when Truman issued an executive order instituting a controversial loyalty program that required background checks on potential civil servants. Under the order, the FBI or another delegated agency could investigate the past associations of prospective government employees to determine if they had a propensity to be disloyal to the United States. This program both increased the investigative scope of the government and served as a baby step on a path that ultimately led to Senator Joseph McCarthy's rise to national prominence in 1950.

Yet there was one other factor: the press and the polls and the pundits. In the late 1940s, the era of modern journalism was just beginning. It would take television to transform the press into the media (just as it would take the cable revolution of the 1980s to blur the line between news, entertainment, and the tabloids). The press was just beginning to exercise its power as the "Fourth Estate." In the past, press barons and editors had placed their stamp on politics and policy. William Lloyd Garrison spread his abolitionist message before the Civil War as an editor of his influential newspaper, the *Liberator.* Horace Greeley, editor of the New York *Tribune,* was the Democratic nominee for president in 1872. In the 1890s, William Randolph Hearst and Joseph Pulitzer created a sensationalist form of news known as yellow journalism that may have been the single most important factor in driving the United States to war with Spain in 1898. During the first decades of the twentieth century, muckraking journalists like Lincoln Steffens and Ida Tarbell exposed the hypocrisy and corruption of big business.

But though journalists and editors and publishers had exerted influence, journalism had never enjoyed a position as a respected profession. In the years after World War I, however, reporters slowly eased their way into the ranks of the elite. Radio certainly helped, and prominent commentators like Walter Winchell and Lowell Thomas in the 1930s, and Edward R. Murrow during World War II, were treated with the kind of adulation that Americans would later extend to network announcers like Walter Cronkite. Winchell alone reached twenty million listeners a week, while Fulton Lewis, Martin Agronsky, H.V. Kaltenborn, and Drew Pearson all had their own loyal followings. Some of these men had been print journalists before making the leap to radio, while others such as Pearson and Winchell continued writing newspaper columns along with their radio jobs. And from the New Deal period onward, a new breed of Washington columnist emerged in the form of what we now know as the pundit. Walter Lippmann, James Reston, Marquis Childs, and Joseph and Stewart Alsop ran in the same social circles as the Washington elite. The Georgetown scene included senators, congressmen, secretaries and assistant secretaries of executive agencies, and leading journalists. It was not uncommon for Roosevelt or Truman to invite some of these journalists to quiet drinks at the White House or informal "off-the-record" meetings. Elite reporters were cultivated for their opinions and for their influence.

During a campaign, these reporters expected to play a role. The relationship between Truman and the press corps hadn't been particularly warm. By the end of the campaign, the camaraderie between Truman and the press on his train was such that it gave him a decisive edge over Dewey, but in the spring, they didn't much like the president on a human level. They thought he was inept and artless, and their coverage of the White House reflected that attitude. While much of the press corps found Truman personally agreeable, they also thought he hadn't lived up to the job that he had inherited. Some publishers, like Robert McCormick of the Chicago *Tribune,* detested Truman. Winchell questioned Truman's ability to govern. Walter Lippmann repeatedly advised Truman to withdraw his name from consideration. Others expressed similar opinions. These views were read by millions who hadn't yet formed such firm ideas. Attitudes against Truman then hardened, and that hardening was soon reflected in the polls.

Clearly, the idea that a journalist could express such opinions runs contrary to the journalistic ethos of objectivity and neutrality, and in the 1940s, most major news outlets were not explicitly linked to one party or the other. Yet men like Lippmann felt totally justified in railing against Truman and urging others to dump him. Years later, he explained his rationale at his birthday party in 1959. "If the country is to be governed with the consent of the governed," Lippmann explained, "then the governed must arrive at opinions about what their governors want them to consent to. How do they do this? They do it by hearing on the radio and reading in the newspapers what the corps of correspondents tell them is going on in Washington, and in the country at large, and in the world. Here, we correspondents perform an essential service. In some field of interest, we make it our business to find out what is going on under the surface and beyond the horizon, to infer, to deduce, to imagine, and to guess what is going on inside, what this meant yesterday and what it could mean tomorrow. In this we do what every sovereign citizen is supposed to do but has not the time or the interest to do for himself. This is our job. It is no mean calling."[8]

Not all of Lippmann's colleagues would have articulated their motives in such grand terms, but most of them shared his conviction. They believed that they served a vital purpose. They believed, though they wouldn't have used the word at the time, that they had the power and the responsibility to "mediate" the election. They believed that they should serve as a bridge between the public and the politicians, and that they should act in loco parentis for an often misinformed and uninterested electorate. In short, they didn't just believe in expressing their opinions; they were convinced that American democracy depended on the expression of their opinions.

It was difficult then and it is impossible in hindsight to gauge the effect of the columnists and the journalists on public opinion. We do not know if person X, leaning toward Truman, woke up one day, read Lippmann, and then decided to vote for Dewey. Or if person Y, supporting Wallace, read a Westbrook Pegler column on the way home from work, and changed his mind. But we can surmise that the tone of the coverage influenced the public climate and, in the spring of 1948, the public climate as measured by polls showed Truman plummeting.

In the 1940s, polling was a relatively new science. Elmo Roper, Archibald Crossley, and George Gallup promised that through rational, careful sampling, they could accurately predict how people would vote in the upcoming election. In the past few elections, Gallup had been right within four percentage points. By May 1948, Gallup reported that Truman's popularity ratings were within 4 percent of the lowest they had ever been. Only 36 percent of voters thought that he was doing a good job as president. In the meantime, other surveys were showing that Truman would lose head-to-head with Dewey in traditionally Democratic states such as Illinois and Pennsylvania. The press seized on these figures as conclusive proof that the president was no longer a reasonable choice for the Democrats, and George Gallup didn't mind one bit.

It wasn't that Gallup disliked Truman. Though Gallup had a reputation as a conservative man, his only ideology was scientific polling. Raised in Iowa, he earned a Ph.D. and taught at Drake University before moving to head the research division at the advertising behemoth Young & Rubicam in New York. He made his mark in 1936 when he criticized the much-vaunted *Literary Digest* poll, which obtained its results by mailing out postcards with questions. Gallup contended that the survey was unscientific in its sampling methods, and he correctly warned that the *Digest* poll was underestimating Roosevelt's strength in the 1936 election. The magazine went out of business after it forecast that Alfred Landon would win. By the late 1930s, Gallup's American Institute of Public Opinion covered not just U.S. elections but foreign elections as well. The group also pretested movies, surveyed radio-listening tastes to see what was popular, and studied the predilections of Book-of-the-Month Club readers.

The pollsters truly believed that the outcome of an election could be known months before it actually took place. They felt that scientific sampling would eliminate mistakes like the *Literary Digest*'s 1936 prediction. They thought that public opinion was only in flux for a short amount of time before it hardened irrevocably, and that long before the actual vote in November, the outcome was already determined. They communicated their views to a press corps that was itself consumed with predicting and pontificating and reporting, and between them, the press and the pollsters helped cultivate a climate of Democratic defeat.[9]

In spite of the beating he was taking in the polls, in the press, and within the party, Truman had loyal friends and strong supporters. He also was preoccupied in April and May with the difficult decision over what to do about Israel. In the end, influenced by his advisers Clifford and David Niles, he chose to recognize the new state, against the strenuous objections of a livid George Marshall, who threatened to resign if Truman went ahead. The president didn't appear that troubled by his political nadir. He told Arthur Krock that sitting all day in the White House left him detached and cut off. Otherwise he appeared in good spirits.[10]

On May 14, as Israel was celebrating its independence thousands of miles away, Truman addressed an enthusiastic group of 1,000 Young Democrats at the Mayflower Hotel in Washington. "I want to say to you that for the next 4 years there will be a Democrat in the White House, and you are looking at him!" He then charged the Republican 80th Congress with multiple failures on foreign policy and domestic legislation, for cutting domestic spending and dodging the mantle of world leadership. "I wish," Truman concluded, "we had a modern Isaiah or Martin Luther to lead us out of this moral despond into which we have fallen. I wish we could bring forth political leaders from you Young Democrats who could preach the gospel of welfare of the country first, and special interest never. That is what we need, my friends, and that is what we must have. . . . It is up to you!"[11]

Men like Clifford and Under Secretary of State Dean Acheson were unwavering in their commitment to the president, and the head of the Democratic National Committee, Senator McGrath, made it clear that he would sink or swim with Truman. Though he looked a bit like a retired boxer, McGrath was a suave, amiable, forty-five-year-old man who excelled at peacemaking and backroom brokering. And it was his judgment that the Democrats would either win with Truman or lose with anyone else. Given his position as chief party fundraiser and political coordinator during the election, McGrath was an ally whom Truman needed.[12]

A few days before Truman delivered his speech to the Young Democrats, the *New York Times* revised its calculations and announced that the nomination of Truman, no matter how unpopular he was in the party, was a virtual certainty.[13] He controlled enough of the party as president and through the efforts of McGrath to obtain a lock on the convention delegates. He was eager to defend his record, and he, like the rest of the country, kept a close eye on what was happening in Oregon, where the Republican primary was scheduled for late May. The outcome there could very well determine who the Republicans would nominate in late June. The Clifford memo had predicted smooth sailing for Dewey, but that had already proved overly optimistic. For a few weeks, it wasn't even clear if Dewey would survive the test posed by the Beaver State.

CHAPTER SEVEN

Dewey Versus Stassen

Dear Mater, I am sure I will overdo it in Oregon but I also am sure now, on the basis of my experience, that I can do whatever is necessary. I am going to go out and have some fun even though the papers report that Stassen is now ahead in the state." At the end of April, Thomas Dewey knew what he had to do. He was going to war, and for those last few days before he set off, he slept nine and a half hours a night, played golf, and put the last touches on his battle plan with advisers Brownell, Jaeckle, and, above all, Paul Lockwood.

The plan was simple, though it called for extensive travel and a punishing speaking schedule. To defeat Stassen, Dewey would use Stassen's methods. He would wage a saturation campaign and blanket Oregon with his name, his picture, his voice, and, as much as possible, his actual presence. He would also pick one theme and hammer away at it day after day. The theme was communism and Stassen's position on outlawing the Communist Party. "My opponent in the Oregon Primary," Dewey declared in a press release, "has urged all over the United States, from New Jersey to Oregon, that the Communist Party of America be outlawed. I am against it. I consider the proposal so dangerous, so destructive of the security, safety and freedom of our Nation, that I have accepted it as the issue of the Oregon Primary campaign." Dewey warned that if America went down the path charted by Stassen, if Americans endorsed an interpretation of the Nixon-Mundt Bill that made it illegal to be a Communist, then the United States would be no better than the totalitarian powers that it had fought against so valiantly during the war. Dewey vowed that he would oppose such a measure to his last breath, even if that meant losing his bid for the presidency.[1]

Staring into the abyss of defeat seems to have focused Dewey's mind. His letters and speeches conveyed clarity and passion, and for the first time, there was fire in his eyes and emotion in his words. He believed in something unequivocally, and he stated it unequivocally. The challenge of Stassen galvanized Dewey and made him confront the task at hand, made him ask himself just how badly he wanted to be president. Judging from how Dewey campaigned in Oregon, the answer was that he wanted it, and he would do whatever he could to vindicate his ambition.

That was how Stassen always seemed to campaign. Indefatigable, people said. Stassen didn't seem to need rest, rather he appeared to gain vigor the more he campaigned, as if he were inhaling the enthusiasm of the crowds and using it as fuel. Pumping hands, working the room, fielding questions, speech after speech, from breakfast until after dinner—that was how he had made his mark in Nebraska and Wisconsin and that was how he campaigned in Oregon and Ohio. Yet listeners were frequently left wondering what Stassen stood for. They liked watching him, with his infectious charm and direct manner, but as the editor of *The New Republic* observed, "Everyone who heard Stassen agreed with all that he said and no one knew quite what he meant."

From the start, Stassen was blessed with remarkably good press. It was difficult not to like him, and his warm charisma appealed even to the usually skeptical press corps. From daily reporters at papers such as the *New York Times* and the *Washington Post* to established columnists such as Arthur Krock, Joseph Alsop, and Cabell Phillips and to opinionated writers at journals such as *The Nation, The New Republic, Time,* and *Newsweek,* Stassen was appreciated for his invigorating style and for adding some spice to what might otherwise have been a dull primary season. They may have disagreed with his views, but they acknowledged that he had experience both as a governor and as an architect of foreign policy. Some wondered if he would be another Wendell Willkie, someone who captured the nomination but who could never actually win the election. But for journalists, whether one respected him or not, Stassen made good copy. Neither Dewey nor Taft offered as much canvas as Stassen, and reporters used what he gave them to paint a picture of high stakes in Oregon.[2]

Meanwhile, the primary fight in Ohio was also warming up. It was spring, and the scent of magnolias and crabapples was beginning to fill the air. Nice weather notwithstanding, Dewey wisely decided not to get involved in Robert Taft's home state, and while he directed his attention to Oregon, Stassen took on Taft in Ohio. Taft had reached the point where a victory in Ohio was essential. If he failed to carry his home state—and carry it convincingly—he would be forced to withdraw from the field. In the last two weeks of April, Taft and Stassen toured Ohio. Taft accused Stassen of being a covert New Dealer; on several occasions, he purposely misstated his opponent's name, and began one speech by denouncing "Stalin . . . excuse me, Stassen." Stassen, in turn, claimed that on every major issue, he was closer to the heart of the Republican Party than Taft. He accused Taft of undermining the vital efforts of respected Republicans like Arthur Vandenberg by clinging to an outmoded isolationism that placed both America and the free world in jeopardy. Though Stassen planned to contest only twenty-three of Ohio's fifty-three convention delegates, he predicted that he would win at least a dozen delegates and thereby show that Taft wasn't just out of touch with the national Republican Party but with Ohioans as well. Going into the final week, labor leaders and workers protested at several Taft appearances by handing out leaflets declaring that any man who would sponsor an "anti-labor" bill like the Taft-Hartley law shouldn't be nominated to lead the country. In spite of these warning signs, Taft boldly asserted that he would sweep the election on May 4, though he conceded that Stassen might get lucky and pick up one delegate.

Taft won, but Stassen managed to get nine delegates. The contest left both men wounded. In fact, James Reston remarked that "one more 'victory' like this would be the undoing of both candidates." Refusing to quit, Taft announced that he would fight until the convention, and Stassen proclaimed himself pleased to have wrested as many delegates as he did from the vaunted Republican leader's home state. But in private, neither was very happy with the way Ohio had gone. Columnists began to write Taft's political obituary, while Stassen was criticized for overreaching. Though the old guard of the Republican Party was lukewarm about Taft, they weren't quite ready to embrace Stassen, and Ohio was a sign that success in primaries wouldn't be sufficient to propel Stassen through the convention. As a result of Ohio, Stassen departed for Oregon needing a victory almost as much as Dewey did.[3]

On May 1, Dewey opened his Oregon campaign by condemning the notion that the Communist Party should be outlawed. Though it was clear to all listeners that Stassen was Dewey's intended target, he refrained from actually using Stassen's name. Even though Dewey was committed to a punishing speaking schedule while crisscrossing the state, he maintained an almost Olympian remove from personal politics. Neither in May against Stassen nor in the fall against Truman did Dewey stoop to attacks on character. At his worst, Dewey treated his opponents with supercilious contempt. However, he rarely impugned their integrity and almost never resorted to ad hominem assaults. He also tried to balance any attack with a positive presentation of his own platform. Having dismissed his opponent's "hysterical suggestions," he proceeded to outline a plan for hydroelectric power in the Northwest.[4]

Dewey never expressed anything resembling despondency, despair, or pessimism about his prospects. In his letters to his mother and in conversations with his advisers, he projected a calm that bordered on the glacial. This may also help explain why so many of his followers were at best lukewarm in their personal feelings for him. As a sympathetic writer in *The Nation* observed, Dewey "pursued such a cautious course and has been so clearly motivated by ambition that he stands for nothing and has no real friends." He was not without attractive qualities and he was a respectful campaigner, but he simply did not fill people with enthusiasm.[5]

In Oregon, at least, he made a stab at being accessible. Like any major candidate, he fielded a wide variety of invitations. Stanley Allyn of Tradewinds Trollers invited the governor to go on a chartered deep-sea fishing expedition in Depoe Bay. An employee of a Portland power station offered to take Dewey on a tour of the plant and then introduce him to the other 1,500 workers. In his letter, he told Dewey that it would be good for him to be seen in the factory, "to show the world that Tom Dewey is not too big to be seen with working people or shake hands with them." Of course, that indicated that some people thought Dewey was "too big" to be seen with working people. Dewey seems to have absorbed the message of these letters, and he went forth and mingled.[6]

Postwar Portland had a population of nearly half a million people. On the banks of the Willamette River, it was an active seaport for shipping everything from apples to lumber throughout the Northwest. Portland was a politically centrist city in a politically moderate state. As both Dewey and Stassen represented the moderate wing of the Republican Party, they had few substantive differences, so the contest came down to individual chemistry: whoever could most impress the most voters would win the primary.

And people throughout Oregon listened. Most may have gotten at best one actual glimpse of Dewey or Stassen, but everywhere there were billboards, photographs, posters, and leaflets. Dewey's voice filled the radio waves, and when it wasn't Dewey himself speaking, it was a local politician or business leader or housewife explaining why he or she was going to vote for the New York governor on May 21. On May 12, Mrs. Paul Skeen, past president of the PTA and the Lioness Club, did a five-minute radio spot on Dewey and women's rights. On May 13, Mrs. Charles Johns, chairman of the State Council of Republican Women, spoke for five minutes on statewide radio on the subject "How Dewey Would Wage Peace." That evening, Bobby Grayson, president of the White Rock Bottling Company of Oregon and vice president of the Multnomah County Republican Club, talked for fifteen minutes on the topic "Dewey and Small Business," while Lee Stidd, past president of the Oregon State Junior Chamber of Commerce, talked for fifteen minutes about young voters and Dewey.

Stidd was only one of the many student leaders who mobilized for Dewey. The Oregon chapter of Students-For-Dewey established three general committees and multiple subcommittees. There were fraternity and sorority committees, and telephone committees to organize phone solicitations, where it was suggested that "boys contact girls and girls contact the boys." There were speakers groups and dormitory groups and groups for signs and banners and groups to organize caravans to speaking events. The students devised their own strategies, but they also established close links with Dewey headquarters in Portland, which aided them in a variety of ways, both organizational and monetary.

As in Wisconsin, the Dewey team also targeted farmers. Though Dewey hadn't won Wisconsin, he did have some success wooing the agricultural vote. Dewey had also benefited from being able to out-spend Stassen by nearly two to one. Though he performed poorly overall in Wisconsin, his campaign managers believed that, at least in terms of the farm vote, they were on to something: Dewey's staff could present a genuine picture of him as a farmer. Granted, the Pawling farm was never his primary source of income, and portraying Dewey as a farm man above all was stretching the truth about as far as the truth could go. But the Oregon Farmers for Dewey, much like the Wisconsin Farmers for Dewey, alerted agricultural workers to the fact that Dewey was as much a farmer as Stassen and promised that he would be better than Stassen on farm issues. A number of Oregon farm leaders endorsed Dewey, and their encomiums were printed and widely distributed. Dewey himself gave speeches announcing that no one knew better than American farmers what should be done about issues such as grain storage and parity pricing, and he vowed that he would listen to what they had to say rather than presume to dictate the answers himself.

Other Oregonians weren't so pleased with Dewey. At one speech, a group of students sat in the front row with copies of *Life* magazine that featured Stassen on the cover. In Portland, Dewey offended a local politician by refusing a shot of bourbon and fetching his own scotch instead. The Anti-Vivisection Association of Oregon was particularly disturbed at the thought of Dewey as a presidential candidate. "Gov. Dewey," their mailing read, "is not genuinely in favor of animal welfare and it would be a calamity to the cause should he be elected President in November. You will recall that the Di Costanza Anti-Vivisection Bill at Albany, New York, was prevented from coming to the floor of the Legislature for a vote in March 1946, by only one man and that man was Gov. Dewey." Dewey had sponsored a bill requiring people to have their dogs inoculated against rabies, but the antivivisection forces doubted that rabies existed and believed that a Dewey presidency would result in "countless animals throughout America . . . suffering the torments of vivisection." Dewey himself was a dog owner, but pictures of him playing with the dog with his sons did not mollify the group.[7]

Dewey's stance on rabies vaccinations did not alienate significant numbers of Oregon voters, but at every turn, he confronted individuals and interest groups who placed extraordinary emphasis on their particular concerns. By themselves, none of these groups had much political power. However, winning a state primary required attending to dozens, if not hundreds, of such small groups. Fifty votes here, a hundred votes there—it all mattered in a close election.

So Dewey roamed the state, surfacing at obscure festivals and some truly bizarre events. In the end, he appeared in front of 100,000 people and covered 2,000 miles. As reported by *Time* magazine, he "hustled down the rain-swept Willamette Valley" and he toured the central Oregon lumber country. He spoke as much as ten times a day and he shook hands as avidly as his rival. He spoke so much that his voice became hoarse and craggy with laryngitis. While both Dewey and Stassen were criticized in the press for a dearth of substance, there was no shortage of coverage. At an event in Coos Bay, Dewey participated in a mock trial by a local pirates' club and then allowed his arm to be pricked so that he could sign his name in blood for the membership rolls. He donned a ten-gallon cowboy hat and was photographed wearing an Indian headdress during a ceremony in which the Warm Springs tribe gave him the ritual name "Eagle Sun." He went to factories and lumber mills and dairy farms and schools and churches. And at Grant's Pass, in a widely publicized event, he was photographed with an organization called the "Cavemen." Clad in animal pelts and animal-tooth necklaces and carrying large wooden clubs, the Cavemen escorted Dewey on a brisk trot. An Associated Press photographer captured the image of him wearing a dark suit and tie, surrounded by these smiling young men. The photo was later reprinted in Leningrad with a caption that expressed sympathy with "the downtrodden masses" in the United States. "Because of resentment toward religious feudalism," the caption continued, "a group of peasants have formed a new organization to return to the old pre-church days."

In conjunction with these events, Paul Lockwood coordinated what later generations would call an intensive "media blitz." There were radio spots and radio interviews and newspaper ads and a small army of publicity men who fanned out across the state. It was widely speculated that Dewey was spending huge amounts of money to pay for the media saturation; estimates ranged from $50,000 to three times that, and Stassen blurted out in a speech that Dewey had spent $250,000, a figure Dewey angrily denied. Still, on one day alone, the state's major newspaper, the *Oregonian,* carried five Dewey ads, and one keen political observer wryly observed that "if all of Dewey's publicity men vote for him, he'll have a sizable start right there!"

For the blitz to be most effective, Dewey had to be appealing not just in person but on radio. To ensure that, Lockwood had placed Ford Bond of New York on retainer to advise Dewey on radio strategy. Bond, who ran one of the most successful radio production companies, recommended that, during interviews, Dewey should keep his answers as brief as possible. People didn't like to hear stump speeches on the radio, he said, and they didn't like politicians to be critical of the questioners. So Bond suggested that "no matter how stupid a question may be, it may appear sensible to thousands of listeners. The listeners cannot see the questioners or know their caliber. To the listeners the questioners are 'big men,' so any hint of sarcastic tinge in a voice, no matter how infuriating the question, will be harmful because it is overemphasized by radio." Gathered around their radios at home, listeners would treat Dewey as if he were "a guest in their living room." Therefore, anything that made him unwelcome would lead to lost votes.[8]

In later elections, the micromanagement of a candidate's media image would be refined. Presidential campaigns would allot significant resources to crafting that image, and most candidates would hire consultants who would go over every gesture, tick, eye movement, and stray phrase for any potentially offensive or off-putting behavior. But in 1948, Dewey's willingness to employ consultants set him apart from someone like Stassen, who had neither the resources nor the inclination. Stassen's attitude toward such advice would have been "The hell with it!" He would win, warts and all—exuberant, careless, boorish, animated—or he would lose. Either way, he would march to the beat of his own drummer. His Paul Revere riders would drive throughout the state, his friends at Pillsbury and General Mills would spend tens of thousands of dollars, and Warren Burger would coordinate. But it was Dewey who would eventually prevail.

The outcome was in doubt until Dewey agreed to debate Stassen on a national radio broadcast on May 18. For months, Stassen had been challenging Dewey to such an encounter but, believing that as front-runner he had more to lose than to gain from such an encounter, Dewey had refused. By mid-May, the dynamics had changed. Stassen wanted the event to be broadcast nationally and held in a large auditorium or stadium with a capacity audience. Dewey would have none of that: his negotiators correctly feared that the sight of the bearish Stassen standing next to the more slightly built Dewey would put the New Yorker at an immediate disadvantage. They insisted on a studio debate with set speeches on the single issue of communism—the one substantive issue that the two men starkly disagreed about—and only a brief period for rebuttal. Stassen, perhaps too confident about his rhetorical skills, agreed to all of the conditions.

At 6:30 p.m., in a Portland radio studio packed with reporters, Stassen opened the debate with a passionate plea to outlaw the Communist Party of America. He said that he supported the Nixon-Mundt Bill, and that a legalized Communist Party gave America's enemies cover to hide "fifth columnists" and "Quislings." Before his response, Dewey took a few moments to consult with his adviser Elliot Bell. He then meticulously deconstructed Stassen's reasoning. As he had in speeches over the previous two weeks, Dewey adamantly opposed outlawing the party, and he even claimed that the Nixon-Mundt Bill, contrary to Stassen's interpretation, did not actually make it illegal to be a member. Rather, Dewey said, the bill placed restrictions and allowed the government to keep tabs on Communists. That was all that was appropriate, Dewey continued. Anything else would mean that the United States had stooped to the level of "Hitler and Stalin." Not only was it morally wrong to outlaw the party, it was strategically wrong. Outlawing the party would only serve to drive American Communists underground, which would make them even more dangerous. He articulated his position with startling clarity: "I am unalterably, wholeheartedly, and unswervingly against any scheme to write laws outlawing people because of their religious, political, social, or economic ideas." The Stassen proposal, concluded Dewey, "is thought-control, borrowed from the Japanese war leadership. It is an attempt to beat down ideas with a club. It is a surrender of everything we believe in."[9]

Dewey had taken a bold position based on conviction. He had no set of public opinion polls to guide what he said, and he even had letters urging him to approve draconian measures against Communists. Reacting to the debate, one woman wrote that Communists were like "vile skunks" who should be exterminated. But in spite of such vehement public sentiment, Dewey refused to pander. He made a strong, principled stand, and he was vindicated. Gauging ratings was a notoriously inexact science at the time, and the audience for the debate was estimated at anywhere from 40 to 80 million listeners nationwide. Stassen had sounded cool and glib, whereas Dewey had at times fumbled over his delivery. But the force of Dewey's words led almost every listener to conclude that he had won the debate. The vague platitudes that often peppered Dewey speeches were nowhere to be found during the debate, and that made the evening all the more dramatic. By the morning of May 18, commentators declared that the tide had turned against Stassen.

On May 21, they were proved right. Dewey won the primary with nearly 53 percent of the vote—111,657 to Stassen's 102,419. Oregon was the last open primary prior to the Republican convention, and Stassen would not have another opportunity to build momentum outside of the party machinery. He had had a glorious run during the primaries, but primaries alone weren't sufficient. The party bosses had never particularly warmed to Stassen, mostly because he hadn't courted them and because he didn't have seniority within the party. Throughout May, there were rumors that, had Stassen been victorious in Oregon, Taft and Dewey would unite in Philadelphia to stop him. But though Stassen had little hope of gaining the nomination, he had successfully kept Dewey from accumulating a majority of delegates. Dewey's viability was reestablished by Oregon, but once the victory had been registered, columnists and commentators turned to handicapping the convention. What they saw was an unpredictable race that might work to the advantage of a dark horse like Arthur Vandenberg or Earl Warren. For the Republicans, Arthur Krock said, it was on to Philadelphia and the "smoke-filled room." The Republican nominee would be chosen not by popular acclaim, primary votes, or radio appeal. He would be picked the way Abraham Lincoln had been picked and the way William McKinley had been picked—by party leaders gathering in hotel suites with the doors closed.

Until then, Dewey strategists plotted out their convention tactics, and Truman headed west on a "non-political" trip to revive his fortunes. Meanwhile, Henry Wallace and his running mate, Senator Glen H. Taylor, began going around the country looking for publicity and hammering both the Democrats and the Republicans for their conduct in the Cold War. The veteran Socialist leader Norman Thomas announced that he would run once more in order, he said, to stop Henry Wallace from assuming the mantle of leadership of the Left. And in the South, the cooling-off period was about to end with the revolt heating up and exploding into a full-fledged rebellion.[10]

CHAPTER EIGHT

Dixie Gets Serious

EVERY DAY, more mail arrived. From Judge A.G. Kennedy of Union, South Carolina: "Please accept my sincere thanks to you for your attitude and stance towards Truman's Civil Rights Program. . . . The Damn Yankees, Jews, Negroes, preachers, teachers and the Scalawags of the South who wish to gain favor with the Negro worshipers of the North and the Negro politicians who are putting pressure on the white people of the country to make white people out of Negroes, do not seem to realize that they will never make white people out of Negroes. . . . If the leaders of the South allow our civilization to be destroyed and a mongrel race to occupy the South it would please the South hating Negro loving people of the country." From Professor C.E. Branscomb of Richmond, Kentucky: "I am interested in the recent action in the South to re-establish the Democratic Party. I am ready to aid in the action. I shall be available to give lectures during the last part of August." From Mr. Jesse Chambers of Salisbury, North Carolina: "I am an old man reared near Valdosta, Ga., where the Negro are generally treated with respect due them. . . . My grandfather owned lots of Negroes. We had no trouble with them." And from Mrs. K.K. Cottingham: "Senator Taft must be a Jew because people who are white want the Arabs as friends and they do not want the Jews going into Palestine and pushing up and joining the Russians."

To each of these writers, Governor Thurmond's secretary sent a brief note thanking them for expressing their views and for their support. To the man who, in two pages of barely legible scrawl, endorsed the Dixiecrats and then proceeded to discuss how sinister it was that "Eisenhower" was pronounced the same in German as in English,

Thurmond's office replied, "The Governor is out of town. . . . I am sure he will appreciate your interest in this important matter and for your thoughtfulness in writing to him about it." To the man from Chicago who sent him an epic poem entitled "Jim Crow Rides at Midnight"—which began "Awake! O Dixieland, Awake! / Your White Man's glory is at stake," and which ended "And God commands the White Man's cry / The Jim Crow law shall never die!"—Thurmond's office sent a polite thank-you note. Obeying the first law of politics, Thurmond tried assiduously to not alienate potential voters, no matter how racist, absurd, or insane their letters may have seemed.[1]

The southern movement was growing, but the goal was still amorphous. Thurmond, Wright, Folsom, and others had no doubt that Truman must not be the party's nominee, but they hadn't yet decided what to do if their efforts to block Truman failed. They were steadfastly opposed to any Democratic platform on civil rights, but they hadn't yet devised a strategy for what to do if the party bosses did not in the end make concessions. Throughout April and May, the protesting Dixiecrats waged a two-tract strategy. They continued to pressure the national party and tried to recruit southern congressmen and senators to stand against Truman. At the same time, anticipating that the party would reject their position, thousands of volunteers, businessmen, local officials, and state party leaders in Arkansas, South Carolina, Alabama, and Mississippi organized to seize control of their states' Democratic Party machinery.

The machinery mattered because state party leaders determined the delegates to the national convention. Only if an overwhelming majority of southern delegates pledged not to support Truman in Philadelphia would Truman be denied the nomination. And if the Dixiecrats could stop Truman from being nominated, then there would be no need to "bolt" from the party. In fact, even the most rabid anti-Truman Dixiecrat preferred staying within the Democratic Party. Controlling the national party could substantially increase southern influence on national politics. The Democratic National Committee was a source of patronage, and it doled out money raised by the party from every corner of the country. A united bloc of anti-Truman, anti–civil rights southern delegates at Philadelphia could wrest control of the party, insert language in the national platform that reinforced Jim Crow, and humiliate the northeastern Democrats. Though their chances were slim, the payoff would be immense.

In Alabama, the state committee was bitterly divided. Split between "loyalists" such as Governor Folsom and Senators Lister Hill and John Sparkman, and States' Righters composed of state senators, former governors, and committee chairmen, the Alabama Democrats spent most of April fighting an internal war. Folsom had railed against Truman, but in the end, he decided that his interests lay with the national party. The States' Righters, however, were better equipped to marshal support at the grassroots level, and in delegate elections in April and May, they won a clear majority. As a result, Alabama's ten delegates were pledged to oppose any Democratic nominee who endorsed the civil rights plank. Boss Ed Crump of Memphis, Tennessee, who opposed Truman but didn't support a bolt, faced one of the toughest political fights of his career, and he barely managed to retain control of the state delegation. Similar battles took place in Georgia and Arkansas.[2]

In Mississippi, Governor Wright solidified his position as the most outspoken and unequivocal defender of the States' Rights position. In a radio address delivered from Natchez, whose faded antebellum mansions nestled on the Mississippi River, he called on Mississippi Democrats—the true "Jeffersonian Democrats"—to support a revolt of state leaders against the national party. That evening, newly printed States' Rights buttons were distributed at a raucous meeting of Holmes County party leaders in Lexington. The buttons featured a serious-looking Thomas Jefferson. Above his head, "States' Rights," below, "Jeffersonian Democrat." As the buttons were distributed, the group was exhorted, "Wear this with pride, from now until November." In mid-April, the Women's Committee of the anti-Truman movement announced that it would sell 75,000 buttons throughout the state in order to raise money for the cause. The Mississippi Democratic Party, firmly controlled by Wright and his allies, printed literature and distributed pamphlets and posters throughout the state. One such pamphlet was called "Know All the Facts about Truman's So-Called Civil Rights Program and What It Means to You." What it meant, the brochure explained, was a triumph for those Reconstruction "scalawags and carpetbaggers that swarmed into the South to prey upon her people when she lay bleeding and helpless at the close of the Civil War. . . . The logical and inevitable result of such policies," the pamphlet concluded, "is anarchy, not law. Political expediency, not a purpose to make better living conditions for any race, is the force behind the movement." Other literature blared, "You Have Been Betrayed," and "Truman's Civil Rights Program Is a Stab in the Back of the South." The state committee called on all Mississippi Democrats to vote for delegates who would stand up for the South in Philadelphia.[3]

Protest was only one aspect of the States' Rights movement. The sentiment against Truman and civil rights was strong, but the Dixiecrat ideology was not purely negative. Fielding Wright articulated a vision of the New South that was at times progressive, at times muddled, at times racist, and occasionally poetic. Addressing a music festival in Walthall County, he gave a long speech that was one part amateur philosophy and one part practical politics. "There seems to be in this nation of ours today so much of the attitude of Let the Government Do It, or, Let Somebody Else Do It. That type of attitude is not the American way. . . . The world needs and the United States needs to return to fundamental principles of individual initiative and individual achievement." He then spoke about the transcendent power of music to connect the listeners to the glory of God and to other people. Music, he continued, is a universal language that brings people together, and when children are taught music in schools, they learn both self-discipline and self-expression. Music soothes humans in their grief, and unites them. "Mississippi is on the march," he said as his speech rose to a crescendo. "We have a vision of even greater progress."[4]

Throughout the South, millions of people were struggling to maintain traditions while simultaneously trying to better themselves economically. The conundrum was how to square modern and traditional values. The cornerstone of those values was racial hierarchy, and it seemed to many that unless that hierarchy was maintained, the last vestiges of the "Southern way of life" would disappear. Family bonds would be weakened and communities would be fractured, and economic progress would then be meaningless. Wright spoke to both the desire to improve the lives of the white people of Mississippi and to the imperative of preserving the values that gave meaning to those lives. Racial segregation was an integral component of States' Rights, the ideological glue, but it was not the sole component.

Most people outside of the South in 1948 found the explicitness and vehemence of the racial prejudice offensive and distasteful. Most people looking back at these attitudes are appalled at the naked expressions of racism. But condemning the past does little more than offer solace in the present that "we" are more moral, more wise, more evolved. In 1948, the Democratic Party endorsed a vision of civil rights that a minority of its members rejected. As the next decades would show, that vision was the shape of the future, even for the South. In 1948, however, the future was opaque and the debate over racial politics was still very much in doubt. Would the Jim Crow vision prevail? Would a federally mandated program meant to redress discrimination be passed? And what were the non-racial consequences of federal power being used to force a white majority in the South to adopt policies that it didn't agree with?

For Strom Thurmond and Fielding Wright and the States' Rights Democrats, the answer was simple. The extension of federal power would destroy the American system of government and lead to a violation of civil rights far more egregious than the violations alleged. In the words of one spokesman for the States' Rights movement, "Our fundamental civil right is individual liberty. . . . My civil liberty, guaranteed by the Constitution, is largely a right to be let alone—a right to speak freely, to practice my religion, to choose my own friends and associates, and to earn my living in any lawful business." Whatever the injustices suffered by southern "Negroes," the federal government was not empowered to coerce southerners to change their morality. Furthermore, said others, trying to change morality by federal dictate actually made the situation for southern blacks worse. According to journalist and political figure Raymond Moley, former New Dealer turned archconservative who gave a national radio address on March 30, "Northern interference in southern problems . . . gives strength down there to those demagogs and clowns who are occasionally elected on waves of prejudice and hate. The enlightened people of the South tell us again and again that they can win if we in the North will only mind our own business."[5]

The claim that American liberty rests on the right to be free from government interference is as old as the Republic. In the second half of the twentieth century, the "freedom from" argument was supplanted by the "freedom to" argument in a series of developments that have been loosely known as the "Rights Revolution." The idea that the federal government has a responsibility to preserve and protect and even facilitate the exercise of rights is a relatively new innovation. The belief that law exists in part to help people be free stands in contrast to the more traditional notion that law exists to protect individuals from the naked exercise of governmental power. Like any substantive dispute in an open society, the argument about the proper role of government is often bitter and intractable, and it is one that is likely to continue as long as there is government. In 1948, those debates were waged openly and explicitly, and they were woven into the center of presidential politics.

In April, while Thurmond and Wright and the other governors were still trying to arrive at the best strategy, Thurmond played coy in public. Responding to a request for an interview from NBC's *Meet the Press,* Thurmond demurred in conversation with the producer Martha Rountree. In an absurd banter, Thurmond repeated more than half a dozen times that he would not make any public statement until after the "big meeting" in Jackson on May 10. Until then, he repeated that, though he was the keynote speaker, he was not an "announced candidate for president" and he was not comfortable giving any interviews about States' Rights goals. He said that he'd be happy to talk to Rountree after the meeting. Suddenly, Thurmond shifted the conversation and invited Rountree to come cover the May 10 meeting. "Come to Mississippi, Miss Rountree," he said for the third time. She replied, "We will be in touch with you then."[6]

Martha Rountree never made it to Jackson, but thousands of States' Rights Democrats did. Fielding Wright made preparations to greet and house the estimated 2,500 delegates who would represent twelve states and the District of Columbia. The presence of so many local party leaders was notable, but the absence of the southern congressional delegation was yet another signal that the States' Rights movement represented a fissure within the southern Democratic Party as well as a split within the national party. The city of Jackson was festooned with Confederate flags, and the Jackson Municipal Auditorium was set up to mimic a national party convention. Blocks of rooms were reserved at three hotels, and information booths were placed in each of the three lobbies, staffed by volunteers who handed out literature, badges, buttons, and guides to local restaurants and attractions.

On Sunday, May 9, on the eve of the conference, Wright delivered a radio address specifically directed to Mississippi "Negroes." He asked them to place their "trust in this innate, uncoerced sense of justice of the white people with whom you live." He warned that nothing but "harm and disaster can come to the members of both races if the program of civil rights is thrust upon us." He promised that as long as he remained governor, he would do everything in his power to protect the individual rights and liberties of the black people of the state. "I am your Governor just as much as I am Governor of the white citizens of Mississippi," he assured his audience. But, he concluded, let there be no mistake: no matter what any president, politician, preacher, columnist, or commentator said, "there will continue to be segregation between the races in Mississippi." And if for some reason the "Negroes" of Mississippi became "so deluded" that they chose to support Truman or the program being advanced, then, said the governor, they would "be much happier in some other state than Mississippi."[7]

On May 10, Strom Thurmond took center stage. To an excited audience of nearly 1,200 in the Municipal Auditorium, Thurmond gave a rousing speech. In his thick South Carolina drawl, he announced that while party bosses and "ward heelers" who currently controlled the national Democratic Party might succeed in nominating Harry Truman for president, they could never force the good people of the South to accept Truman. "Harry Truman has never been elected president of the United States," Thurmond said, "and he never will be." Thurmond didn't claim that every aspect of the civil rights program was morally wrong. In fact, he stated that he agreed wholeheartedly that lynching was both illegal and repugnant. But that didn't mean that federal government had a right to legislate against it. "The Federal Government," he continued, "does not have the right to deal with crimes occurring within the states." And lynching, like almost all forms of murder, was a state crime and should be dealt with by state law. As governor, Thurmond himself had aggressively pushed the conviction of those found guilty of murder by lynching, and he could point to a strong antilynching record. Yet he denounced what he saw as an unjust encroachment of federal power on the rights and privileges of the states.

During the speech, Thurmond alluded to the numerous candidates who could serve both the nation and the South, but he gave no indication that he himself was among that group. That didn't prevent the press from anointing him the likely standard-bearer of a rump convention. The national media gave extensive coverage to the meeting, and spun it as a symbol of the breakup of the Democratic Party. Most commentators concluded that any chance of healing the party breach was now impossible. The only question was what the States' Righters would do next. One rumor held that the more moderate faction of the southern Democrats would ally with the ADA and throw the nomination to Eisenhower or Justice Douglas. There was scant evidence that such an outcome was even remotely likely, but the very fact that there was speculation demonstrates the depths of the internal crisis afflicting the Democratic Party.[8]

The meeting in Jackson adjourned without any definite plans for what to do when, as seemed likely, the Democratic Party met in Philadelphia and selected Truman. The leaders of the movement did, however, engineer a resolution that they would hold a separate nominating convention in Birmingham on July 17 if the national convention adopted a platform that was inconsistent with southern views on states' rights. But in the weeks after the meeting, a mood of despondency settled over the leaders, though Thurmond himself maintained his usual equilibrium. In Charleston he donned a convict's uniform and smeared his face with paint and paraded through the streets as one of seventy men to be initiated into the Omar Temple, Nobles of the Mystic Shrine. For several hours, he stood in his striped outfit and peddled peanuts in order to raise money for a Shriner's hospital for crippled children.[9]

Throughout late May and June, States' Righters watched as the movement slowly lost steam. They had hoped in Jackson that eleven states would support the initiative against Truman. After Jackson, only four—Alabama, Mississippi, South Carolina, and Arkansas—were solidly committed to a convention bolt. The representatives from Georgia had actually walked out of the Jackson meeting, making it clear that their delegation wasn't planning to walk out of the

Philadelphia convention. In Louisiana, Governor Earl Long gave no indication that he would endorse an anti-Truman splinter group. And at a meeting of the States' Rights "steering committee" in Jackson, Ben Laney tried to find a graceful way to back down. He suggested that it was time for "a face-saving compromise in the caucus" that would unite the States' Righters with the national party in exchange for some token concessions by party chairman Senator McGrath. In return for a softened stance on civil rights, the States' Righters would remain in the Philadelphia convention hall and would not convene in Birmingham on July 17. Of course, the steering committee had its own extremists to consider, and in Mississippi, the state Democratic Party was utterly committed to bolting if Truman were nominated, regardless of whether he altered his positions. Though Wright was the leader of the Mississippi Democrats, if he had compromised, they would have charged ahead without him.[10]

If the national party leaders had had their way, not one southern state delegation would have left the fold. There would have been no meeting in Birmingham, and Strom Thurmond and Fielding Wright would never have become candidates for president. The men who controlled the national party were even prepared to let civil rights slip to the back burner to prevent that. But as adamant as some southerners were in opposing civil rights, some northerners were just as determined to advance civil rights. In July 1948, few people had heard of the young dynamic mayor of Minneapolis. After the Democratic convention, Hubert Humphrey would never again suffer from political obscurity.

CHAPTER NINE

Wallace Hits His Stride

THE EVENTUAL TRIUMPH of liberal anticommunists such as Humphrey came at the expense of Henry Wallace and his new party. Wallace, however, believed throughout the spring of 1948 that his movement was on track. Attendance at his rallies steadily increased, and only a few weeks after his bitter exchange with Truman, more than 20,000 paid to hear him speak at Chicago Stadium.

After several months of touring, the Wallace camp had further refined the art of the rally as fund-raiser. Perhaps their most important tactic was using radio commentator and ex-rabbi William Gailmor as master of ceremonies. Bald, stocky, and six feet tall, Gailmor was always neatly dressed and, in the words of *New York Times* reporter Cabell Phillips, "his voice was sharp and incisive. His delivery modulates easily from an infectious chuckle to an arrogant challenge, to shouted, impassioned invective. Twenty minutes of this usually induces a state of ecstasy in his audience." In Chicago on April 10, Gailmor played his routine to perfection, a routine designed not simply to get the crowd primed for Wallace, but to raise more money.

Gailmor asked the crowd if it was worth their while to belong to a people's party. He asked them if it was worth $250 to anyone in the room. He looked around imploringly. Then he pointed to a distant spot and an usher rushed to where he pointed. "Here we are!" Gailmor shouted. "A check for $250 from Mrs. William T. Smith." He told the crowd to give Mrs. Smith a round of applause for her generosity, and then it was back to the pitch. Who's next? He asked. Who's going to show Henry Wallace that you believe in him? Who's going to demonstrate just how important the people's party is, how much it is valued? Henry Wallace, continued Gailmor, didn't have a national committee with party bosses in every county and every city. He didn't have the advantages of the established parties. He needed money for radio time, for printing posters and pamphlets, for renting halls like Chicago Stadium. And his running mate, Senator Glen Taylor, needed money as well. If you can't afford $250, how about $100? If you can't afford $100, how about $50? And down he went, until finally he asked everyone in the audience to reach into their pockets and take out a dollar bill and place it on the tray that the ushers were passing around. At Chicago alone, Gailmor coaxed almost $20,000 out of a crowd that had already paid admission.

In a Chicago speech broadcast by CBS, Wallace lamented the "hysteria" that was being generated by the "big business–military alliance," which he claimed was running the country. This alliance wanted to suppress his message and his movement. They controlled the press and radio, and through those media, they spread stories of "mysterious submarines, the dangers of free elections in Italy, and grossly distorted reports of every international incident," all with the goal of using mass hysteria to control thought and make sure the public was so scared that no one asked questions that might lessen the profits being made by the big business–military alliance. He called for public control of military industries, saying that only when no one could profit from war would war become less profitable. Finally, he reiterated his refusal to join in the "highly emotional attacks on Communists," attacks which he believed served only to weaken civil rights and thereby strengthen the monopolists and those in government who did their bidding.[1]

This was classic populist rhetoric. The critique of monopolists and Wall Street had been made before, by William Jennings Bryan and his doomed Cross of Gold campaign in 1896, by the more marginal James Weaver in his run for the presidency in 1892, by the Wisconsin La Follettes in the first decades of the century. The same interpretation of American politics was advanced by Father Charles Coughlin in the 1930s when he condemned the New Deal as a smokescreen that allowed big business to extend its control. The suspicion that a secret big business–military alliance was wielding undue power had led Senator Harry Truman to convene a senatorial committee during the 1940s, a committee whose success helped propel Truman to the vice presidency in 1944 in lieu of Henry Wallace. The rhetoric of populism and progressivism was often extreme, yet it spoke to millions who believed that somehow, someone had robbed them of the American dream.

That was also the message of Wallace's runningmate, Glen Taylor. The forty-three-year-old senator was the ultimate political maverick, a man who had held no elected office until his surprising victory in 1944. They called him "the singing cowboy," because he'd spent several years during the Great Depression strumming a banjo as a tent-show cowboy. Three times he ran for office, and each time his most distinctive campaign gimmick was to take out his banjo, hook it up to a rickety sound truck and play hillbilly songs next to potato farms throughout Idaho. Even after he was elected to the Senate, he kept the banjo close by and, in the fall of 1947, he rode up the steps of the U.S. Capitol on a horse, waving his white ten-gallon hat to the stunned journalists who had assembled for the photo opportunity. The stunt was meant to generate attention for Taylor's "peace tour," but the press paid more attention to the horse and the hat than to Taylor's earnest calls for an end to the military buildup and a return to what he claimed was the true legacy of Franklin Roosevelt and the New Deal.

Taylor believed that his mission was to fulfill that legacy. That meant staunch support for Truman's domestic policy through 1947, but with the sharp turn in the Cold War, Taylor decided that the New Deal was being abandoned. After trying unorthodox tactics like the horse-ride up the Capitol steps, Taylor concluded that the Democratic Party was a lost cause. On February 23, 1948, in a speech broadcast by CBS, Taylor announced that he would stand with Henry Wallace. "I, no more than Roosevelt," he declared, "could remain in the party which has betrayed the principles in which I believe. . . . I am going to cast my lot with Henry Wallace in his brave and gallant fight for peace. I am convinced that Henry Wallace is the only leader capable of ending the Cold War and re-establishing even the beginnings of international goodwill." Along with Wallace and the rest of the new party, Taylor pledged to fight Taft-Hartley, Universal Military Training, the drive toward war, inflation, and racial discrimination. He promised that he would never embrace corrupt bosses like New York's Ed Flynn, Kansas City's Tom Pendergast, or Boston's Jim Curley. And in one of the more memorable lines of his speech, he explained, "I am not leaving the Democratic Party, it left me. Wall Street and the military have taken over."

Taylor was welcomed into the Wallace camp. The Progressive Party churned out mini-bios of the largely unknown senator: "Glen Taylor of Idaho rode into American life on horseback, wearing cowboy clothes, strumming a banjo and singing ballads in a very pleasant tenor voice." The Progressive Party extolled his liberal record on price controls and his years of deprivation, wandering from one job to another during the Depression, but Taylor never quite emerged from the shadow of the gimmick that got him publicity in the first place.[2]

Once the press had him pegged as a singing cowboy, they looked for other absurdities, and for the rest of the campaign, the most coverage Taylor received was for getting arrested in Birmingham. Venturing south of the Mason-Dixon line, Taylor wanted to dramatize the commitment of the new party to racial equality, for he certainly didn't entertain any serious hopes that the people of Alabama would rally behind the Wallace-Taylor ticket. Invited to speak at a black church, Taylor decided to flaunt the local Jim Crow laws and enter the church through the "Negro entrance." Taylor made sure to give the municipal authorities advance warning and the police chief of Birmingham wasn't one to pass up the bait. In fact, "Bull" Connor got a perverse thrill from locking up and roughing up anyone who challenged segregation. Taylor was promptly arrested and put in jail. He later claimed that the police had shoved him against a wire fence and that he had suffered multiple scratches. Quickly brought before the judge, Taylor was convicted of disorderly conduct, fined $50, and sentenced to 180 days in jail, which the judge suspended after lashing out at Taylor and "his publicity stunt." Editorializing on the incident, the *Shreveport Journal* sardonically observed, "Obviously, Mr. Taylor's reason for his offensive gesture was to attract Negro support of the Wallace ticket. . . . But, as he learned in Birmingham, it's different here in the South. . . . Shame on you, Senator Taylor."[3]

The bemused tone of much of the commentary hid one rather striking reality. Taylor wasn't, like Wallace, simply the leading representative of an upstart party: he was a United States senator. The impunity which with Connor had arrested Taylor is less startling than the muted reaction of Taylor's senatorial colleagues, or the lack of public outcry that one of the most powerful elected officials in the country should have been treated like a county drunk. This spoke volumes about the dwindling support for Wallace and the Progressive Party. Unless you knew better, it would have been easy to assume that Taylor was simply a buffoon or political hack. If a senator could be dismissed so utterly because he had allied himself with the Progressive Party, then Wallace, C.B. Baldwin, Elmer Benson, Rexford Tugwell, and the other party leaders should have realized that, enthusiastic crowds notwithstanding, their movement was in serious trouble.

But Wallace didn't see it that way. Like the biblical prophets that inspired him, he interpreted the intensity of the attacks on him as a sign that he was touching a chord that needed touching. He believed the rumors of a Roper poll that he might win more than ten million votes, even after pollster Elmo Roper himself went on record calling the poll a myth. Wallace donned army coveralls, grabbed a gardening spade, and planted three dozens gladiolas next to the front door of the national headquarters of the Progressive Party at 39 Park Avenue. He also prepared the tiny plot for a few corn plants. His message: the third party would thrive and grow as the year evolved just as surely as the gladiolas and the corn. And as he listened to the mounting assaults on him personally, he was more convinced than ever that the future was bright.[4]

In March, the columnist Westbrook Pegler went on the warpath against Wallace. Pegler managed to obtain a series of letters that Wallace had exchanged with Nicholas Roerich in the 1930s. Pegler had already made use of these letters in 1947 to embarrass Wallace, but he dredged them up again in the spring of 1948 now that Wallace was even more high profile. Pegler detested Wallace and relished his destruction. And if anything would destroy Wallace, it was the "Guru letters."

Roerich was an eclectic White Russian painter and mystic who attracted a small but devoted circle of followers in the 1920s. He portrayed himself as a teacher of the ancient wisdoms of Theosophy and Buddhism, and he attracted Wallace's notice in 1933 when Wallace was secretary of agriculture. The first known letter was dated March 12, 1933, when Wallace responded to Roerich's "Banner of

Peace" initiative for ending war. "Dear Guru," the letter began, "I have been thinking of you holding the casket—the sacred most precious casket. And I have thought of the New Country going forth to meet the seven stars under the sign of the three stars. And I have thought of the admonition 'Await the Stone.' " Wallace signed the letter "G" for "Galahad."

Not surprisingly, Pegler had little trouble turning these letters into a weapon against Wallace. In 1934, Wallace, with Roosevelt's full knowledge, authorized the use of Department of Agriculture funds to send Roerich on a journey to Inner Mongolia, presumably to locate a strain of drought-resistant grass. Yet Roerich spent considerable portions of the journey trying to locate the kings of the semimythical Buddhist Kingdom of Shambhala. In subsequent letters, Wallace used ever more elaborate codes, referring to Roosevelt as "the Flaming One," and to Churchill as "the Roaring Lion." In short, Wallace looked to Roerich as a spiritual master. Americans then and now tend to not trust political leaders who are engaged in nontraditional religious endeavors. Wallace was hardly alone in his curiosity about Eastern religion, but the letters were damaging nonetheless. Their appearance only added to the conviction shared by many that Wallace wasn't just wrong—he was also dangerous.[5]

Wallace himself was unfazed by the publication of the letters, and he refused to engage Pegler during press conferences. Judging from his demeanor, he actually seemed to be gaining inner strength from the increasing virulence of the external attacks. In April and May, the ADA racheted up its anti-Wallace activities. On April 28, the national chairman, Leon Henderson, sent out a letter with a pamphlet titled *Henry Wallace: The First Three Months,* which traced what it claimed was an insidious communist network underlying the new party. The report had been prepared in collaboration with the Research Division headed by William Batt, and it was favorably received by the ADA membership, and by prominent people such as James Loeb, Arthur Schlesinger, and Eleanor Roosevelt.

At a "Town Meeting" held in Charlotte, North Carolina, and broadcast by ABC radio, Taylor debated Dwight Macdonald and syndicated columnist Dorothy Thompson. Macdonald accused Wallace and Taylor of appeasement; Thompson was less kind. Never known for her subtlety, Thompson had exposed Hitler in the 1930s, and she had ridiculed Thomas Dewey in 1944. Ever ready with a devastating bon mot, she eschewed clever phrases in her evisceration of Wallace. "The Communist Party—let's tell the truth—initiated the movement for Wallace." She went on to say that nowhere had an alliance between the Communist Party and a left-leaning party not ended in total communist domination. "A Communist alliance," she asserted, "is a macabre joke. Wherever Communists and their allies triumph, the population is reduced to utter pauperism." Thompson was unusually blunt, but her stinging accusations over national radio (with Taylor present) show just how unfettered campaign rhetoric could be in 1948.

Wallace also continued to be hammered by the national press. The *Washington Post* lead article on May 2, written by Alfred Friendly, alleged that the Wallace movement was the direct result of a plot hatched in Moscow in order to foment opposition to the Marshall Plan, which had finally won passage after months of debate by the Republican 80th Congress. In her columns for the *Washington Daily News,* Eleanor Roosevelt labeled Wallace as "politically inept," and she described his Chicago speech as simplistic and distressingly reminiscent of Neville Chamberlain's appeasement policy toward Hitler. Even more damning, she stated that "the American Communists will be the nucleus of Mr. Wallace's third party."[6]

Wallace's next major initiative only solidified that impression. On May 11, he dispatched an "Open Letter to Premier Stalin." Unveiled during a speech in front of a packed Madison Square Garden—another event kicked off by an impressive Gailmor fund-raiser and songs by Paul Robeson—the letter outlined Wallace's steps to achieve "the Century of Peace." He suggested a reduction of armaments, an end to the international arms trade, the resumption of unrestricted trade between the United States and the Soviet Union, the free movement of citizens between the two countries, and the free exchange of ideas. He called for a policy of peaceful coexistence and noninterference in internal affairs of other nations. While he acknowledged the likelihood of an ongoing competition between communism and capitalism, Wallace flatly rejected the notion that such competition had to entail cold war between the United States and the USSR. "There is no American principle or public interest," he concluded, "which would have to be sacrificed to end the Cold

War and open up the Century of Peace which the Century of the Common Man demands." He spoke to thunderous applause from the Garden crowd, and ended the speech urging the immediate recognition of the new state of Israel.

The reaction to the letter was swift. Within the government, there was some question about whether Wallace had violated any law against private citizens conducting state diplomacy. In the press, the letter was treated as an incontrovertible sign of Wallace's misguided loyalties, though some newspaper reporters saw the episode as an opportunity to relate a good story. Wallace visited Detroit two days after his New York speech, and the *Detroit Free Press* advised all reporters to "stay very close to the third party candidate. Who knows," the editors wrote, "after Stalin gets that letter he may just grab the telephone and call Henry—right here in Detroit. Think of that!" Stalin didn't telephone, but he did answer Wallace's letter a week later, saying that peaceful coexistence was both possible and desirable and that negotiation along the lines established by Wallace was acceptable to the Soviet Union. The State Department quickly distanced itself from Wallace's action and Stalin's response, stating, correctly, that Wallace no longer spoke as an official representative of the American government.[7]

Throughout May and into June, Wallace was in perpetual motion. From New York to Michigan, from Illinois to California, from Oregon to Washington, he spoke at large rallies and small gatherings. He spoke in open fields, with loudspeakers set up on trucks and cars, and in high-school auditoriums, athletic field houses, and gymnasiums. In New York, he addressed the founding conference of the New York State Women for Wallace Committee and lauded the efforts of suffragettes and of women workers during World War II. In Moline, Illinois, he met with Rock Island County officials. In Detroit, he ventured onto the turf of labor leader Walter Reuther and greeted striking auto workers at the Dodge plant and at the main plant of Chrysler Motors. He told workers they were entitled to a larger share of the profits. Under heavy police escort, he then spoke in the Mirror Ballroom, sharing the stage with state senators, a few heads of the union locals, and Coleman Young, then an official in the Wayne County CIO who later became the mayor of Detroit.

He addressed a huge crowd of 30,000 at Gilmore Stadium in Los

Angeles, and the stars turned out to meet him. He shook hands with Charlie Chaplin, the aging, controversial screen actor, while Chaplin's wife Oona wrote a $1,000 check. Edward G. Robinson, looking like the hard-boiled characters he played in the movies, listened, his face drawn in a mask of consternation, as Wallace blamed monopolists for Americans' troubles. Actor Burt Lancaster and director Fritz Lang turned out as well. Earlier in the day, Wallace had met with students who then went out to petition for him at intersections. That evening, behind closed doors at the exclusive Beverly-Wilshire Hotel, the glitterati pledged $29,000 to his campaign. The next morning, he spoke in Spanish to Mexican laborers assembled in Lincoln Park. And then it was on to the Bay Area.

One rally at the Oakland Auditorium was followed by another at the fabled Cow Palace in San Francisco, where he delivered a canned version of his Madison Square Garden speech, plus an encomium to Stalin for his response. He attended a luncheon the next day at the Fairmont Hotel, and then rushed to the airport to catch a flight to San Diego for one day. Then he traveled to Seattle and down to Oregon, where Dewey and Stassen were busily campaigning. The University of Washington forbade political speakers, so the Wallace team set up a truck and platform on the edge of the campus. Students stayed on campus, across the street, while Wallace spoke from the platform. Behind him was a sign: RALLY TO DEFEAT THE NIXON-MUNDT BILL, AT HIGH SCHOOL MEMORIAL STADIUM, MAY 21, 7:30 PM. There was a brief photo opportunity, including a picture with State Treasurer Russell Fluent, who wore a necktie that read "Wallace '48."

A thousand people trundled through a dreary night to the Spokane ice arena to listen to Gailmor and Wallace. They paid one dollar to sit on folding chairs that had been placed on a mat over the skating rink. A gospel quartet opened the evening, and Wallace talked about hybrid strawberries and his great-grandfather's voting record. Then, at 11:00 p.m., he drove with his entourage to Diamond Lake and spent the night in Shaw's Lodge. In Portland, he talked for more than an hour, saying that Americans had forgotten their noble history of freedom from oppression and that now the government was doing the oppressing, domestically and internationally. He said that Americans had forgotten their history of championing the good of the many; now the few, the greedy, and the shortsighted were promoting cold war for their own petty profit.

Days later, he went to Washington, D.C., to testify for the Senate on the Nixon-Mundt bill, then to Albuquerque, New Mexico, to be interviewed by hookup for a prominent national radio broadcast with Edward R. Murrow. Murrow: "How's the weather out your way, Mr. Wallace? Crops look good?" Wallace: "Oh, it's beautiful weather and the crops are pretty fair." Murrow: "How much support are you getting from the Communists and do you welcome it?" Wallace gives a long answer, but never specifically says yes or no. Murrow: "Do you believe that American Communists are dedicated to the overthrow of our Government by violence?" Wallace diverts the subject, says that there are laws against any group advocating the violent overthrow of the U.S. government.

Attacks against Wallace continued. Eleanor Roosevelt said that Wallace was "being fooled" by Stalin. Pamphlets were issued by the White House and the ADA, including one titled *The Man on the Merry-Go-Round—Henry Wallace,* which called him "the Great Wanderer of American politics" and harped on the "dangerous men" who surrounded him.[8] Yet more signatures came in from more states, and the Progressive Party was on the ballot in almost every state. Supporters called him a savior; they told him that he must run and that he would win. They told him that he was blessed, that he carried the voice of the people. And Wallace—the mystic, the preacher—embraced what he saw and what he heard. "All of you who are within the sound of my voice tonight have been called to serve."[9]

Day in and day out, the speeches blurred and the dinners melded into one another. On a campaign, time passes so swiftly that it's almost impossible for anyone involved to notice the bigger picture. Stassen must have felt the same way Wallace did as he stared out into adoring crowds week after week, as he listened to the fulsome praise of local officials who introduced him at breakfasts, lunches, and dinners. In Oregon, Dewey knew the sensation of nonstop politicking, of meeting, greeting, and smiling. It was hard not to get swept up in the enthusiasm of the crowds. It was hard not to translate the smiling faces, the adulation and the awe, into votes. It was almost impossible not to feel that the rapt attention was for them alone, and not for their opponents.

For Wallace, whose campaign schedule was more grueling than any of the major candidates except Stassen, it was even harder to distinguish between campaign popularity and electoral strength. The men who surrounded him wanted the movement to be strong, and even the more realistic were not immune from looking for evidence to support their desires. Wallace himself was especially vulnerable. He had the weakness of a true believer in his own rhetoric. When he spoke, his voice rang with conviction, and when the crowds cheered, it only reinforced the sense of mission. Those who observed that Wallace was politically tone-deaf might have gone one step further. He heard what he wanted to hear, and he didn't want to hear that his refusal to disavow the Communist Party was drowning out everything else he was saying and coloring it, in the eyes of most Americans, a deep and alarming shade of red.

CHAPTER TEN

Truman Goes West

Harry Truman's problem was the opposite of Wallace's. If Truman believed what people in Washington were saying, he ought to have conceded in May. If he listened too closely to the reporters he met with or if he paid too much heed to the clamoring of the liberals in the ADA and the Dixiecrats in the South, he should have sent his wife, Bess, back to Independence to get their old home ready for his retirement.

Presidents have frequently complained that the White House feels like a prison. Truman was no exception. The most powerful man in the country, and arguably the most powerful man in the world, was trapped in a mansion and surrounded by staff, butlers, advisers, and Secret Service men. By 1948, the White House was undergoing significant transformations. The dual pressures of the New Deal and the Cold War had led to a sizeable increase in the number of people working for the Executive Office. Woodrow Wilson had only seven full-time aides, and on weekends, visitors could stroll up to the White House and peek inside to say hello. During the Hoover administration, the White House staff consisted of fewer than fifty people. In the early years of Truman's first term, the White House staff numbered more than two hundred.[1]

The bureaucratization of the White House had the unintended consequence of further isolating the president from the public by placing him at the center of a complex, layered "court." In 1948, it was harder than it had ever been for an ordinary person to reach the president, and that made it more difficult for the president to get a sense of what people were thinking or saying outside the corridors of the White House. Like many politicians, Truman thrived on direct contact with people, and he chafed under the restrictions that the White House placed on him. Feeling stifled and helpless as his reputation rose and fell, he looked for a way to get some air, and in early May, after consultation with his advisers, he decided to do what frustrated Americans had traditionally done: to head west.

In his memoirs, Truman reflected on the origins of the western tour. "Early in May I had an idea—perhaps the only one that the critics admitted was entirely my own. In order to circumvent the gloom and pessimism being spread by the polls and by false propaganda in the press, I decided that I would go directly to the people." Truman overstated his autonomy. For months, Clifford and others had recognized the need for Truman to get out of the White House; only the excuse had been lacking. In addition, Truman had recently begun to experiment with a new style of speech making, and his advisers felt that in order to hone that style further and to assess its efficacy as a campaign technique, he needed more practice and more exposure. Earlier in the year, the president of the University of California, Robert Gordon Sproul, had invited Truman to receive an honorary degree at Berkeley and speak at commencement. Under the pretext of accepting Sproul's invitation, Truman planned to take a two-week trip to California, by train.[2]

During several speeches in April and early May, Truman departed from the prepared text and talked extemporaneously. The change was long overdue. The president had never been a scintillating speaker, and when he read from a text, he had a tendency to sound flat and uninspiring. At the same time, he was folksy. He didn't use big words and he didn't like abstractions. He liked to tell stories and speak plainly, like the former farmer he was. The experiment went well. His speechwriters wondered how the new Truman would come across to a radio audience, and at the suggestion of several staffers, he tried the extemporaneous style again at an event for the National Conference on Family Life that was to be broadcast live on May 6. For nearly thirteen minutes, he acted as if he were in a local barbershop giving the patrons an earful of his opinions, and the audience repeatedly interrupted him with laughter and applause. It worked perfectly, and the radio audience loved hearing this relaxed, direct, and charming Truman. The president himself recognized the difference; as he noted in his private diary, "Responses from the radio audience on Family Life speech are very satisfactory. Looks like as if I am stuck for 'off-the-cuff' radio speeches. It means a lot of new work."

This different speaking style focused on Truman's strengths and allowed him to connect directly to his audience. The professional radio consultants hired by the DNC staff were at first uncomfortable with the innovation. The 1940s saw the emergence of radio image professionals such as Bruce Barton, who was a pivotal strategist for the Dewey campaign; J. Leonard Reinsch, who worked for Cox Broadcasting in the early 1940s and then was hired by Roosevelt in 1944 to help Truman refine his rapid, monotonic delivery; and Madison Avenue promoter Edward Bernays, who adopted the same approach to selling politicians that he had to selling products. These men and their agencies staged mock interviews, had candidates speak into a microphone as if they were conducting a live broadcast, and then analyzed the performance. In subsequent decades, the image industry became much more sophisticated, but already in 1948, Truman was surrounded by professionals such as Reinsch, DNC Radio Director Ken Fry, and publicity man Jack Redding, all of whom offered advice and critiques.

Truman wasn't very receptive to the image men. He didn't like being told how to speak, and he instinctively distrusted attempts to manufacture a persona. That helps explain why he took so readily to "off-the-cuff" speaking, for it allowed him to be more natural, not more packaged. At the same time, it created the sense that he was indeed natural. Radio audiences liked the staccato simplicity and the directness. As the professionals might have said, the conversational tone played well, and it had the added advantage of allowing Truman to feel liberated from the straitjacket of "expert" advisers and consultants. Henceforth, he wouldn't try to be an orator; he would be Harry Truman, man of the people.[3]

The western tour gave him an opportunity to try out his new style on a wide range of audiences. It put him in touch with the public, or at the very least with a wider range of people than he tended to encounter in Washington. It also served a more banal purpose, which Truman preferred not to dwell on. The Democratic Party was severely pressed for cash, and two weeks of presidential speeches was one of the only surefire methods to raise money.

For all of the organizational skills of the White House and the campaign staff, the trip was haphazard. Outbound stops were scheduled in advance, but few plans had been made for the return trip. Charlie Ross even considered having the president fly back from California. The sloppiness stirred up some resentment among the staff, and Eben Ayers, the assistant press secretary, sniped at Ross in his private diary, saying of the proposal to fly Truman back, "Not many people see him when he's in an airplane a mile in the air." In the end, it was decided that the whole trip would be completed by train.

The train was sixteen cars long and anchored by a specially equipped Pullman coach called the Ferdinand Magellan, in honor of the Portuguese explorer who traversed the known world. It had been used by Roosevelt, and it was every man's fantasy, with an oversized bed in a suite with a shower, a private dining room, a lounge for poker and bourbon, a kitchen, and a platform on the back for speeches. The rest of the train, which was dubbed "the Truman Special," had its own press room with typewriters, tables and chairs, dining rooms, parlor rooms, and a public address system. When the train pulled out of Union Station on the evening of June 3, it carried the president, his staff, Secret Service men, Western Union men, Signal Corps men, and nearly sixty reporters, each of whom paid $450, excluding food, for the privilege of riding on the train. These reporters were informed that Truman would make five major addresses in places such as Chicago, Omaha, and Los Angeles as well as more than forty brief speeches from the back of the train. They were told that the president intended to keep his remarks informal, friendly, and homey.

The two-week swing was called an "official, nonpolitical trip," and Truman therefore paid for his staff out of official White House funds, and not out of DNC moneys. No one in the press believed that the 8,500-mile trip was truly "nonpolitical," and the Republicans were furious at this naked use of presidential power to advance a presidential campaign. Then as now, incumbent presidents enjoy distinct advantages over challengers, and the western tour was a perfect example of how easily Truman could use the prerogatives of office to pursue his personal ambitions.[4]

He even joked about it. On the first morning, he woke up at 5:45 a.m., shortly before the train arrived in Crestline, in the heart of Republican Ohio. A crowd of 1,000 milled around the station while the high-school band struggled through the national anthem. Truman kissed babies, shook hands, smiled, and took local politicos on a tour of his train. "On this nonpartisan, bipartisan trip we are taking here," he laughingly told the townspeople, "I understand there are a lot of Democrats present too." He was just passing through, he said. "I am going down to Berkeley to get me a degree." As the newsmen wired these remarks around the country, Republicans fumed and Truman laughed.[5]

Chicago was next, where he had a frosty meeting with Chicago boss Jake Arvey and then addressed the Swedish Pioneer Centennial Association, reminiscing about Swedish settlers and denouncing communism and dictatorship in the Baltic states of Estonia, Latvia, and Lithuania. The next morning it was on to Omaha. Omaha was staunchly Republican, but Harry's old friend Ed McKim lived there. McKim, Truman, adviser Harry Vaughan, and Treasury Secretary John Snyder had for years spent a few weeks each summer together as officers in the Reserves, and McKim wanted to host Harry as a guest of the 35th Division Association. He booked a hall about fifteen miles from downtown Omaha, a Shriner's auditorium called the Ak-Sar-Ben, which, as everyone knew, was Nebraska spelled backwards. Truman proudly accepted the invitation; he had been McKim's captain in France during World War I, and he was looking forward to marching with members of his old wartime division.

But McKim must have let the occasion go to his head, because he jealously guarded the invitations to the talk. The hall could have held 10,000, but McKim never publicized the event and restricted the list to veterans of the 35th. Harry arrived, walked on stage, and stared out at barely 2,000 people in the dark. In the words of correspondent Robert Nixon, "the auditorium was as empty as Soldier's Field in Chicago at midnight with nothing going on." The press were all assembled, and they immediately spotted a good photo op. Shots of the president in a nearly empty hall made their way across the wires, and columnists gleefully interpreted the foul-up as a further sign of Truman's dwindling fortunes. But Truman didn't seem to mind, and he refused to publicly rebuke his old friend. He made some stinging criticisms of the Republican abandonment of farmers, and he happily marched with the former soldiers, clowning around and laughing.

The train made an arc north to Idaho. At a stop in Carey, in southern Idaho, Truman was scheduled to dedicate the small Willa Cotes airport. He solemnly rose to praise the brave young man who had given his life for his country. To honor him, Truman said, we are naming this airfield. Suddenly, a tearful woman burst through the front of the crowd and said, No, no, Mr. President, Willa isn't a young man, she's a girl, my daughter, and she died in a plane crash. She died during a joyride, hedgehopping. Truman had been misinformed by his press secretary, and while Charlie Ross turned various shades of crimson, the president tried to make amends for his gaffe. Once again, the press corps gleefully publicized the episode.[6]

Thankfully, that was the last major blunder, though at a platform talk in Eugene, Oregon, he did say of Stalin, "I like Old Joe! He is a decent fellow. But Joe is a prisoner of the Politburo." This was not the most acute analysis of the Soviet leader whose collectivization programs and purges had cost the lives of millions of Russians and Ukrainians and Poles and assorted others. For the mistake at the Carey airport, Truman gave Ross a tongue-lashing and then prepared for his appearances in Berkeley and Los Angeles. One hundred thousand people turned out to catch a glimpse of the president in Seattle. People were eager and animated, which was in itself a good sign, but better was yet to come.

In Spokane, the president stood near one of the wonders of New Deal engineering, the Grand Coulee Dam, and bitterly labeled the Republican 80th Congress the worst in the country's history. For two years, Truman's domestic agenda had been almost completely stymied by the 245 Republicans in the House and the 51 Republicans in the Senate. On foreign policy, there had actually been consensus, but Truman chose to attack the Republicans for their domestic shortcomings. Most Americans cared far more about the rising cost of living than they did about aid to Germany. They felt directly and personally the consequences of more expensive fruit and vegetables and homes and cars; few experienced the threat of Italian Communists or Czechoslovak coups. At the Grand Coulee Dam,

Truman conceded that the Radical Republican Congress headed by Thaddeus Stevens in 1868 may have been slightly worse. After all, that Congress tried to remove a president simply because it didn't like his politics. But Truman lambasted the current Republicans as a "do-nothing" Congress. He didn't know it at the time, but his campaign had found a theme.[7]

In retrospect, Truman's harping on the "do-nothing" 80th Congress looked calculated. It seemed planned, as if campaign managers had sat up late nights in the White House, as if speechwriters and advisers like George Elsey, David Niles, Phileo Nash, and Clark Clifford had loosened their ties and gone through packs of cigarettes in order to come up with that perfect angle. But this was not the case. The theme that would define Truman's acceptance speech at the nominating convention, that would permeate his campaign speeches all fall, the one issue that Truman would return to again and again— that theme emerged, casually, one afternoon in Spokane. After weeks of hammering at the Republicans and their congressional majority, it just gelled. The "do-nothing" Republicans would be Truman's ticket to a second term.

Robert Taft was outraged. As one of the leaders of that Congress, he felt personally libeled by Truman's attacks. Do-nothing? Taft correctly felt that the 80th Congress had achieved remarkable things, particularly in passing the labor bill that bore his name. And what Congress hadn't achieved could be squarely blamed on a president who refused to work with the Republicans on any major domestic legislation. Truman, Taft said the following evening during a radio broadcast, was a bungling, inept politician who would stop at nothing to hide his incompetence behind a smoke screen of scurrilous lies. "The President," Taft protested, "is blackguarding the Congress at every whistle stop in the country."

A whistle-stop was a town so small and insignificant that it had no regularly scheduled train service and had to signal the train by whistle if any passengers wanted to board. How would those towns and cities on Truman's route react to being referred to as whistle-stops? The publicity man for the Democratic National Committee, Jack Redding, immediately polled thirty-five communities that Truman had visited to get their responses. Most replied that they resented the term. Said the president of the Laramie, Wyoming, chamber of commerce, "Characteristically, Senator Taft is confused, this time on whistles." Said the mayor of Seattle, "Seattle is not a whistle stop, but everyone who sees her stops and whistles." Said another mayor, "Senator Taft is in very poor taste to refer to Gary as quote whistle stop unquote. 135,000 citizens of America's greatest steel city resent this slur." Taft was put in his place, but he had bequeathed to the nation a label and an idea. The original context of the expression soon faded, but the moniker stuck; ever since, Truman's has been known as the whistle-stop campaign.[8]

The early miscues in Omaha and Carey couldn't obscure the fact that, overall, the tour was proving to be a huge success. The crowds were enormous. At each place, a higher percentage of the local populace came out to hear Truman than had ever come out for any politician. Thousands trekked, drove, or hitched to meet the president. Fifty-five thousand packed the Berkeley stadium to listen as Truman laid out the foreign policy of his administration. In Los Angeles, nearly one million lined the flag-draped route between the railroad station and the Ambassador Hotel. The L.A. County Sheriff's Department provided a yellow and black honor guard, and the throng showered the president's motorcade with confetti and torn telephone books as Truman sat in his car and waved. At the Los Angeles Press Club, Dinah Shore serenaded the president with "You Made Me Love You," after which Truman looked around and grinned.

In his prepared remarks, he amended some of his accusations and acknowledged that Congress included many good men, Republican and Democrat. As a whole, however, it was awful. "The 80th Congress has said that prices would adjust themselves. Well, the prices have adjusted themselves and are adjusting themselves. They have almost gone off the graph adjusting themselves in favor of the man who controls the goods, and the consumer pays through the nose." He wanted a housing bill, a health care bill and a social security bill. He was against class legislation that privileged the few and against policies that helped those few at the expense of the many, and that was why he was so opposed to the Republican Congress. But he reminded his audience that he wasn't trying to impugn the integrity of the people's representatives. "I know the majority of the Congressmen," he said in conclusion. "As individuals they are fine people . . . but this Congress has not done very much for the benefit of the people."

Los Angeles also presented another challenge: James Roosevelt. The California party leader still hadn't reconciled himself to a Truman nomination. He didn't believe that the president could win the general election, and he watched Truman's progress through California with some concern. If the president was as popular as the turnout seemed to suggest, it was going to be difficult for Roosevelt to prevent his nomination in Philadelphia. For his part, Truman preferred to make an ally of the powerful son of FDR, and he met with him after his engagement at the Press Club. Greeting the president in a suite at the Ambassador, Roosevelt tried to cow the president with his greater size. Truman wouldn't back down. "Your father asked me to take this job," he told the younger man. "I didn't want it. . . . But your father asked me to take it and I took it." FDR, Truman continued, would "turn over in his grave" if he knew what his son was up to. "But get this straight," Truman said as he jabbed his forefinger into Roosevelt's chest, "whether you like it or not, I am going to be the next president of the United States. That will be all. Good day." And with that, Truman walked out of the room.[9]

Truman's populist rhetoric was a hit in Hollywood. In addition to Dinah Shore, Lauren Bacall, Lucille Ball, Desi Arnaz, and numerous other movie stars turned out to say hello and to give money. But Truman's words alienated many in the business community. In San Francisco, the Union League Club, across the street from the Fairmont Hotel, purposefully turned down the blinds on the side facing the president's suite. By excoriating Congress for helping the rich, Truman made it clear that he wasn't going to be the friend of the wealthy the way Taft and others seemed to be. By talking about farming and dams in the Northwest and at stops in the San Joaquin Valley, he endeared himself to farmers and agricultural laborers, but in the process, he threatened the men who controlled the estates. Hollywood may have loved him, but the business side of California considered him an enemy.[10]

The return trip was made more swiftly, though Truman stopped in his hometown on the way back. Greeted by 5,000 at Kansas City's Union Station, he was serenaded by an AFL band playing "The Missouri Waltz" and "Hail to the Chief." Then he was driven in a convertible to his house in Independence. Along the way, he smiled and waved happily at people carrying signs that read WELCOME HOME HARRY. It seemed as if the whole town had turned out to say hello, and he and Bess hosted an impromptu reception on their front lawn for about 500 friends and neighbors before heading out to Grandview to drop by his brother's farm and to visit the home of his mother, who had died the previous summer.[11]

The next day, the train sped back to Washington, D.C. It would take a few weeks before the magnitude of the trip sunk in. Truman had redefined his campaign style. He had energized his staff. He had cultivated a no-nonsense rhetoric that made it clear who he was fighting and what he was fighting for. He had shown the normally cynical press corps that he could deflect criticism more quickly than they could generate it, and that he was an indefatigable campaigner. He had sent a warning shot across the bow of Congress, and he had made a strong statement that he and no other Democrat would lead the party in the fall. James Roosevelt couldn't have gotten three million people to turn out and listen to him at stadiums and whistlestops along a nearly 9,000-mile route. In fact, no one else in the United States' political arena could have done what Truman did that spring.

Some commentators were impressed. Listening to Truman during the trip, said one reporter, was "a revelation even to the correspondents who covered Truman at the White House. A new Truman, a real Truman has emerged from the cocoon of self-consciousness. This new Truman is folksy, hearty, and humorous. He dares to come from church and use the word 'damndest' on Sunday." That side of Truman still didn't come across during major addresses, but in informal settings, he blossomed. Another reporter observed that "Truman's campaigning lexicon is based on words that American political campaigns haven't seen since frontier days: 'lie,' 'total misrepresentation,' 'suckers,' 'special interest Congress,' 'rich man's tax law.' Truman well understands that these are terms most voters will understand." Some reporters admiringly noted that the president had been tough on the voters, lecturing them about their responsibility for the current Congress and enjoining them to exercise their power by voting on election day. If they didn't, he told them, they'd have no one to blame but themselves if things didn't go the way they hoped.

Yet the verdict of most observers was that, while Truman had put on an impressive show, he was still cooked. Hurting Taft and humiliating the Republicans couldn't mask the divisions in the Democratic Party, nor could Truman obscure the fact that he had been forced to campaign the way he had because the local Democratic machinery was everywhere in collapse. The president couldn't rely on city and county bosses to get out the vote. He had to whip up enthusiasm himself, or no one would. One astute commentator even observed that by helping himself in the short term, Truman might be hurting himself down the line. Before the trip, it was thought that any Republican could triumph in November. Now, the race seemed tighter, and the Republicans would have to nominate the strongest candidate. And then Truman would definitely lose. Others acknowledged the president's skill at this new type of campaigning, but they discerned a note of desperation. Cheering masses, they said, would not necessarily translate into votes.[12]

The reactions of the press were carefully analyzed by the White House. In its post mortems, the White House staff concluded that the East Coast press were still jaded and had not treated Truman fairly. For the future, the campaign would need to do a better job cultivating the press corps. Too frequently, reporters had not been provided with sufficient background material, briefing books, schedules, and speech drafts. According to one White House memo, reporters "were left to their own devices which frequently led to mischief. . . . Efforts should be made constantly to create news items to feed back to the press cars. Recognition of a hostile press should emphasize the importance of furnishing as much constructive material as possible." As a result of the trip, the Truman campaign began to think about manipulating the press in much more systematic ways. Truman had found a public style that was both a throwback to an earlier era and uniquely his own, and the campaign had benefited from a trial run.[13]

Pouring off the train, the press corps might have taken stock and turned a critical eye to the polls that said Truman was doomed. But they didn't take the time, in part because they didn't have the time. The Republican convention was about to convene in Philadelphia, and they had only a few days before the first gavel sounded.

CHAPTER ELEVEN

The Republicans Decide

THE FIFTEEN-FOOT-LONG rubber elephant was on its knees and its ears were pinned back. Drenched during a morning thunderstorm, the elephant now lay half-supine over the hotel marquee. A deflated GOP elephant was not exactly the harbinger that Thomas E. Dewey was looking for as he and his staff set up their war room in the Bellevue-Stratford Hotel in downtown Philadelphia on June 19. Throughout that Saturday, the elephant continued to deflate until it was whisked away, patched up, vulcanized, and then replaced the following day, replete with a GOP banner draped over its sides. And there it remained for the week.

Dewey huddled with his forty-four-year-old campaign manager Herbert Brownell Jr. In the seventeen years that they had known each other, they had switched roles. In 1931, Brownell unsuccessfully ran for the New York State Assembly, and a young lawyer named Thomas Dewey had managed his campaign. In 1932, Brownell tried again and this time he won, and for the next six years, he helped craft legislation that aided District Attorney Dewey in prosecuting mob bosses for racketeering. Brownell took some of the blame for Dewey's defeat in 1944, but he had been a skilled organizer and fund-raiser as chairman of the Republican National Committee. Often described in the press as colorless and annoyingly precise, Brownell's personality meshed well with Dewey's, and he proved to be a superior campaign manager during the convention.

Dewey was also joined by foreign affairs adviser John Foster Dulles, by the dapper and austere sixty-one-year-old Nassau County boss J. Russel Sprague, and by the Buffalo political operative Edwin Jaeckle. The strategy was simple: try to generate at least 400 votes on the first ballot and, at all costs, avoid going to more than three ballots. Dewey would need 548 votes out of 1,094 delegates in order to secure the nomination, but though he had the early lead with somewhere between 300 and 400 votes, the odds were still dicey. In past conventions, early leads often evaporated, as had Dewey's in 1940 when his position during the first ballot steadily eroded until Wendell Willkie won on the sixth ballot. The more ballots, the more likely it would be that neither Dewey nor Taft, the other front-runner, would be selected. History dictated that when the convention could not agree on the early leaders, dark-horse candidates emerged. That was how James Garfield had been nominated in 1880 after thirty-six ballots, and how Warren G. Harding had been chosen in Chicago in 1920 after ten ballots. Observers predicted that with each passing ballot, men like Arthur Vandenberg, Earl Warren, and maybe even Harold Stassen would rise at Dewey's expense. In fact, several handicappers believed that the third ballot would be the make-or-break point for Dewey.[1]

The fourteen primaries had given Stassen a chance to shine, Dewey a chance to campaign actively, and Taft a chance to alienate more people. But the primaries didn't select the nominee; the convention did. The public didn't pick who would represent the Democrats or the Republicans; the parties did. In 1948, the people may have selected a president, but the party bosses established the menu of options. The United States was a fully functioning democracy, monitored and maintained by an exclusive club of politicians and businessmen. Other than election day itself, the nominating convention was the most important moment of a presidential election year.

The convention had a schedule of a keynote address and other speeches, platform committees and platform adoption, prayers and pageants and roll calls, nominating speeches, and state-by-state voting. But the real business of the convention didn't take place on the floor of the Municipal Auditorium. It occurred in hotel suites, on the telephone, in corridors off the main hall, and during heated discussions between leaders of the various state delegations and representatives of the candidates. It happened at odd hours, in a twilight zone of loosened ties and whiskey. Preparation was everything. Knowing the delegates—their preferences, their divisions, their rivalries—that was essential. Knowing the factions—who hated whom,

who craved what, who was loyal, and who was ready to betray—
that was the key to victory. And on all of these counts, Dewey and
the "Triumvirate" of Brownell, Sprague, and Jaeckle were by far the
most skilled.

The reforms instituted after 1968 were designed not just to minimize conflict during the era of televised conventions but also to
democratize the nominating process. By the 1970s, the idea of a
thousand people, mostly men, gathered together to determine one of
the two options that the American people would have for president
seemed to violate the spirit of democracy. In 1948, however, the consensus was that unmediated democracy was far too risky, and that
the best way to select the man who might be president was to leave
the choice to the professionals. The 1,094 delegates who assembled
in Philadelphia for the Republican convention were composed of
governors and members of Congress, state and national party officials, party workers, and various others who had been appointed as
a reward for work done. Though many of these delegates were
"pledged" to one candidate or another, that pledge was negotiable.
State delegations were often committed to a favorite son candidate
for the first ballot. For instance, in 1948, the Pennsylvania delegation was pledged to Senator Edward Martin. By the second day of
the convention, however, Brownell had negotiated with Martin, and
Martin agreed to release his delegates to Dewey. Delegates were bar-
gaining chips, and operatives such as Brownell spent most of the
conventions trying to collect the 548 chips that their candidate
needed to win.

Before the convention began, the Dewey team spent weeks in
preparation. They printed a glossy pamphlet called *The Philadelphia
Story* that touted Dewey's record and detailed the rationale for his
selection as the party's candidate. They printed 10,000 copies of a
special tabloid with pictures of Dewey and his family. They published
5,000 copies of a "Dewey sketchbook" with portraits by famous
artists. They reprinted Dewey's Oregon speeches on communism,
and they printed special invitations to the Dewey headquarters.
They conceived of the headquarters as a multimedia theme park
designed to seduce delegates. They had 5,000 balloons made with
Dewey's face on them; they spent $650 to commission 300 Dewey
neckties; they planned to distribute thousands of buttons and fans

and cigarette lighters and banners.[2] Brownell arrived with note cards on every single delegate. On these cards were details about the delegates' political positions, their business interests, family life, favorite movies, and whatever information could be used. Vote for Tom Dewey, Brownell might say to one, and we'll help you with that road you want to build through your county. Throw your state delegation to Dewey, he might say to one of the power brokers, and we'll offer you a cabinet post once he wins the general election in November. Select Dewey, and we'll have Walter Annenberg, the multimillionaire publisher, give your favorite charity a hefty donation. And so it went.[3]

There was also an elaborate game of chicken. Different camps put out rumors to different newsmen. As the front-runner, Dewey needed to maintain his position in the lead; no contender who had lost votes between the first ballot and the second had ever won the nomination. Taft and Stassen had to work to make sure that their delegates remained firm even if the initial ballots broke in Dewey's favor. Given that the balloting wouldn't occur until four days into the convention, each day consisted of furtive meetings and public announcements and constant gossip. Taft, for instance, announced on Sunday, June 20, the day before the convention opened, that he was teaming up with Stassen to stop Dewey's nomination. The Chicago publisher Robert McCormick also met with Stassen and then circulated the news that he personally would work for Dewey's defeat. McCormick alluded to various state delegations whose support for Dewey, he said, was wavering. Brownell countered with daily news conferences, hinting at defections from Taft and discussions with Stassen supporters, who, he claimed, would shortly declare that they were switching sides. And some then did, and that sent ripples through the hall and into the lobby and across town to the Bellevue-Stratford and other hotels.

For the previous two decades, convention halls had been lit to facilitate the creation of newsreels. These reels would then be shown at movie halls throughout the country, serving as visual publicity for the party and the candidate. But for this convention, the hall had been renovated with new lighting that would allow for cameras of a different sort. Newsreels required high-powered carbon lighting, but television needed low-powered fluorescent lamps. Thousands of dollars were spent to rewire the hall to allow for both types of lighting. The result was a brilliantly lit convention floor on which delegates were warned to wear sunglasses against the glare.

"Meet your next president on RCA Victor," blared an ad in newspapers and magazines throughout the Northeast. "For a real Eye Witness view of the Conventions, see and hear the candidates, the parades, the action on RCA Victor Eye Witness television!" All for only $325 plus an Owner's Contract fee of $55. The most polished television coverage was produced by a joint venture between *Life* magazine and NBC, but even that broadcast was fairly primitive. The five cameras caught much of the action on the floor, but the images were fuzzy, and the focus was rarely sharp. Even worse, television had a way of transforming people's appearances. "Good looking women turned into witches and dapper men became unshaven bums," reported *Time*. Makeup artists were called in by the various managers, and people soon discovered that unless they applied heavy makeup, television was going to make them look bad.

Television was a factor in Philadelphia's selection as host city not just for the Republicans, but for the Democrats and Progressives as well. Philadelphia was in the middle of the coaxial transmission belt, and from there, almost all of the 500,000 television sets in the eighteen cities stretching from Richmond to Boston could be reached. Four networks—the American, National, and Columbia Broadcasting Systems and DuMont—and a smattering of local stations pooled resources in order to pay for round-the-clock coverage, lighting, five cameras, and the control room. The parties sensed that in the future, television could alter the way conventions were staged. Alf Landon, party elder and one-time nominee, observed that widespread use of radio during the campaign of 1928 had trimmed the length of convention speeches by two-thirds, and he looked for television to have a similar effect. Others wondered whether television would penalize serious but unphotogenic candidates and reward good actors who knew when to smile and when to look serious. In 1948, it was too early to tell, but these forecasts have since proved eerily prescient.

Looking back, we can see 1948 as the end of one political era and the beginning of another. It was the end of a particular type of backroom politics, the end of the hidden convention. Even before the reforms of the late 1960s, 1952 was the last time either the

Republican or the Democratic convention went to more than one ballot. In 1948, television was a novelty. The producers and anchormen and directors and cameramen who worked the convention floor that year went about their jobs with the same frantic, seat-of-the-pants intensity that has characterized television news ever since, but the public who watched didn't respond much differently to television in 1948 than they did to radio or newsreels. Perhaps the medium was simply too new for people to assimilate it fully. Perhaps the fact that only a small percentage of the populace watched diluted the effect. When asked about how they felt about television, people expressed delight and amazement, but the actual coverage was rarely exciting or "mediated." Watching the conventions in 1948 was much like watching C-SPAN coverage of debates in Congress in the 1990s: occasionally interesting and very often tedious. So little of substance actually took place out in the open that the coverage consisted mostly of endless speeches, prayers, marching bands, campaign songs, and a few hours of genuine drama as the public balloting took place on Thursday, June 24. The networks were so busy with basic logistics that they had little energy to think about making the conventions an interesting show. Aside from the studio interviews in Room 22, the most complicated aspect of the convention coverage was shot selection. The producer sat in a dark room in front of all five camera pictures and made snap decisions about which to air when, whose reactions to broadcast, when to show a floor-wide shot, and when to focus on the speaker. Other than that, the conventions were not mediated by television.

That would change dramatically in the 1950s and 1960s. By then, people had developed a relationship to the images on the screens in their homes, and network news established protocols that would serve their ratings and get more viewers. A symbiotic relationship evolved between the networks and the party managers. Networks wanted drama and personalities, and they wanted to give more play to news anchors and analysts like Walter Cronkite, who would act as intermediaries between the viewing audience and the parties and guide people through the conventions. Party leaders wanted publicity—free publicity—for the candidates and for their issues. The conventions became transparent, overproduced, and prepackaged. Speeches were shortened, just as Alf Landon predicted, and issues were simplified. The purpose of the convention ceased to be nomination. Instead, it became a public spectacle for mass consumption. The background politicking continued, but at a far less intense pitch.[4]

But back in 1948, commentators noted the presence of television, and delegates took advantage of the overflow rooms with television screens. When the main hall became too hot, they were able for the first time to retire to their hotel rooms and follow the proceedings on TV while sitting back and sipping a cool drink. Dewey, who appreciated the potential importance of television, instructed his managers not to let themselves be caught on camera negotiating with rival camps. He was concerned that pictures of Brownell or Bell or Jaeckle huddled with a senator or state delegate might make the Dewey campaign look suspicious to television viewers who did not know about the jockeying that normally took place on the convention floor.[5] But these concerns were not all-consuming, and for the most part, the convention continued much as conventions had for the previous decades. Some sensed the coming revolution, but most of the delegates and candidates went about their business unaffected and unconcerned by those five innocuous cameras on the convention floor.

One other change noted by the commentators at the convention was the presence of more women. There were 113 female delegates out of the 1,094. Sam Koenig of New York's Sixth District was believed to be the most veteran of all the delegates, having attended eleven previous conventions. In 1900, he remembered, the Republican convention that renominated William McKinley was also held in Philadelphia, but the delegates were all men. The reporter who interviewed Koenig said that, in 1900, "A man could air his purple profanity in thicker cigar smoke and liquor reek, without fear of offending." Koenig replied, "They've limited our stronger language a bit." To the male reporters, women seemed to be everywhere, in the lobbies, on the streets, in the bars, and in various aspirants' headquarters. In Stassen's headquarters, women passed out iced tea with lemon accompanied by crackers and Wisconsin cheese. During the first few days, Stassen volunteers trundled through the lobby carrying a rowboat and a comely woman who held up a sign that read MAN THE OARS, RIDE THE CREST, HAROLD STASSEN, HE'S THE BEST. At

Dewey headquarters in the Bellevue-Stratford, women redecorated the grand ballroom and offered handouts of nylons, face cream, emery boards, Lifesavers, chewing gum, Coca-Cola, and silver polish to get women to visit the exhibits touting the campaign. Mrs. Dewey held a reception for 4,000 guests, while Mrs. Taft made the rounds giving interviews. *New York Times* reporter Meyer Berger announced that as a result of the feminine touch, "the smoke-filled room had surrendered to the Coke-filled room."[6] As it turned out, the convention was far less "feminized" than the male delegates had feared, though a number of women played prominent roles. Mrs. Dewey met with reporters and refused to discuss any political issues; instead she talked about her two sons and their military academy in Albany. The ex–Republican congresswoman Clare Booth Luce gave a stirring speech, announced that Harry Truman was a "gone goose," and acted as a behind-the-scenes power broker.

Finding a room was another convention concern. The city's hotels were filled to capacity, and delegates were bused in from as far away as Trenton, Atlantic City, and Wilmington. Some of the participants stayed in private homes, and others doubled and tripled up in single rooms. Sleep was hardly a priority, as the convention was one vast, constant party. Each headquarters had its own diversions, and music and alcohol were omnipresent. Souvenir peddlers roamed the streets selling buttons, photographs, dolls, and banners. As many as 200,000 tourists and gawkers milled around the various sites, flirting, laughing, dancing, talking. Near the Taft headquarters at the Benjamin Franklin Hotel, a baby elephant named Little Eva, imported from India, paraded back and forth. And everywhere, bands played the convention song, "Date in '48."[7]

Working from his suite at the Benjamin Franklin Hotel, Robert Alphonso Taft believed that he had Dewey stopped. Stassen was working with Taft, Colonel McCormick was rounding up delegates, and Vandenberg was keeping his own counsel. Governor James Duff of Pennsylvania hated Dewey, and the Georgia delegation was in dispute. The platform committee headed by Senator Henry Cabot Lodge Jr. of Massachusetts was divided, and Governor Earl Warren of California made it clear that he was going to fight for the nomination and that he wouldn't accept or even consider a vice presidential spot. Throughout the hall, the mood was jubilant. The delegates were convinced that regardless of whom they nominated, their man would win in November, and they expressed elation at the number of viable options.

The next day, Tuesday, brought the stunning announcement by Martin of Pennsylvania: he was releasing his votes to Dewey. Duff, Taft, and Stassen were all caught off guard. Hearing of Martin's decision, New Jersey governor Alfred Driscoll, a Vandenberg supporter, decided to switch sides, and one veteran handicapper opined, "There goes the ball game." It appeared that a Dewey avalanche might be beginning. Dewey held a four-pronged press conference, with radio men and reporters and newsreel cameras and television lenses fixed on him. "How do you feel, Governor?" In his baritone, Dewey replied, "I feel swell," and then told the conclave about the state delegations that had been calling to inform Herb Brownell that they would vote for Dewey on Thursday.[8]

Sensing that the convention might be slipping permanently out of their grasp, the anti-Dewey forces caucused on Tuesday and Wednesday. Taft, Stassen, McCormick, Duff, Governor Kim Sigler of Michigan, and Earl Warren's representatives tried to stanch the flow of defections to Dewey. Meanwhile, Vandenberg scored a victory in the platform committee, a victory that was at least as important to him as securing the nomination: as a result of his efforts, and of Henry Cabot Lodge's support, the Republican platform did not kowtow to the isolationist wing of the party represented by Taft. Instead, the platform bound the GOP to an internationalist position on foreign policy and guaranteed that the general election would be fought almost entirely on domestic issues. The platform committed the party to support the European Recovery Program and the United Nations, and it affirmed the principle of collective security. It also urged continued friendship with nationalist China, and called on the government to assist Israel. Not only was the platform a victory for Vandenberg and Dewey; it also marked yet another triumph for the emerging bipartisan Cold War consensus.

On domestic issues, the platform was filled with vague promises and vapid language. It called for the reduction of inflation and of the public debt, for fiscal prudence and conservatism, for "aggressive antimonopoly" action to help small businesses, for lower taxes, good labor relations, support for veterans, statehood for Alaska and

Hawaii, equal rights for women, restoring the right of states to dispose of tidelands and other territorial waters, vigorous enforcement of existing laws against Communists, preserving minimum prices for agricultural commodities, protection of civil rights, and self-government for the residents of the District of Columbia.[9] The platform reflected the big-tent philosophy of Dewey; it also mirrored his low-key approach. There was nothing radical or flashy in the language or in the proposals. The clear commitment to internationalism was the most surprising element, but for the rest, it was a platform designed to unite the party and not ruffle the feathers of any one constituency. It was the platform of a party that expected to govern.

On Wednesday, the various candidates were nominated, and the hall was packed. Wild applause, jeers, boos, hoots, and laughter could be heard in equal measure as speaker after speaker rose to put forth the names of Dewey, Taft, Stassen, Warren, Vandenberg, and MacArthur. Meanwhile, the Dewey "bandwagon" was gathering momentum, and most delegates believed that only a sudden, unexpected development could prevent Dewey from gaining the nomination by the third ballot. Brownell, Sprague, and Jaeckle understood the psychology of a convention; they recognized that the perception of victory was an essential prerequisite to actual victory. And by Thursday morning, they could taste it.

But they also knew that conventions were mercurial. They realized that the nomination could slip away suddenly, and that Taft wasn't giving up. Hoping that no one in the press would call his bluff, Taft announced Wednesday morning that "the Dewey blitz has been stopped."

Dewey woke up early and ate bacon and eggs in his room. Then he met with a stream of visitors, had a chicken sandwich for lunch, and sat down in front of his television set to watch as the balloting began. The first ballot went pretty much as the Triumvirate had predicted: Dewey 434, Taft 224, Stassen 157, Vandenberg 62, and Warren 59. There was a brief break before the second ballot, and then the process began again. Typically, favorite son candidates dropped out during the second ballot, and 1948 was no exception. Dewey picked up most of New Jersey's votes while Taft gained most of Illinois's. By the end of the second ballot, Dewey had 515 votes, 33 shy of victory.

The anti-Dewey forces staged one last attempt to halt the march. Governor Duff put forth a motion to adjourn. Things were moving quickly on the floor, and Brownell didn't have time to step outside and call Dewey in his hotel room. He made a spot decision to instruct the Dewey delegates to support the recess motion. His reasoning was that if they opposed and lost, that would be interpreted as a sign of weakness. He recognized the danger of a break in the action—after all, momentum was fickle, and in that interim any number of things could happen to endanger Dewey. But Brownell preferred to risk the unknown to a public defeat on the motion.

Watching the happenings in his hotel room, Dewey felt sure that he would win on the third ballot. In later years, he confessed that he was "horrified to hear that we had consented to an adjournment. This seemed like an act of the highest folly. We had no direct telephone line to the floor where I was, so I was sweating blood for a long time. Finally, somebody called me to say that the other side had agreed that I was about to be nominated. It was one of the longer waits of my life until I got that telephone call." In the space of a few hours, the opposition collapsed. Taft simply didn't have enough support, and Vandenberg expressed no desire to challenge Dewey. One by one, the major delegations caved. Senator William Knowland of California, Governor Sigler of Michigan, and House Majority Leader Charles Halleck of Indiana all announced for Dewey. The third and final ballot was unanimous: Dewey was the Republican candidate for president of the United States.[10]

"I thank you with all my heart for your friendship and confidence," Dewey told a hushed and exhausted convention audience that evening. "I am profoundly sensible of the responsibility that goes with it. I accept your nomination. In all humility, I pray God that I may deserve this opportunity to serve our country." He did not mention Truman, or communism, or any specifics. To reassure the delegates who had opposed him, he then said, "I come to you unfettered by a single obligation or promise to any living person." He was saying that his victory had not been engineered by secret guarantees or by promises of postelection favors. Whether or not that was true, only Dewey and his immediate advisers knew, but no one contested the statement at the time. With the petulant exception of Colonel McCormick, there seemed to be little ill will for Thomas Dewey. His main rivals all conceded graciously, and each promised to work with the Dewey team to ensure a Republican victory. The only remaining decision was to select a running mate.[11]

The contenders included Stassen and Halleck, but after hours of discussion during the evening of June 24 among Dewey, Vandenberg, Foster Dulles, Driscoll, Edward Martin, Brownell, and several others, both names were discarded. Halleck was powerful in the party, but his isolationism and crusty demeanor disqualified him. The group debated until four in the morning, and then Dewey picked up the telephone and asked a man who had earlier said he wouldn't consider the job. But when he got the call, Earl Warren changed his mind and accepted the offer.

Earl Warren, fifty-seven years old, was a popular governor. Tall, silver-haired, and distinguished, he looked the part of a statesman. Republicans and Democrats supported him in California. He was affable, centrist, and bland. He had barely campaigned in the spring, and when asked what his strategy was before the convention, he said, "Sure, I'd like to be president. My strategy is no strategy." He thought he was good at being California's chief executive, and he felt that he'd be a good chief executive for the nation. He evinced a desire "to serve well" in his chosen field of politics. In 1948, no one would have guessed that this was the man who would almost unilaterally transform American civil rights as chief justice of the Supreme Court. His selection as running mate to Dewey was greeted quietly. One paper dubbed the vertically challenged Dewey and the lanky Warren "Mutt and Jeff," after the popular cartoon duo. The addition of California to the Republican ticket made good electoral sense, but Warren filled no one with giddy enthusiasm. He acceded to the pressure from Dewey because, he told a friend, he "felt an obligation to the party."[12]

The convention came to an end that Friday. It had been a hot week, so hot that delegates and newsmen had christened the hall "the Steam-heated Iron Lung." All of the rest rooms in the auditorium ran out of paper towels because people doused themselves with cold water and used the towels as cold compresses. After a week of arguing, partying, dancing, drinking, and deliberating, the delegates returned to their home states for a brief respite before preparing for the fall campaign. *The Nation* described Dewey as "the Nominee

Nobody Loves," and indeed, the mood of many of the attendees was that they had made a politically smart choice but not an especially inspiring one. As the encomiums from columnists such as Dorothy Thompson, Arthur Krock, and Ernest Lindley of *Newsweek* poured in, Dewey returned to his farm in Pawling. For the first time in nearly a year, he felt relieved. He believed that the hard part was over.[13]

CHAPTER TWELVE

The Democrats Assemble

THE MOOD DURING the Republican convention had been triumphant; the tone of the Democratic gathering three weeks later was anything but. "We are here to honor the honored dead," said New York's mayor William O'Dwyer to a reporter. "Won't you please act accordingly?" Most of the nearly 1,600 delegates seemed to feel that they were at a funeral, not a nominating convention.

Even when Truman was actually nominated, the evening was marred by mishaps. It was sweltering, and the voting had taken far longer than expected. A national committeewoman from Pennsylvania, Emma Guffey Miller, sister of former senator Joseph Guffey, planned a surprise tribute for Truman. She had the Pennsylvania Florists Association create a liberty bell made of flowers. They had given one to Dewey, and naturally Miller wanted to make Truman's bouquet even more impressive. She had the florists place a cage of several dozen pigeons inside the bell, and at the appointed time, she intended to release the pigeons into the hall as symbolic "doves of peace."

The problem was that the pigeons had been placed inside the bell hours before. By the time Miller brought the bell to the podium, two of the birds had died and the rest were desperate for relief from the heat. The minute she opened the cage, they darted out as fast as they could and flew directly toward the thirty-six-inch pedestal fans that surrounded the stage. Sam Rayburn, the former Speaker of the House and chairman of the convention proceedings, started swatting at the low-flying pigeons. His craggy voice carried to the radio and television microphones, and he could be heard shouting, "Get those goddamned pigeons out of here!"

But they could not be contained. One of them briefly came to rest on Rayburn's head, while another landed on the fan right next to Bess Truman. Other pigeons were flying toward the ceiling and, in their nervousness, started to splatter the delegates with droppings. Watching the absurd scene, Jack Redding turned to Congressman Mike Kirwan and said, "What damn fool could have thought of a thing like that? In this heat, they could all be dead. It's bad enough having the Zionists, the Dixiecrats, and the Wallace-ites after us, now we got to have somebody arrange for the SPCA to have at us." By the time Truman came onstage, the surviving birds had retreated to the balconies and the overhead lights, where they watched as the president addressed the recently strafed delegates.[1]

Emma Guffey Miller's pigeons symbolized the chaos of the Democratic Party. The convention was marked by last-ditch efforts to remove Truman from the ticket and by internecine divisions over civil rights that threatened to further weaken an already battered party. Truman was one of the few who didn't view the Dewey-Warren ticket as a strong one, and as would be true for much of the campaign, he seemed more optimistic about his chances than almost anyone else in the Democratic Party. When he heard the news from the Republican Convention, he was apparently pleased, and assured his stunned associates that Dewey was easily beatable. At the end of June, as the Republicans were coronating Dewey, Truman was authorizing the largest airlift ever conducted in order to supply West Berlin with food, fuel, and medicine. Given that he didn't blink in the face of the challenge posed by Stalin, Truman was hardly about to be intimidated by Thomas E. Dewey.

But some members of the Democratic Party still wanted the convention to nominate a candidate other than Truman. The delegations from Alabama and Mississippi were pledged to walk out of the hall if a civil rights plank were adopted, and it was common knowledge that Truman would endorse a mild civil rights statement in the party platform. James Roosevelt had retreated in the spring, but in the hot July days before the convention, he made a final attempt to draft Eisenhower. The ADA also harbored hopes that the Truman nomination could be halted, and Leon Henderson joined forces with Roosevelt to try to convince Eisenhower to put forth his name.

In early July, recognizing that time was limited, the anti-Truman coalition redoubled its efforts and united around Eisenhower. The movement brought together groups that ordinarily wouldn't have spoken to one another. The ADA made fast friends with machine bosses such as Jacob Arvey and William O'Dwyer, while the Roosevelts, the patrician Connecticut liberal Chester Bowles, and Mayor Hubert Humphrey were suddenly working side by side with Senator Claude Pepper, Senator Lister Hill, and Strom Thurmond. In New York City, ADA supporters picketed in front of Eisenhower's Columbia University home with signs that read, IKE, YOU FAVOR THE DRAFT, WE FAVOR IT FOR YOU. Eisenhower was told that he could write the Democratic Party platform and name his running mate, if he would only consent to be the nominee.[2]

On July 9, Eisenhower made one last unequivocal statement that under no circumstances would he accept the nomination. That finally deflated the Eisenhower balloon, but rather than embracing Truman, the forces arrayed against him turned to the next option, Supreme Court Justice William O. Douglas. Taking a break from a trout-fishing vacation in Oregon, Douglas quashed expectations that he would be available to run. This left the ADA, the southern delegates, and the various anti-Truman party bosses at the altar for a second time in less than three days. It also severely damaged James Roosevelt, and his own delegation started to question the appropriateness of his continuing as leader. Stated California delegate John McEnery, Roosevelt was "a hypocrite beyond all doubt, because he went all over the state trying to wreck President Truman and the Democratic Party." A weak Roosevelt was good for Truman in the short term, but not good for the Democratic Party's prospects in California come November. In addition, a number of the southern states vowed never to support Truman, and they announced prior to the convention's opening ceremonies that they would either bolt from the hall or vote for Senator Richard Russell of Georgia. However, by Sunday, July 11, most southern delegates understood that Truman was in control, and they turned their energies to making sure that the party platform included no more than an anemic reference to civil rights.

In the week before the opening day, the platform committee hammered out a civil rights plank. Though Truman didn't dictate the language, the committee was composed of allies selected by McGrath, and the chairman of the subsection dealing with civil rights had been quietly informed of the White House's desires. The initial civil rights plank was almost exactly what the Democrats had adopted in 1944, and it differed little from what the Republicans had endorsed at Philadelphia a few weeks earlier. It stated that the Democratic Party was committed to "continuing its efforts to eradicate all racial, religious, and economic discrimination. We again state our belief that racial and religious minorities have the right to live, the right to work, the right to vote, the full and equal protection of the law. . . . We again call upon Congress to exert its full authority to the limit of its constitutional powers to assure and protect these rights."

To liberals and centrists, that language gave the illusion of vigor, but to southerners opposed to any federal action on civil rights, the last clause was sufficiently mollifying. If it was unconstitutional for Congress to legislate state civil rights, then the last clause acted as a guarantee that the federal government could do no more than exhort the states to adopt laws that were consonant with the principle of equality. Having made a rhetorical stand on civil rights in February, Truman had no incentive to alienate the South or to provoke a bolt. He wanted to keep the party together, not split it apart, and if modest civil rights language would keep the South inside the party, that was a price Truman was willing to pay. The only problem was that the ADA refused to cooperate.[3]

In addition to dealing with a brewing storm over civil rights, Truman had to select a vice-presidential running mate. Once again, Douglas's name surfaced. For the liberals who disliked Truman, the addition of Douglas to the ticket would at least be a consolation prize. But Douglas was no more willing to accept the number-two spot than he had been to contend for the number-one position. As the convention convened on Monday, July 12, Truman still had not come up with a running mate; the delegates were at best apathetic and at worst actively hostile to Truman; the party bosses like Arvey and Flynn no longer had the power they used to; and the labor unions were divided. Overall, the Democrats were in a sorry state.

The only marginal good news was that, having studied the Republican convention, the Democrats made better use of the television cameras. According to Arthur Krock of the *New York Times,* in the aftermath of the Republican gathering, those Americans who had watched television expressed dismay that the most serious national political decision took place in an atmosphere that reminded them of the ungainly melange of a country circus, a street carnival, or a Fourth of July picnic. After watching the Republicans, William Batt, the astute director of the Research Division of the DNC, observed that "the speeches at the Republican Convention were long, deadly, and uninteresting." Yet the Republicans still managed to get more coverage than "any news story in history, thanks in large part to television." He recommended that the Democrats keep their words brief and to the point, and that they target their remarks to the liberal and independent voters who were thought to be the key to the election. Kenneth Fry, the DNC radio director, suggested that the Democrats could improve on the Republicans by "timing the convention better, providing better staging and eliminating clumsy timegaps and general sloppiness showman-wise on the platform." Television captured not just the speakers but also the bored expressions on the faces of the delegates, and Fry issued a memorandum enjoining attendees to avoid any "traces of boredom, insecurity and petulance." They were also advised not to read magazines or newspapers, not to yawn, and not to scratch themselves in embarrassing places.[4]

Though the delegates did not in the end do much to comply with these exhortations, there were some exceptions. One of the first speakers on July 12 was India Edwards, of Harwood, Maryland. Edwards, the executive director of the women's division of the DNC, believed that women held "the balance of power and will elect the next President of the United States. . . . Remember," she added, "there are 1,700,000 more women voters than men." Edwards was acutely sensitive to the fact that her speech would be televised. A rather nondescript woman in her fifties, she choreographed her talk with the viewing audience in mind. To emphasize a point about rising prices, she released some balloons. When she discussed how much more expensive basic foodstuffs had become under the Republican 80th Congress, she pulled items from a shopping bag. She was followed at the rostrum by Frances Perkins, the former labor secretary, who was somewhat less entertaining.[5]

The highlight of the first day was the keynote speech by Senator

Alben Barkley of Kentucky. A southerner who refused to join the Dixiecrat revolt, Barkley was seventy years old and had spent thirty-five years in Congress. He was deeply respected in the party, and he had given the keynote address at both the 1932 and 1936 conventions. A tall, jowly man with a lined face that showed the effects of drink and weather, Barkley was an unrepentant New Deal liberal and a masterful orator. In the small world of the American political elite, one of his daughters had married Douglas MacArthur II, the nephew of the general who was then governor of Japan. Even though his home was in rural Paducah, the senator had never learned to drive a car, and he and his wife lived much as they had at the turn of the century.

His speech that evening electrified the moribund delegates. He stirred up memories of New Deal glory. "I am not an expert on cobwebs," he said, "but if my memory does not betray me, when the Democratic Party took over the Government of the United States sixteen years ago, even the spiders were so weak from starvation that they could not weave a cobweb in any department of the Government in Washington." In response, the audience began laughing, shouting, and hooting, while one of the bands played "My Old Kentucky Home." Barkley also struck a note of caution. The Republicans had arrogantly predicted victory, but he declared that it would be the height of folly to announce "the result of a contest four months in advance." When he finished his speech, the 1,596 delegates broke into a "spontaneous" demonstration and marched around the hall with signs and banners inscribed with BARKLEY FOR VICE-PRESIDENT.

And indeed, soon after the speech, Truman asked Barkley to join the ticket, and Barkley agreed. Though several party leaders were concerned that Barkley was too old, too liberal, and too similar to the Missouri-born Truman to add much to the ticket, on the whole Barkley was immensely popular within the party, and his presence would do much to cement the fractious Democratic coalition. Given what was about to happen over the civil rights plank, that cement was essential.[6]

The Democrats had somewhat different rules and procedures for their conventions than the Republicans. Though there were 1,596 delegates, only 1,234 of those could vote. The Democratic delegates were also more heavily weighted to congressional districts. Then there was the difference in mood. Some of the only color was provided by the Hawaiian delegation, who brought along a group of women who gave out leis and orchids while dressed in *holoku,* the traditional grass skirts. Whereas the Dewey campaign had given away more than $20,000 in party favors, the Democrats limited themselves to manila envelopes with the slogan "Here's Your Truman Victory Kit." The envelopes contained a notepad, some thimbles marked "Sew Right With Truman," an automatic pencil, and a campaign button. The contrast between the frugality of Truman's campaign and the largesse of Dewey's was not lost on the press, nor was the unfolding drama over the language of the platform.[7]

As their convention spokesman, the ADA selected Hubert Humphrey. He was a rising star in the party, and he was running for the Senate. His liberal credentials were impeccable, and as a midwesterner, he was free of the taint of northeast liberalism. He could count on the support of both the populist wing of the party and the liberal intelligentsia, and along with former Wisconsin congressman Andrew Biemiller, Humphrey led the charge against the initial civil rights language adopted by the platform committee. On Tuesday, July 13, he and the ADA leaders debated whether or not to offer a minority plank when the full convention took up the party platform the following day. The southern delegates had already put forward a minority amendment that was even more watered down than the language proposed by Truman and the committee. The ADA decided to offer a more stringent clause, and Humphrey was nominated to make the speech. But that evening he balked, worried that he would harm both the party and his own chances at winning a Senate seat. Joseph Rauh of the ADA told Humphrey that he was popular because he was so closely identified with liberal causes such as civil rights and that compromising those views would hurt his electoral prospects more than taking on Truman and the South would. Humphrey finally agreed to make the speech, but only if language were inserted that praised Truman's "courageous stand on civil rights."

The moment after Senator Myers read the civil rights plank from the podium, southern delegates rose in protest. Delegate Walter Sillers of Mississippi shouted, "Give us the right to govern our own fundamental affairs," and presented a minority platform to that effect. That was the cue for Humphrey. "I say the time has come to walk out of the shadow of states' rights and into the sunlight of human rights," he declaimed. As the floor began buzzing, delegates from New York and Pennsylvania suddenly donned yellow skullcaps with propellers on top, and a beautiful woman carrying a TRUMAN FOR PRESIDENT sign paraded through the various state delegations. Humphrey continued his ringing defense of equality for all, quoting everyone from Thomas Jefferson to Alben Barkley. In order for the United States to defend the free world against communism, Humphrey stated, Americans could not "use a double standard." America had to be morally sound and consistent. It could not guarantee rights for some while denying rights to others. "To those who say that we are rushing the issue of civil rights, I say to them, we are 172 years late." And with that rhetorical flourish, he asked the assembled convention to ratify the minority plank, which called on Congress to "wipe out discrimination."[8]

The speech helped secure Humphrey's senate victory in November. His rise continued for the next two decades, until he became vice president and then the Democratic nominee in 1968, and his career like that of so many of his liberal colleagues was crushed in the mortar of Vietnam.

Though the ADA had engineered the minority plank, northern bosses like Arvey and Flynn decided that their liberal, urban constituents would support the Humphrey position, and the minority plank narrowly passed, 682 to 651. That was the final straw for Alabama and Mississippi. Alabama's chairman, Handy Ellis, along with thirteen of Alabama's twenty-six delegates, shouted, "We cannot participate further in this convention," and walked out the door as the hall erupted in a cacophony of boos, hisses, and howls. Mississippi followed, waving the Confederate flag. As they were leaving, Hardy Lott of Mississippi tried to get the band to play Dixie and offered the leader $50. "Gosh, I could use that $50," the leader replied, "but I have strict orders not to play Dixie, or anything else when the march takes place." The "marchers" intended to head back to their hotels, but a director from the Life-NBC television broadcast convinced them to stage something a bit more dramatic for the cameras. With the lenses fixed on them, several southern delegates ripped off their badges and tossed them into a pile.[9]

Most of the South stayed in the hall, however. The remaining southerners realized that the battle was lost, and though they put forth Richard Russell as a protest candidate, delegates such as Senator Lister Hill of Alabama and Charles Bloch of Georgia believed that little good could come from walking out. Later that evening, as the balloting began, the southern delegates sat glumly in their seats as Russell was overwhelmed by Truman. The final tally was 947½ votes for Truman, 263 for Russell, and half a vote for former Indiana governor Paul McNutt.

Not until nearly 2:00 a.m. did Truman and Barkley emerge from the stiflingly hot room in the back of the hall where they had been sitting for nearly four hours. Wearing a double-breasted white suit and a black tie, Truman looked surprisingly cool and unrumpled. Using the same extemporaneous manner that had won over crowds during his western tour in June, the president stepped up to the podium with only a rough outline of a speech. After more than half an hour of demonstrations, after a brief statement by Barkley, after the band had played "Hail to the Chief" and "The Missouri Waltz" numerous times, after the cheers and applause, Truman gave an electrifying acceptance speech. "Senator Barkley and I will win this election and make those Republicans like it," he declared. "Don't you forget that. We will do that because they are wrong and we are right."

Then, in a gesture that stunned and excited the bleary-eyed assembly, Truman went on the offensive against the Republican Congress. He described them as the worst Congress ever, and he assailed their hypocrisy. "The Republican platform cries about cruelly high prices. I have been trying to get them to do something about high prices ever since they met for the first time. . . . The Republican platform urges extending and increasing social security benefits. . . . I wonder if they think they can fool the people with such poppycock as that." Well, he continued, he wasn't going to let them get away with it. "On the twenty-sixth of July, which out in Missouri they call Turnip Day, I am going to call that Congress back and I'm going to ask them to pass laws halting rising prices and to

meet the housing crisis which they say they're for in their platform."
He also called on them to pass legislation on a national health program, on civil rights, on education, and on an increase in the minimum wage. "What that worst 80th Congress does in its special
session will be the test. . . . The American people will decide on the
record." And with that, he accepted the nomination of his party to
be president of the United States.[10]

In the end, the speech that appeared improvised was actually the
product of weeks of discussion and several days of intensive writing
and rewriting. Murphy later estimated that at least three-quarters of
the speech was verbatim from the outline. Only after having hashed
out the general contours of his speech with Clark Clifford, Sam
Rosenman, Charles Murphy, George Elsey, and others, did Truman
himself add such homey expressions as the line about "Turnip Day."
The story of how the acceptance speech came to be shows that Truman's off-the-cuff campaigning required intensive staff work. During the campaign of 1948 and in the telling of it by Truman and
others in later years, Truman crafted an image of a simple man
speaking in simple language to good, honest Americans. While his
words and actions may have stemmed from genuine beliefs and
heartfelt positions, he was no more natural than Dewey, if by natural
one means unrehearsed and unfiltered. As the fall campaign would
demonstrate, Truman needed a team of fact-finders and writers in
order to speak extemporaneously. His staff enabled him to be himself, to take chances, and to go off on tangents. As a result, he was
seen as the plain talker that he was.

The idea of calling a special session of Congress was a novel and
risky notion—it had been discussed and debated by Truman's advisers for several weeks. Not since 1856 when Franklin Pierce ordered
Congress back to pass a military appropriations bill had a president
exercised this unusual constitutional prerogative. At the end of June,
an unsigned memorandum was prepared on the issue. Later filed in
the papers of Judge Samuel Rosenman, who had been a major player
in the Roosevelt White House and who offered occasional advice to
Truman, the memorandum posited the pros and cons of a special
session. "This election can only be won by bold and daring steps," it
began, "calculated to reverse the powerful trend now running

against us. The boldest and most popular step the President could possibly take would be to call a special session of Congress in early August." Doing so would force the press and the public to focus on the 80th Congress rather than the White House and it would force Dewey and Warren either to defend the Congress or criticize it. Either way, the action would drive a wedge through the Republican coalition. On the other hand, the Republicans could aid and abet a southern filibuster on civil rights, or they could pass toothless bills on housing, price controls, or national health. Those bills might fool the people, and force a Truman veto, which would then make the president look like a hypocrite. The greatest danger, however, was that the Congress would actually pass meaningful legislation in these areas and thereby allow Dewey and Warren to take credit for what were Truman's initiatives. Still, the memorandum stated that the president could counter most of these risks and that the benefits more than outweighed them.[11]

The convention had gone better than many Democrats had feared, and the press responded favorably with some notable exceptions. Ever the contrarian, columnist H.L. Mencken noted in his diary and in his articles that "the convention was inconceivably idiotic." He also might have noted that the drama of the conventions obscured the fact that, for many Americans, the differences between the Democrats and the Republicans seemed negligible. (In the popular film *State of the Union*, Spencer Tracy, playing a presidential hopeful, is asked to detail the distinction between a Republican and a Democrat. His campaign manager answers, "There's all the difference in the world. They're in and we're out.") The Republicans purportedly stood for enlarging the area of individual opportunity and decreasing the role of the federal government, while the Democrats supposedly stood for those Americans who weren't at the top of the economic heap. Yet the centrist Dewey had engineered a platform that in key respects mimicked the Democrats and accepted the core of the New Deal. The result was that the line between the two candidates was blurry, even if the line between the two parties was not.[12] This presented more of a problem for Truman than for Dewey. Truman was unpopular and lagging in the polls. He needed to put to rest the predictions of his defeat and to overcome public apathy to his candidacy. Dewey simply had to coast on a fairly popular noncontroversial set of issues. This basic reality ended up dictating campaign style for both candidates.

THE TWO major party conventions of 1948 were television's political baptism. Looking back, the NBC commentator John Cameron Swayze remembered the thrill of this early television experiment: "One night I called my wife and asked her how I looked. 'Dead,' she said. 'You'd better get new make-up.' But it was lots of fun. Everything we did was innovative. We couldn't plan because we didn't know what to plan for."[13]

Soon, everything would be planned with television in mind, but for the remaining months of the presidential election season, television remained a sideshow, its importance overshadowed by radio and print journalism. As many as ten million people had watched the conventions on television, but few commentators believed that the act of watching made much of a difference in whom they would vote for. Assessing the effect of television, some predicted that it would be a passing fad. Others warned that unless government stepped in, television would destroy radio, Hollywood, book publishing, print media, and American culture. "It is imperative for the government to evolve a comprehensive television policy before it is too late," warned Bernard Smith in *Harper's Magazine*.[14] But television regulation was not high on either party's agenda, and these warnings went unheeded. If Truman and Dewey had been handed a crystal ball and shown that the future consisted of massive television advertising, along with packaged and test-marketed candidates, perhaps they would have given some thought to the relationship between television, money, and politics. As it was, television appeared to be a curious novelty—interesting, primitive, perplexing, and uncertain. In 1948, the task of winning in November and passing laws on housing and catching spies and containing the Soviets and following baseball and arguing over civil rights seemed far more imperative than a national debate about television.

After the conventions, Truman and Dewey retreated for a few weeks to recover from the draining spring and early summer. They went over fall strategy with their advisers at a leisurely pace that they soon would be unable to afford. In the interim, the last pieces of the campaign were falling into place as the southern rebels prepared to nominate their own protest candidates and as the Progressives gathered in Philadelphia so that Henry Wallace could once again make his case for a new party.

CHAPTER THIRTEEN

Dixie Rises

W HEN HANDY ELLIS of the Alabama delegation marched out of the Municipal Auditorium, he triggered the next stage of the Dixiecrat rebellion. The angry departure of half the Alabama delegates and all of the Mississippi representatives was a brief, albeit dramatic moment during the Democratic convention, but seen from the point of view of the South, the walkout was the culmination of months of speculation and weeks of planning. For people in the Deep South, the walkout was the only news of significance, and civil rights was the only issue of consequence. According to one news report, on July 13 and 14, as the civil rights drama was acted out, "every radio [in Mississippi] was tuned in one direction. . . . In every home, in every car, coffee shop, office or garage the same voices, the same shouts and the same monotonous drone of the roll call came from every set. . . . There was bitter disappointment when the Southern group failed to push through its States' Rights declaration. There was hot anger when the liberal democrats rammed their Truman Civil Rights platform down the South's throat." And as a reporter from Jackson put it, " 'Alabamy Bound' replaced 'The Missouri Waltz' as the theme song of democracy today as the Southern delegates made it plain that they are all set to walk out of the national convention and hold their own States' Rights convention in Birmingham on Saturday."

Nothing about the movement was simple, including the logistics of the convention walkout. It had taken Ellis several hours after the passage of the minority plank to get Chairman Sam Rayburn to recognize him, as Rayburn tried to prevent a spectacle. Ellis finally managed to be recognized, and he then staged the long-anticipated walkout. The reporter from Jackson expressed relief that "the Southern boys were keeping things alive. . . . I repeat that if it had not been for the Southern revolt, this convention would have gone down in history as the most uninteresting ever held." The Mississippi delegates had planned for their escape by reserving two special Pullman cars to take them to Birmingham the following day. Senator Eastland and several of his friends caught a train to Washington, picked up Eastland's car, and then drove to Birmingham. Governor Laney and the Arkansas contingent as well as Thurmond and the South Carolinians stayed for the last day of the convention and cast their ballots for Russell. They would have departed with Alabama, but internal divisions in the South Carolina and Arkansas delegations made that impossible. Laney was described as "horse radish strong against Truman," and Thurmond made it clear that he would never support the Democratic nominee.[1]

Still, Thurmond claimed he wasn't sure he'd be able to make it to Birmingham. He explained that prior engagements might keep him from attending. "I would like to go to Birmingham," he said, "but I just don't see right now how I can. I wish those in charge of the meeting had waited a week or so before calling it to give us folks a chance to make our plans." By all accounts he had known well in advance that the States' Righters intended to hold their own meeting in the wake of Philadelphia. Strangely, Thurmond had scheduled a review of the South Carolina National Guard that weekend, and he initially turned down the invitation to attend the rump convention in Birmingham. His vacillation made good political sense. In the South, naked ambition was a liability. If Thurmond was to lead the Dixiecrat revolt, he had to be perceived as an unwilling leader, one who served when called and not one who craved power and position. So he briefly played at Cincinnatus, and then "reluctantly" canceled his engagements in South Carolina and made the trip to Birmingham.

Commentators in the North decried the bolt, though not necessarily on principle. Some reporters noted that in departing, the Southerners had squandered reservoirs of good will among northern delegates who were just as zealous about states' rights though not so adamantly opposed to civil rights. Had the Dixiecrats been able to moderate their stance, some news stories suggested, they might have cobbled together an acceptable compromise and been able to remain within the party. Once they left, however, compromise was no longer an option.[2]

The convention weeded out the States' Rights moderates. After months of fulminating, most of the South had grudgingly and glumly accepted that it was Truman or the Republicans, and they chose the devil they knew. For all of the letters and telegrams in February from southern representatives, only Alabama and Mississippi officially bolted. As of mid-July, therefore, the Dixiecrats commanded just a small portion of the South, and only South Carolina and Arkansas showed signs of potentially joining the two Deep South states. Armed with the strength of zealotry, the true believers in states' rights gathered on Saturday, July 17.

In 1948, Birmingham symbolized the New South—industrial, polluted, and booming. It was the South's answer to Pittsburgh, all steel and factories and furnaces, and iron mills in the surrounding Red Mountains that left the landscape scarred. Among the cities of the South, only New Orleans had more people, and Birmingham was far more raw, violent, and ridden with class struggle. It was the logical place to inaugurate a purely southern party, and the resulting convention was a raucous, edgy, chaotic combination of wealth, power, and rabble-rousing. That Monday had been Birmingham's wrestling night, and the red-brick City Auditorium was quickly refurbished for the convention. The wrestling ring was removed, and the ceiling fans were oiled in anticipation of the swelter. The only oddity was the absence of Confederate flags. The States' Righters wanted to give the appearance of being the one, true, national Democratic Party. The hall was decorated with the Stars and Stripes and the flags of the forty-eight states instead. Of course, that didn't stop hundreds of people in the audience of 6,000 from unfurling their own Confederate banners and waving them at every opportunity.

The lobby was full of scowling men in seersucker suits, puffing on cigars, looking, as the *Birmingham News* put it, "like a Yankee thinks Southerners ought to look." Bands played "Carry Me Back to Old Virginny" and "Deep in the Heart of Texas." After an invocation and a lusty rendition of "Dixie," the convention opened. The keynote speaker was former Alabama governor Frank Dixon, and other bigwigs included Thurmond, Wright, Governor William

Tuck of Virginia, Senator Eastland, and the nearly blind and partly deaf eighty-seven-year-old former governor of Oklahoma, William "Alfalfa Bill" Murray. Known for pithy racist aphorisms such as "this country became great through Christian principles and the white man's brains," Murray was a white supremacist folk hero. Wearing an old battered hat and a dirty shirt, he walked through the hall with a copy of his book, *The Negro's Place in the Call of Race,* and occasionally stopped and read portions out loud. Also prominent were Wallace W. Wright, the fifty-four-year-old president of Mississippi's largest wholesale grocery company, and Birmingham's police chief, Bull Connor. Most southern states were there, but North Carolina and Kentucky were absent while Georgia, Virginia, and Tennessee were represented by college students. Many of the so-called "official" delegates were either low-level state bureaucrats or businessmen who happened to be in Birmingham for other reasons. The audience was composed largely of people looking for a good political show, and their allegiance to the cause was no deeper than their allegiance to a traveling circus.

One of the least palatable attendees was Gerald L. K. Smith, author of several virulently racist and anti-Semitic tracts. To his credit, Thurmond publicly distanced the States' Rights movement from the likes of Smith. He didn't want the convention to be identified with the radical separatist fringe, nor with conspiracy theorists such as the author of *Jews Have Got the Atom Bomb,* who meandered through the crowd warning people of the looming danger of a Zionist nuclear attack. But Thurmond wasn't exactly a racial moderate, and he did not voice any objection to the comments of Bull Connor that, in contrast with Philadelphia, "You will not find a Negro lawyer speaking on this platform, nor an ex-convict from Boston." Connor was referring to George Vaughan, an Ohio attorney who had tried to unseat the Mississippi delegation in Philadelphia, and to former Boston mayor James Curley, who had had a number of brushes with the law. Dixon, the keynote speaker, gave an ugly address in which he decried the creation of a "federal gestapo" and characterized the States' Rights movement as a defense "against those who would destroy our civilization and mongrelize our people." In response to Dixon, the hall erupted in demonstrations. Students from Ole Miss started chanting "To hell with Truman," and undergraduates from Birmingham-Southern College hoisted pictures of Robert E. Lee.[3]

When the meeting adjourned for lunch, most of the delegates wandered around the hall or just outside, smoking and drinking. The leaders remained inside trying to decide what the platform would be and who would be nominated. Even more problematic, no one could agree on tactics. Should the convention call on the delegates to leave the Democratic Party? Or should they urge the assembly to try to take control of their state Democratic machinery and replace Truman's name with the States' Rights candidate? Should the movement be defined by animus toward civil rights or by the principle of state power?

By late afternoon, the inner circle had drawn up a brief, thousand-word declaration that would serve as the party's platform. It stated that in order to protect "the American people against the onward march of totalitarian government," all citizens must abide by Article X of the Constitution, which holds that the powers not delegated to the United States government are reserved for the states. The statement also unequivocally endorsed segregation and rejected the notion that the federal government had the authority to legislate relations between the races. Document in hand, Alabama segregationist Horace Wilkinson rose to nominate both Thurmond and Wright for president. Wright, who had called the meeting and whose Mississippi contingent was the most organized and unified of the southern delegations, declined the nomination. He didn't want anyone to accuse him of using states' rights as a vehicle for his personal ambition. He agreed to be the vice presidential candidate, however, and in his acceptance speech, he reminded the gathering that the southern party "is not a bolt ticket." Rather, he proclaimed the States' Rights Party the legitimate representative of the Democrats in the South. He promised to do his best, and he thanked the assembly for their support.

Governor Thurmond didn't share the qualms of his running mate. Thurmond was presented to the crowd, and by acclaim, he was chosen as the nominee. The whole process appeared informal and improvised. An uninformed spectator could have been forgiven for mistaking the gathering as a good old boy rally. But Thurmond had prepared some remarks, which he read at about six in the evening. "If the South should vote for Truman this year," he began, "we should petition the national government for colonial status. The South has been stabbed in the back by the President." Under the banner of civil rights, Thurmond continued, the federal government sought to destroy local autonomy. He predicted that in order to protect themselves, voters would turn toward the States' Rights position in November. "I did not ask to be recommended for this place," he concluded. "I did not seek it, but I would be no less than a traitor if I did not help the Southern people."[4]

The one-day convention then came to an end in a final flurry of "Dixie" and frantic cheers. The Dixiecrats had crossed a Rubicon of sorts, and Birmingham marked a clear-cut break from the mainstream Democratic Party. But the Dixiecrats suffered from severe internal divisions, beginning at the top of the ticket with Thurmond and Wright. Thurmond intended to campaign throughout the South. He eagerly anticipated the weeks of stump speaking, and he dreamed of extending the movement at least to the border states of Kentucky and Missouri and perhaps even into West Virginia, Pennsylvania, Maryland, and elsewhere. Wright, however, insisted that the Dixiecrats were not the fourth party and that he would only campaign in those states that selected Thurmond-Wright as the Democratic Party candidates.

Even more telling, Thurmond, disturbed at the impression that Birmingham was a racist rally, distanced himself from the idea of white supremacy. In a widely reported interview the day after the convention, Thurmond, speaking from his home in Columbia, South Carolina, described himself as a "progressive Southerner" who had no sympathy for white supremacists or racists. He decried lynching as one of the most ugly forms of murder, and he reiterated that his enemy was the unconstitutional extension of federal power, not the black inhabitants of the South. Newspapers throughout the Northeast gave Thurmond a clean bill of health after this interview. The *Hartford Courant* declared that the governor was conducting himself with "dignity and intelligence," while the *Washington Evening Star* stated that Thurmond's record as a progressive advocate for fair treatment of "Negroes in South Carolina entitles him to a respectful hearing."[5]

Conversely, most major papers in the South dismissed the Dixiecrats as an exercise in futility. Said the editorial board of the *Norfolk Virginian-Pilot,* "Our own guess is that the Birmingham war dance will amount to practically nothing." Even the usually pro-States' Rights *Memphis Commercial Appeal* raised doubts. "The indignation of the States' Righters is understandable," the editorial commented. "Nevertheless, the Birmingham method is not the best either for the Democrats or for the American political system. One of the reasons we oppose Wallace so bitterly is that he is following the European pattern of many small parties that leads to utter confusion and invites Communism to take over. The two-party system must be preserved." Better to lose with Truman, the paper announced, than splinter the party and the political system.[6]

The notion that third parties imperil the stability of American democracy was not new in 1948, nor has it dissipated in the decades since. Whenever a new party attempts to muscle its way into the national spotlight, the established parties respond with a variety of weapons, and among the most potent is the charge that these parties strike at the foundation of the American political tradition. According to defenders of the two-party system, once new parties proliferate, American democracy becomes dangerously factional. The authors of the Federalist Papers warned against this, and Americans have been wary of small parties ever since. This hasn't prevented groups that feel unheard and unrepresented from trying to create new parties. As the Dixiecrats and the Progressives of 1948 demonstrate, new parties arise even though the political deck is stacked.

The States' Rights movement effectively channeled the grievances and the ideology of a disgruntled minority into politics. In the absence of the States' Righters, that minority might have fumed and then voted for Truman, or it might have festered until it exploded in an orgy of new lynchings, Klan gatherings, and assorted acts of terror and violence. The Dixiecrats, unappealing and utterly reprehensible as some of their beliefs may have been, can be seen as a positive force in American politics. Through the mechanism of a third party, more than two perspectives were voiced during the general election. Voters—at least in the South—had several options. In that sense, democracy was well served. When voters today complain about the lack of choice in presidential politics, they often romanticize what those choices would be in an ideal world. In reality, more choices mean a greater number of objectionable views. That is the trade-off. More options, more engagement, but also more divisions. Fewer options, more consensus, but also less passion.

In later years, Thurmond clung to the conviction that if there had been widespread television coverage in 1948, the States' Rights movement would have fared better. He believed that the inability of his party to get its message to a wide array of voters doomed it to be a fringe protest movement. He claimed that because few people heard or saw the Dixiecrats outside the South, voters never had the opportunity to make their own choice as to the merits. Instead, the Dixiecrat message was mediated through a variety of not-so-friendly news sources. For the next three months, Thurmond went by car from hamlet to hamlet, from tiny local festivals to tiny local theaters, to improvised stump speeches at farms and plantations. His talks were rarely carried on national radio for the simple reason that the Dixiecrats couldn't afford to purchase the airtime. One reporter from the *New York Times,* John Popham, covered his campaign, while the correspondents from the major southern dailies such as the *New Orleans Times-Picayune,* the *Charlotte Observer,* and *Atlanta Constitution* were either lukewarm or antagonistic.[7]

It was widely believed that the Dixiecrat movement would further hamper an already mortally wounded Democratic Party. The confident predictions of Truman's advisers at the end of 1947 that the South would have nowhere to go now seemed shallow and foolish. As of early August, the Dixiecrats seemed certain to capture Alabama, Mississippi, South Carolina, and Arkansas. Other states were so disenchanted with Truman and the national party that it was hard to say with any certainty what they would do or for whom they would vote. Thurmond and Wright obviously didn't mind if the Dixiecrats split the party, and they avidly hoped for Truman's defeat. Yet, after the flurry of activity surrounding the Philadelphia and Birmingham meetings, the coalition was left with very little money, a skeleton staff of volunteers and local officials whose commitment to devote time and energy was at best shaky, and a national press corps that was either hostile or apathetic and very often both.

The States' Rights campaign had to raise money. The volunteers at campaign headquarters in Jackson, Mississippi, made calls, organized luncheons and dinners, and distributed buttons. These activities generated some income, but in the desperately poor South of 1948, these operations were almost literally nickel and dime. Thurmond and Wright didn't need thousands; they needed millions. Though the movement was never well funded, from the moment the campaign began, rumors circulated that one source of money was the real reason for the revolt.

During any presidential election, politics occurs on at least two levels. One level is occupied by the public positions of the candidates. Democrats took a public position for the repeal of Taft-Hartley; Republicans came out in favor of internationalism. Such statements may reflect deeply held beliefs or they may be the consequence of multiple negotiations between competing interests within the party. Yet there is another level that rarely sees the light of press scrutiny or public discussion. That level is occupied by money and influence. In most campaigns, an intrepid reporter or clever political operative from the opposing camp manages to disclose some information on this rather private, and usually secret, second level. But for the most part, presidential elections in the United States have been conducted on the first level, and candidates rarely assail one another with any consistency or specificity on the second. The principle is simple: you don't attack my questionable links with particular businessmen and industries and I won't attack yours. In Oregon, Dewey never harassed Stassen for his connections to the Pillsbury fortunes, and Stassen never criticized Dewey for his links with political machines throughout New York State. They stuck to the issues, which meant that the campaign was waged on a fairly high level of rhetoric and ideas.

Tidelands oil was the Dixiecrats' sordid secret. In 1947, the Supreme Court ruled against the state of California in its dispute with the federal government over who owned the three-mile belt of water along its coast. That ruling reversed more than a century of precedent that gave states jurisdiction and ownership over the tidelands areas off their coasts. For Louisiana, Texas, and Mississippi, losing jurisdiction over the tidelands of the Gulf of Mexico meant ceding control over miles and miles of oil fields, and that meant a huge decline in tax money as well as substantial losses of under-the-table income that would flow from oilmen to state legislatures. The shallow waters off Louisiana and Texas were rich in petroleum deposits, and politicians in those states were furious not just at the court decision, but at President Truman's decision to veto a Republican resolution reaffirming the precedent of state control.

The Republican Party platform included a statement supporting the principle of state control of "submerged lands and territorial waters." The Democrats made no such pledge. At no time did the States' Righters make the tidelands dispute an explicit part of their ideology, yet several of the largest donors to the Dixiecrats were Texas oilmen, and one of the most vociferous advocates of the movement was Governor Beauford Jester of Texas. It was estimated that as much as $30 billion in oil lay just off the coast of Texas and Louisiana, and that was $30 billion that oilmen from those states were determined to have. Jester played a clever game in the summer and fall of 1948. He urged oilmen such as H.R. Cullen of Houston to give generously to the Thurmond-Wright campaign, and he spoke as if he were part of the movement. Yet Texas never broke with the national Democratic Party and Jester never officially renounced his affiliation. Meanwhile, there were loud rumblings that the Dixiecrats were nothing but a sinister tool of tidelands oil interest, rumblings of such disturbing intensity that Thurmond and Wright felt the need to make public pronouncements about things that normally remained hidden in the background of electoral politics.

In response to a query from the editor of the *Birmingham Post,* Thurmond issued a statement on July 26 denying any links. That followed an equally adamant denial by Governor Wright that he too knew nothing of the supposed conspiracy. Yet the rumors wouldn't die. Throughout the South, there were whispers that the States' Rights drive was simply a smoke screen for a few wealthy men like Wallace Wright (the Mississippi businessman who was one of the Dixiecrats' principal financial backers) and a few angry governors and local politicians. "I know nothing of any attempt by oil interests to make any contribution whatever to the States' Rights Democrats," Thurmond informed the editor. "Not one dime has been contributed by such persons, and so far as I know there has been no suggestion of any kind to come from oil interests. We consider the tidelands oil question as a matter for the states just as we consider so-called civil rights legislation and many other like questions to be reserved to the states by the Constitution. Anyone who insinuates that there is any other intention in the States' Rights Movement than that of protecting and preserving this Constitutional guarantee must undoubtedly be attempting to smear our movement."

Thurmond's denials both at the time and in retrospect have a "the lady doth protest too much" quality to them. In one of his first major campaign appearances, in Houston in August, he and his wife, Jean, were photographed smiling and waving in front of the private plane on which they had arrived. Standing next to them was the portly, ruddy-faced H.R. Cullen, the owner of the plane. Wright arrived in Houston by private train, paid for by Cullen. One of Wright's main contributors was EBASCO, the largest electric power company in Mississippi, which had designs on tidelands petroleum, and one of his craftiest advisers was George Godwin, who was an advertising man and politico whose clients included some of the largest oil companies in the region.

It is difficult to determine just how much money these groups gave. The Dixiecrats kept very poor records, perhaps by intent, perhaps because they were disorganized and decentralized. Throughout the campaign, the Dixiecrats operated on a shoestring, and the fact that they were so evidently underfunded undermines the most outrageous accusations that the whole movement was a sham to camouflage oil interests. If the oil barons had in fact been the primary factor behind the States' Rights movement, they could have spent far more money and thus been far more effective. It is probably most accurate to say that the Dixiecrats, like all major political parties, had angels in the background, and that their particular angels seemed to many to be not so angelic.[8]

IN THE WEEKS following Birmingham, Thurmond returned to South Carolina to rest, plan, and speak at the Watermelon Festival in Cherryville, North Carolina, and then at the Mullins Tobacco Festival in South Carolina in order to crown the local "Queen for a Day." Meanwhile, various States' Rights leaders met in Atlanta, Birmingham, and Jackson to establish some sort of coherence for the coming campaign.

One of the oddest groups to attend the nominating convention in Birmingham had been the People's Progressive Party of Alabama. Led by Robert Travis, the small group picketed in front of the City Auditorium with pro-Wallace placards. Though the Dixiecrats and the Progressives shared certain critiques of the two main parties, Travis was treated with contempt, and his exhortations that the people of Alabama wake to the message of Henry Wallace fell flat.[9] He would have been better received had he made the journey north, to Philadelphia, where Wallace and Taylor and the true believers of the Progressive Party gathered for the last of the major political conventions of 1948.

CHAPTER FOURTEEN

The Progressives
Congregate

FREDERICK SCHUMAN arrived at Philadelphia's 30th Street Station at 9:45 a.m. on the morning of Friday, July 23. Two days before, he had driven to New York City from his home in Williamstown, Massachusetts, where he was the Woodrow Wilson Professor of Government at Williams College. For some months, Schuman had been active in the new party. An authority on foreign relations, he gave frequent public lectures critiquing American foreign policy and propounding his vision of world peace. And so he was asked by Henry Wallace and Rexford Tugwell to be a member of the platform committee that would meet just before the convention began.

Schuman was anxious and excited. He had never been to a meeting like this one, and he felt jittery. He wasn't just attending the convention; he was a member of the small, select group responsible for crafting the new party's message. On his arrival, he caught a taxi from the train station to the Broadwood Hotel and checked in. Then he took a cab to the convention hall in order to attend the second session of the platform committee. He arrived at a largely empty space of endless rooms and seats and a few young people wandering around aimlessly. Nobody at the hall knew where the committee was meeting, and Schuman began to worry he had gotten the day and time wrong. He enlisted the aid of the young women at the reception desk, who finally located the meeting. It was at the Bellevue-Stratford, almost back where he had started, a few blocks from the Broadwood.

Hundreds of people stood outside the hotel, and policemen paced warily under the marquee that had recently been home to rubber elephants and papier-mâché donkeys. The professor nudged his way through the crowds and up the front steps, only to be stopped by a suspicious cop who demanded his delegate credentials. Schuman presented them, and then rushed as quickly as he could through the lobby, past the signs for various open houses hosted by affiliated organizations, including the Stern Gang, the Israeli underground paramilitary organization that had blown up buildings and assassinated British officials in Palestine and whose allies included future Israeli prime minister Menachem Begin. In the conference room, Rexford Tugwell, the brilliant Columbia economist and former governor of the Philippines who was part of the early New Deal "brain trust," was chairing the meeting, along with the controversial Lee Pressman, the heavy-set, sardonic former general counsel of the CIO, whose communist sympathies made him unacceptable to organized labor. Dozens of others participated in the discussions, including Mrs. Paul Robeson.

After a quick break and a much needed lunch in an air-conditioned restaurant, the larger meeting concluded and Schuman joined the eight-person drafting committee to go over the 9,000-word platform plank by plank. He successfully argued for putting the "economic planning" article before "anti-monopoly," thereby offsetting the more Marxist rhetoric that some of the committee preferred. The meetings at the hotel dragged on, and so Schuman didn't hear the stirring speeches during the opening session that night by Shirley Graham McCanns, a "Negro woman come to Philadelphia to help write a platform for me and my children"; by Josiah Gitt, editor of the York *Gazette* (the only daily newspaper in the country to endorse Wallace) and head of the Pennsylvania Progressives; and by keynote speaker Charles Howard, attorney, publisher, graduate of Tuskegee Institute, and a Republican Negro leader until his defection to the new party. The drafting group became increasingly ornery in the smoky, stuffy, poorly lit room. Louis Adamic held forth on the pernicious effects of fatigue, while some members started to argue over where to place punctuation marks. They worked through the night. Schuman managed to extricate himself at 6:15 a.m. on Saturday and catch two hours of sleep in his room before the phone started ringing. A group from Chicago wanted him to stage a floor protest against a rules clause in the platform. He told them that he'd call them back when he was fully awake.

In mid-afternoon, Schuman injected himself with multiple cups of coffee and a heavy lunch and headed to the convention hall just as Wallace was nominated. The hall was filled with plainly dressed women. Even the wealthy ladies present wore distinctly humble clothing; Mrs. Elinor Gimbel was clad in a gingham frock. The men were clothed mostly in shirtsleeves of a nondescript character, their suspenders on display. Schuman noticed a large number of musicians, playing banjo or guitar or harmonica, and a choir of boys and girls in white shirts and green scarves standing behind the speakers' platform. Every twenty or thirty minutes, one band or another broke into music.

The Progressives, more than any other major political movement, had a feeling for music, especially folk and gospel, with their lyrics of suffering, protest, and redemption. Bands played "John Brown's Body," the chorus performed "Great Day," and the whole hall sang hymns and ballads for a half hour before each new session. Schuman saw delegates from Iowa struggling with ten-foot-high stalks of Wallace corn. West Virginians wore plastic miner's helmets. The Idahoans all had cowboy hats, and some carried placards in the shape of potatoes with the slogan AN IDAHO POTATO IN EVERY OVEN— WALLACE AND TAYLOR IN THE WHITE HOUSE. In one corner, a small group waved banners urging ARMENIA FOR THE ARMENIANS. Pictures of Wallace and Taylor were everywhere. As Wallace's name was placed in nomination, Schuman heard the chant of "One, two, three, four, we don't want another war," while the organist started playing "The Battle Hymn of the Republic" followed by "The People's March Is On," complete with hallelujah chorus. The crowd erupted in shouting, banner waving, singing, and general exaltation. Though part of Schuman's brain told him that all political conventions were raucous, exciting affairs no matter how right or how wrong the candidates, the other part was swept up in the fervor of the moment.[1]

It didn't last. Schuman was asked to redraft a section of the platform dealing with the United Nations and world government. He suggested that the language include an exhortation for world government that criticized both the United States and the Soviet Union for destabilizing international politics. That was unacceptable to Wallace, but there wasn't time that evening to hash it out. Schuman had paid $2.65 for a ticket to the mass meeting at Shibe Park, the home of the Philadelphia Athletics baseball team. In the crowd of 30,000 Schuman estimated that a third of the people were Jewish, a fifth black, and more than a third very young. The stadium was brilliantly lit with floodlights, and Schuman listened to the actor Sam Wanamaker narrate the program. By the time Wallace and Taylor gave their acceptance speeches after 10:00 p.m., Robeson had again stirred the crowd with songs and a speech, William Gailmor had once more wrung another $50,000 from the crowd, and Vito Marcantonio had given a rousing, demagogic speech. Taylor, all grins, denounced the Marshall Plan and Wall Street. And then Wallace, who stirred even the staid Schuman with his intonation: "All of you who are within the sound of my voice tonight have been called to serve."

The next morning Schuman had a prebreakfast meeting with Wallace. The candidate and his campaign manager, C.B. Baldwin, greeted Schuman warmly, and they went over the final draft of the platform. Wallace liked everything except the passage about "Left totalitarianism." He sternly told Schuman that the Progressive Party "must not, cannot and will not, engage in any form of Russophobia or Red-baiting." Schuman didn't agree that criticizing Stalin's excesses constituted red-baiting, but he knew that this was one fight he couldn't win.

After breakfast, he met with Glen Taylor. Taylor went over the draft, and the argument continued. Taylor contended that the Cold War was almost exclusively the fault of the United States, and Baldwin worried that if any hint of criticism of the Soviet Union appeared in the platform, Paul Robeson would rise to object. The final language read, "Responsibility for ending the tragic prospect of war is a joint responsibility of the Soviet Union and the United States." Baldwin still fretted that Robeson and others would be offended.

That afternoon, Schuman arrived back at the hall just after Gailmor had begun to read the platform language to the assembly. The new clause did indeed provoke objections, and several hours of debate ensued. Even more divisive was the amendment proposed by Vermont farmer James Hayford, who suggested the inclusion of the clause "Although we are critical of the foreign policy of the United States, it is not our intention to give blanket endorsement to the foreign policy of any nation." A brief smattering of applause greeted the modest-looking Hayford, and then a chorus of boos. The amendment was voted down, and the platform was then adopted.

By this time, Schuman was utterly exhausted. Not happy with the rejection of both his language and the Vermont resolution, he still felt that the party was sound, full of good people who would work for what was best for all Americans. After what he had seen, he was confident that the Communists were not running the party and that no matter what happened in November, he had played a small part in the founding of a new political force that would last for many years to come.

Astute observer that he was, Professor Schuman was a bit too sanguine about communist influence in the movement. They certainly weren't in control, but the defeat of the moderate Vermont resolution had been engineered by delegates who were members of the American Communist Party, and portions of the international relations sections of the platform had been crafted by Pressman with the interests of the Communist Party in mind. By late July, as more people around the country defected from the Progressives, the number of Communists in the movement grew in proportion to the whole, and they assumed a larger role, though they had little direct influence over Wallace, Taylor, or Baldwin.

All of the conventions in 1948 were a mix of high politics, low politics, and entertainment. The stage-managed convention lay in the future, and television had not yet worked its strange destructive magic. Politicians still staked out clear positions on issues, even on specific issues, even when those positions were so unambiguous that some voters were alienated even as others were attracted. The Republican platform of 1948 was the most modern in that it was the least explicit and most designed not to alienate the various wings of the party and the various blocs across the country. But for the most part, the language of politics and of the conventions was often dramatic, occasionally boring, and frequently substantive.

In his role as a delegate and member of the platform committee, Schuman witnessed many of the key moments of the Progressive Party convention, but not all. He wasn't present for the discussions on the party's name, for instance. Until July 24, the party did not have an official title. It had been known simply as the "new party," but in Philadelphia, the decision was made to label the movement "the Progressive Party," and thereby link Wallace to a long line of American progressives from Theodore Roosevelt to Robert La Follette. Schuman also had little contact with the inner circle of the party. Though he knew Wallace casually and Rexford Tugwell and C.B. Baldwin somewhat better, he didn't interact with the other leaders, like Albert Fitzgerald, the cochairman of the National Wallace for President Committee; Elmer Benson, the elderly former Minnesota governor who represented the link between the new party and the old Midwestern Progressive movement; Clark Foreman, the obscure party treasurer; John Abt, who had formerly served as counsel for the Amalgamated Clothing Workers; Lew Frank, one of the primary speechwriters; the sculptor Jo Davidson; and of course, Robeson.

He also wasn't present for the charged confrontation between Henry Wallace and several hundred reporters. At the beginning of the press conference, Wallace read a letter from recently murdered journalist George Polk, whose mysterious death in Greece was a cause célèbre. He used the letter as a way of lecturing the assembled journalists about their responsibilities to the truth. Some of the reporters were vaguely sympathetic; most were hostile or simply amused. Almost all wanted a dramatic story to report, perhaps a repudiation of communism or an embrace of it. Wallace told them he would not repudiate any who supported him and he would not pander to any group, Communists included. The venerable Norman Thomas, who had already announced his intention to run against Wallace in order to demonstrate that the Old Left would have nothing to do with a new party that included Communists, was present in his capacity as a reporter for the Hoyt syndicate controlled by the publisher of the *Denver Post*. Asked if he would accept an invitation to debate Dewey or Truman, Wallace said yes. Asked if he would debate the Socialist candidate Thomas, Wallace

answered no. "Why?" someone asked. "Because I believe in conserv-
ing my strength," Wallace replied. Reflecting on the episode later in
the day, the stentorian Thomas commented, "He shows a certain
prudence."

Also at the press conference were veteran journalists like H.L.
Mencken of the *Baltimore Sun,* who had covered the Scopes monkey
trial in 1925, the Alsop brothers from the *Washington Post,* and
Wallace's obsessive nemesis Westbrook Pegler. Pegler asked Wallace
to comment on the Guru letters, but Wallace wouldn't bite. "I never
discuss anything with Westbrook Pegler," he said again as he had
said before. Another reporter rose to Pegler's defense and asked the
same question. "I never discuss anything with stooges for Westbrook Pegler," replied an icy, angry Wallace. Mencken then rose to
ask the candidate to define stooge. The conference deteriorated from
there, with a visibly irritated Wallace responding curtly to palpably
hostile questioners such as Dorothy Thompson.[2]

Unlike at the two other Philadelphia conventions, only one television network, NBC, decided to cover the Progressive conclave,
and sporadically at that. On the whole, the press treated the Progressives with derision and hostility. Though the platform was the
most complicated of the major party statements, it received only
cursory discussion. It stood against Universal Military Training,
against the "anti-Soviet hysteria" sweeping the nation, and against
segregation and racial discrimination. The party called for disarma-
ment, public financing of twenty-five million new homes, amnesty
for World War II conscientious objectors, and negotiation with the
Soviet Union. Yet the press focused largely on the Guru letters and
suspected communist control of the proceedings. Mencken referred
to the "swarms of crackpots" who attended and the "slick Communists" who dominated. Marquis Childs focused on the rivalries
between Tugwell and Pressman, and on the not-so-hidden communist agenda. Cartoonists from across the country took great pleasure
in skewering Wallace. One depicted him standing at a conference
table shaped like a hammer and sickle, another had him in a kitchen
washing dishes for Stalin, while another showed him banging a hammer and sickle gavel on a podium. Rube Goldberg drew a buck-
toothed Wallace reminiscent of Mao in front of delegates holding

signs with the names of various states, and one sign with the word "Moscow."[3]

Elated in the aftermath of the gathering, Progressive Party leaders allowed euphoria to get the best of them and predicted that they would gain as many as ten million votes in November. They pointed to the hundreds of thousands of signatures they had obtained in California to get on the ballot, and they made note that representatives from almost every state had come to Philadelphia. The party also planned to run candidates for gubernatorial, senatorial, congressional, and state assembly seats throughout the country.[4] Wallace envisioned an intense autumn that mirrored the frenetic pace of his spring campaigning. He even planned to take his message into the heart of the South, where the Dixiecrats had the edge and where Harry Truman dared not venture. After months of defections from the movement, Wallace in late July was surrounded by men and women who believed so utterly in the cause that they were inclined to interpret any criticism as "red-baiting." Though the Communist Party was actively working for Wallace's election, Wallace preferred to look the other way. He genuinely thought that democracy was strong enough to allow for communism, and he was convinced that the moral price of denouncing the Communists in the Progressive Party was higher than the political price of accepting their support.

The Progressive Party was notably egalitarian, and though Wallace was treated as a messiah figure, his supporters were eclectic and representative of the diversity of America. More than the professional politicians who made up a significant percentage of the Democratic and Republican Party leaders, the Progressive Party was truly grassroots. The participants were young and not particularly affluent. Many were well educated, including writers such as Norman Mailer; publishers such as Angus Cameron of Little, Brown and Company, who headed the party in Massachusetts; and editors such as Josiah Gitt.

Traveling to Philadelphia in itself was an odyssey for many of those thousands who were present in the convention hall. J.A. Ruccio, a labor leader and a committeeman of the Pennsylvania Progressive Party, wrote to Gitt, the state chairman, to explain why he was having a hard time attending meetings. "Dear Mr. Gitt, I hope this doesn't sound as though I am making excuses or placing blame for my absence at both the Pittsburgh and Harrisburg meetings of the Committee. The bold truth is I was broke, tho I could have borrowed some money, the best connections I could make out of here that day was a bus which would have arrived in Pittsburgh at 10:19 p.m., too late for the meeting. I could have flown by plane, but don't like to fly, never have. Besides this, I had some domestic difficulties, my arm was bothering me a great deal and I was feeling pretty low about things generally, that is, all except our movement—which, I assure you, I am dedicated to. . . . P.S. My phone is reconnected—thanks to a check I received today." No professional member of either the Democratic or Republican Party would have written their state chairman with such a series of excuses, but the Progressives defined themselves as being a compassionate, nonjudgmental, inclusive force in American society. Ruccio was a fairly ordinary man living a difficult life that was by no means atypical in 1948. He and thousands like him were the lifeblood of the Progressive Party.[5]

Gitt himself gave an earnest speech on the opening night of the convention. He recalled the spirit of Washington, Jefferson, Lincoln, and others who had defied the conventional political wisdom of their day to pursue politics they believed in. Among the many strengths of the new party, he said, one stood out: "Our Party will give the American People the chance to choose. . . . Without it, the People would have no choice but to accept the Bi-Partisan program." Whether or not the Progressive Party fulfilled its potential in 1948, Gitt was right. Its presence meant that the public was given another choice, an alternative that was in every way distinct from the two major parties, and equally distinct from the Dixiecrats.[6]

The Progressives received highly negative press coverage, and that helped dilute their support. At the same time, negative press was still press. Both the Progressives and the Dixiecrats were covered in print and on radio. Though both parties complained vociferously that they weren't being covered as much or as fairly as the two established parties, in retrospect, it is striking how much attention they received, not how little, and how much reaction they generated, not how few people voted for them. If you cared about politics in 1948, you couldn't escape reading about or hearing about Wallace and Thurmond, and though you would have had a difficult time believing that Wallace wasn't a communist tool, you still would have been exposed to the ideas of the Progressive Party. That made the fall campaign dynamic—perhaps not more dynamic than the major campaigns of 1800, 1832, 1860, or 1912, but more dynamic and more ideologically diverse than anyone of political age in 1948 would experience again in their lifetimes.

CHAPTER FIFTEEN

The Calm Before
the Storm

IN LATE JULY the candidates took a much-needed break. They went home, to their families and friends, and enjoyed a few weeks of summer at their farms, estates, and houses. They spent some concentrated time with their families, knowing that such time would be almost nonexistent after Labor Day. By August, it was hot almost everywhere, and in a world without much air-conditioning, there was a natural tendency to slow down, to focus a bit on the baseball pennant race among the Cleveland Indians, the Boston Red Sox, the New York Yankees, and the Philadelphia Athletics. Babe Ruth, one of the heroes of his generation, fell ill and died.

The pollsters were busy, however. Elmo Roper and George Gallup tried to get a read on the national mood. They both discovered that people were most concerned about the rising cost of living, and about whether they would be able to keep pace. Dewey was ahead in every poll. Forty-eight to 45 percent were for Dewey, 31 to 37 percent were for Truman, and barely 3 percent were for Wallace. In the South, the Dixiecrats had the support of 14 percent of the population, though that figure was even higher in the Deep South. Truman's support showed little of the postconvention "bounce" that devotees of the modern televised convention are familiar with. In fact, his poll numbers in July and August were actually lower than in June after his western trip. Commentators believed that the wide gap between Dewey and Truman, and the extremely narrow support for the third parties, would dictate campaign strategy, and they were right.[1]

With their large lead, the Republicans would try not to take any chances, while the Democrats would have to campaign aggressively to win over indifferent or wavering voters. Meanwhile, the Dixiecrats and the Progressives needed to rely on dramatic gestures, schedule major speeches when the two main parties were inactive, and pray that something Wallace or Thurmond said or did would be sufficiently controversial to sway public opinion. Dewey was considered personally popular with the electorate, but his strength in the agrarian Midwest was suspect, and the overall popularity of the Republican Party still lagged behind the Democrats. Truman was regarded as so unpalatable in the Deep South that no one believed it even worth his while to campaign south of the Mason-Dixon line. Almost all radio and newspaper people wrote off the Democrats as a disintegrating coalition and expressed grave doubts about Truman's chances of victory. Again and again, columnists or radio personalities announced that Truman faced "almost certain defeat" in November.[2]

Truman didn't plan to fulfill those prophecies. He was still president, and he made sure that both the Republicans and the country knew it. Just as the special session of Congress convened, he issued two executive orders. One desegregated the armed forces, while the other set up an agency to monitor fair employment practices in the civil service. The executive orders were a bold display of the powers of the presidency. In issuing them, Truman set the stage for being able to attack the Republicans and the 80th Congress for their inability to pass meaningful legislation on civil rights. Even if the special session magically managed to overcome the resistance of the southern representatives to civil rights legislation, Truman could still say that the Republican-controlled Congress had been a laggard.

Republicans were frustrated that they had been trumped. They dutifully assembled on July 26 and spent the next twelve days deadlocked. The attempt to pass federal anti–poll tax legislation foundered on the shoals of southern Democrats, while housing, education, and Social Security bills ran into Republican opposition. Dewey and his managers desperately wanted the congressional Republicans to pass at least some token bills that would allow

Dewey to rebut Truman's claims of the "do-nothing" Congress. Instead, the divided congressional Republicans passed one hollow housing bill sponsored by Senator Joseph McCarthy, who was an obscure junior Republican from Wisconsin, and then proceeded to question Elizabeth Bentley about an alleged Soviet spy ring that reached into the very core of the U.S. government.

First in front of a Senate subcommittee and then before the House Un-American Activities Committee, Bentley, a former courier for Russian intelligence services, testified about the extensive penetration of the State Department by Soviet agents. She claimed that Harry Dexter White, a Truman appointee to the International Monetary Fund, was a Soviet spy, and his was only the most prominent of the names she provided. Several days later, an editor at *Time* magazine, Whittaker Chambers, testified that Alger Hiss, an influential State Department official during World War II, had also served as a Soviet agent. The combined testimony of Chambers and Bentley, followed later in August by the outraged denials by Hiss, was the most dramatic development of the special session, and one that would have long-term ramifications. Congressman Richard Nixon would eventually make a reputation for himself as a vigorous anti-Communist who brought down Alger Hiss, and less than two years later, Senator McCarthy would launch his first salvo against purported communist infiltration of the Truman administration.

Neither Truman nor his party knew it at the time—nor did Republican leaders—but the special session would come back to haunt the Democrats. When Truman went on the warpath against Dewey and the Republicans in the fall, he unleashed a torrent of vitriolic rhetoric that was often unconstrained by factual validity. So embittered were the Republicans by Truman's success that they vowed revenge, and looking for the best method to achieve retribution, they lit on the spy hearings of August 1948. Truman's short-term gain inadvertently sowed the seed for the assault on his presidency and on his party that would occupy much of his second term.[3]

In the midst of these goings-on, Truman and Dewey briefly met at New York's Idlewild Airport for a dedication ceremony. They shook hands for the photographers, made brief speeches, and acted like fighters greeting each other warily in the ring just before the bout is to begin.

Dewey was both calm and complacent that summer. He rested at his Pawling farm with his family and advisers, attended to the voluminous correspondence he received each day, and planned tactics for the fall. In one of his "Dear Mater" letters, he wrote, "I am getting in fine shape. I've paid a lot of attention to farm matters and, of course, some to politics. We think the Special Session is a nuisance but no more." A few weeks later, in an August 9 missive, he bragged to his mother that he had shot the best golf score of his life at a local Pawling course, making a forty-one in nine holes. He took the opportunity to help his elder son Tommy with baseball, and he was pleased that the farm was actually making a profit. Apparently, his life was neither stressful nor arduous, though he knew he had some work to do. "I guess my vacation is over. We will have to start writing speeches in earnest soon though I do not expect the campaign to start for a very considerable time—not until middle or late September." In a footnote, he answered what must have been an earlier query. "I do not know about accommodations at the White House for the family at Inauguration," he informed his curious mother. "You . . . would of course stay there with us if we moved in after the Inauguration but I doubt there would be much room for any others."[4]

Dewey clearly believed that the election was his to lose. Based on that assumption, he and his advisers designed a campaign that would minimize risk. Dewey would act presidential. He would refuse to belittle his opponent, though he would at every opportunity remind voters that the Democrats had been in power for sixteen years, that they were a tired, divided party with no vision, and that it was time for a fresh approach in the White House. At the end of the special session, he met with a group of young Republicans in Albany and chided the Truman administration for stooping to "easy remedies and quack solutions." Under a Republican administration, Dewey said, the nation could look forward to new ideas rather than back to the "dim, departed, almost forgotten and never to be recovered past."[5]

The men around Dewey were working hard during these weeks.

A shift took place in the hierarchy of advisers. Whereas Sprague, Brownell, and Jaeckle had been preeminent at the convention, by August, Elliot Bell, the New York State banking superintendent and a former *New York Times* financial writer, had assumed a more central role, as had Paul Lockwood. Brownell continued as campaign manager, but the other two members of the convention Triumvirate had less influence. Bell and Lockwood, working from Albany, dispatched advance scouts throughout the country to prepare for the fall. These scouts met with local Republicans in important states to coordinate appearances and to discuss what message Dewey should convey in order to galvanize the electorate. Many Republicans thought that Dewey, as a former federal prosecutor, would hit Truman hard during the campaign, and they hoped to see a vigorous Republican effort to attack the record of the Democrats.

Dewey, however, did not wish to wage an aggressively negative campaign. He felt that his interests would be better served by making general criticisms of the Democratic Party and referring to Truman by name as infrequently as possible. He wanted to convey a positive message about the brave new world of a Republican administration, rather than harp on the specific shortcomings of the Democrats. Dewey also wanted the press to pay attention to Earl Warren. Throughout August, the Dewey team stressed that Warren would be a key component of the Republican campaign, and Warren himself gave several speeches and press conferences in which he promised a campaign free from "bitterness toward opponents."

In mid-August, Dewey and Warren met in New York to finalize plans. They would campaign separately, each by train, each beginning in late September. Both would make coast-to-coast tours, and though they would visit some of the same states, they did not intend to be in the same state at the same time at any point during the fall. According to Brownell, the goal was "to reach the maximum number of voters," and that goal could be best met by splitting up. The two also agreed to make special efforts in states where Senate seats were closely contested, states such as Tennessee, where Democrat Estes Kefauver was competing against former chairman of the Republican Party Carroll Reece, and Minnesota, where Humphrey was running to capture the seat. Dewey and Warren didn't just want to gain the White House; they wanted to ensure Republican control of Congress for years to come.[6]

While Dewey was enjoying a respite in Pawling, Truman was in Washington blasting the special session and charting the coming weeks with his campaign staff. By early August, it was clear that the public was disenchanted with the 80th Congress, and while Truman's chances at election appeared slim, the fortunes of the party as a whole appeared to be improving. Barring a Dewey landslide, the Democrats believed that they had a good chance of retaking the Senate in November, and for that reason alone it was necessary for Truman to wage a credible campaign. Of course, the president and his inner circle hadn't conceded anything, and they designed a campaign that would catapult Truman and Barkley over Dewey and Warren.

The campaign began with the spin put on the special session. Even before Congress met on July 26, White House staff briefed reporters and issued press releases in order to put the 80th Congress in the worst possible light. In a memo to Clark Clifford, William Batt provided an overview of the challenges and how Truman might meet them. "All of our resources must be used to make it overwhelmingly clear that the coming special session of Congress will be a battle between the forces of the people, led by the President, and the forces of special privilege, represented by Republican leaders." Batt warned that in this struggle, the press would be largely against the president. Therefore, both in August and after Labor Day when the general campaign began, Truman "must be in continuous close contact with the people. He must arouse their confidence and make them aware of their strength, by showing them his courage, his coolness, his determination, his sincerity, and his fighting spirit." In addition, he should demonstrate his humanity and simplicity, which would draw voters even closer to him and highlight the contrast between him and his rather dull opponent. Batt also advised that the best way for Truman to maintain contact with the people was through constant use of the radio.

Responding to Batt's suggestions about intensifying the attack on the 80th Congress, the Democratic National Committee printed leaflets urging people to "Remember in November the Congress That Forgot You!" Not only had Congress done nothing, the Democrats claimed, but it had stood by while inflation eroded the standard of living for tens of millions of Americans, while prices rose faster than wages, and while ordinary workers and farmers suffered even as rich Republican businessmen prospered.[7] The Democrats knew that this message could resonate if Truman and the party repeated it over and over. They knew that populist, anti–Wall Street, anti-elite rhetoric had played well before, and that if anyone could sing that song effectively, it was Harry Truman. Truman's confidence was based not just on some internal, personal muse, but on various bits and pieces of evidence that an easy Dewey victory was far from a certainty.

For instance, on August 1, Truman's man Leslie Biffle was dispatched on a reconnaissance mission to take the pulse of the people. Starting in Virginia, Biffle disguised himself as a chicken farmer, complete with a beat-up, rusty truck and crates. He drove through West Virginia, Kentucky, and Ohio and stopped and talked with people at gas stations, roadside diners, farms, stores, motels, bars, movie theaters, malt shops, coffee shops, barbershops, haberdasheries, department stores, police stations, post offices, and grain depots. From these conversations, he concluded that the support for Dewey was much more tentative than the mainstream press were reporting and that Truman was held in more personal esteem than people in Washington or in the party thought.[8]

Truman's advisers evaluated the situation carefully. They spent weeks coming up with a rough blueprint for victory, and then implemented it. Once again, Clifford's was a potent and acute voice. He summarized the thinking of the campaign staff in an August 17 memo for the president. "The first objective," he began, "is to win a large majority of the 15,000,000 independent voters who overwhelmingly followed the liberal leadership of the Democratic Party in the last four elections." In order to do this, Truman should continue the drumbeat about the miserable 80th Congress and then link Dewey to it. "The second objective is to win support from three large groups . . . which can swing the election . . . : workers, veterans, and Negroes. This does not mean that farmers, small businessmen, and other groups should be overlooked. . . . The third objective is to cut through all party lines by showing that the President's policy has kept the nation on a road leading to peace, and that changes in this policy may lead to war." During speeches and interviews, Truman should, Clifford advised, point to the dismal legacy of the Republican presidents in the 1920s and to the current Republican record on labor and the party's reluctance to embrace an internationalist foreign policy. Clifford also underscored the importance of seventeen states where the 1944 margin of victory was slim. These states, including New York, Pennsylvania, Ohio, Illinois, Michigan, Missouri, and Wisconsin, shaped Truman's itinerary for the fall. Clifford recommended three major tours, beginning with the Midwest and a Labor Day speech in Detroit, then heading west and finally to the East, including a swing through rural New York State and a speech in Harlem. The one question was whether he should venture south at all, and as of mid-August, many of his advisers, watching the States' Rights campaign unfold, were inclined to write off the Deep South entirely. Finally, Clifford strongly recommended that "a trained observer should precede the President at every stop he is scheduled to make. This man should prepare a brief on the town the President is scheduled to visit, explaining the local issues of importance and how they tie in to national issues. . . . This man should start his circuit at least two weeks before the President's tour begins."[9]

After the startling outcome of the election, many writers heralded the Truman victory as an example of the way honest, simple, straight talk will ultimately triumph in American politics over glib, packaged, and calculating politicians. Yet as was true for the June tour, Truman's spontaneity was at once genuine and calculated. The idea of having Truman emphasize that he was a man of the people, of having him speak informally, of having him give short speeches and travel by train—all of these techniques were carefully developed, rigorously debated, and honed by what we now call "advance men" and "market research." On the campaign trail, Truman did speak simply, he did focus on issues, and he did stress substantive differences between the Democrats and the Republicans. But this didn't mean that his campaign was simple or that his advisers weren't as coolly calculating as Dewey's. If anything, as the autumn would prove, they were more calculating, and better at the game of politics.

What they weren't as good at was raising money. The financial health of the Democratic Party hadn't improved much by August. In order to conduct the campaign, McGrath and his staff estimated that they would need somewhere in the area of $50 million. By law, the party's national committee could only spend $3 million. In order to make up the difference, Truman-Barkley clubs were set up in every state. Technically, these clubs were private organizations and were not under any legal constraints as to how much they could spend. The clubs became the main conduit through which the campaign was financed, and the primary recipient of donations, whether from labor organizations or from private individuals.[10]

"I DID NOT risk my life on the beaches of Normandy," Governor Thurmond announced on August 1 as he began his journey, "to come back to this country and sit idly by while a bunch of hack politicians whittles away your heritage and mine. As for me, I intend to fight!" The Dixiecrats may have been poor; they may have been shunned by most of the leading Democrats of the South; they may have seethed with anger and resentment; but they certainly didn't lack enthusiasm. The campaign was directed by Judge Merritt Gibson. From headquarters in Jackson, Gibson tried to organize a regional campaign on a negligible budget. At the end of July, the Dixiecrats were boldly predicting that they would vie for the presidency in all forty-eight states. Then reality slowly set in: that would be impossible.

In too many states, the southern rebels were thwarted by the Democratic Party election machinery. In North Carolina, the States' Rights Party was barred from the ballot by a board of electors controlled by Democrats faithful to the mainstream party. In Georgia, much of the state machinery was dominated by Senator Russell, who, for all of his fulminations against Truman, would not endorse the States' Rights movement and made sure that the balloting would not fall into the hands of the Dixiecrats. By mid-August, the States' Righters had pared down their expectations. Instead of forty-eight states, they would aim to get on the ballot in thirty-five. In spite of the optimistic projections of Thurmond and Wright, of campaign manager Gibson and campaign cochair Wallace Wright, polls showed the Dixiecrat ticket commanding only 14 percent of the vote throughout the thirteen southern states. Truman polled 41 percent, Dewey 34, and Wallace a mere 2. Only Mississippi, South Carolina, and Alabama were pledged to the Thurmond-Wright slate.[11]

Fund-raising was a chronic problem. The Dixiecrats were cut off from the traditional sources of Democratic money. They were based in the least affluent region in the United States, and they were without an infrastructure. In a matter of weeks, they had to raise a minimum of $1 million, and though oil money helped and Mississippi and Alabama businessmen contributed, that wasn't enough. One scheme was to designate September 11 as "States' Rights Dinners Day." Throughout the South, the party planned to sell box lunches for $10 apiece. People were urged to spend this substantial sum in the interest of combating the creeping "totalitarianism" of the federal government. In addition to this regional drive, the Gibson team in Jackson appointed county chairmen throughout the South, and each of these chairs was responsible for raising money through dollar-a-plate lunches, rallies, button sales, and banquets. The National States' Rights Democrats Campaign Committee also mailed pamphlets enjoining people to "Support These Courageous Men," Thurmond and Wright. Not only would a vote for the States' Righters possibly prevent Truman from achieving a victory in the electoral college, this pamphlet informed voters, but it could also send a clear message to a Dewey administration that the South would not accept any federal legislation on civil rights. Attached to each mailing was a form that said, "Invest in the Fight for Local Self-Government and States' Rights," complete with a donation slip with the address of the committee printed on it.[12]

After opening the race in Cherryville, North Carolina, on August 1, Thurmond traveled to Houston, courtesy of H.R. Cullen. Upon his arrival, a twenty-six-piece band played Dixie favorites before Thurmond and his party were whisked away in a motorcade to the Rice Hotel. That evening, Thurmond socialized with the local press corps at a buffet dinner at the Houston Club, and he was seen glad-handing the attorney general of Texas. He chided the press for continuing to use the name "Dixiecrat" when the party was actually the legitimate embodiment of the Democratic Party and when its main issue, states' rights, was of national concern. The next morning, Thurmond and Wright held a press conference in preparation for the major address Thurmond would give that evening in the Sam Houston Coliseum.

"Destiny brings us to the great State of Texas," Thurmond began. "On this battleground for freedom, we sound a call for a return to constitutional government in America." He then rehashed his condemnation of the Democratic convention in Philadelphia and accused Truman of taking the first steps toward the creation of "a police state in this country." He lumped Truman, Dewey, and Wallace together in a cabal that wished to strip the South of her rights: "States Rights' Americans resist this shameful betrayal of our national character. States Rights' Americans are ready to stand, even at the expense of life itself, as Crockett, Bowie and Houston stood in Texas, for individual liberty and freedom, and for the right of the people to govern themselves." The governor continued in this vein. He asserted that the usurpation of state power by the federal government was a national issue that should worry Arizona as much as Alabama, and he painted his struggle as a struggle for "human rights." Hitler, Thurmond said, "gained power by advocating human rights for minority groups. Under his plan, the constitutional rights of the people were destroyed." Then he included Mussolini and Stalin as other dictators who had used a federal police force to usurp power. Thurmond used the words "police" and "police power" repeatedly during the speech, and time and again, he returned to the central theme that the States' Rights campaign was about freedom versus tyranny. He depicted the Fair Employment Practices Commission (FEPC) as something "admirably suited to the Russian form of government, where the thoughts, activities and ambitions of the people are controlled from Moscow." The FEPC would prevent average Americans from choosing "his or her associates," and it would empower "a federal Gestapo" to enforce its regulations. "With humility, with the knowledge that the greatness of the cause must overshadow all its servants, I accept the nomination for president."[13]

This overblown rhetoric set the tone for the subsequent campaign. In the three dozen major speeches Thurmond gave during the next ten weeks, he would vary little from the text he read in Houston. Thurmond was not a deep thinker and he lacked an extensive speech writing team. Unlike Dewey and Truman, he had neither the time nor the staff nor the intellectual inclination to develop a series of nuanced speeches. Instead, he and Governor Wright went from place to place and gave only slightly different versions of the same message, hoping that people would be so alarmed and aroused by the evocations of police states and Nazism and the end of freedom that they would awake from their complacency and vote against Truman and for the States' Rights platform. Yet even in Houston, there were signs of creeping recidivism. Beauford Jester, who had earlier pledged to fight the Truman-Barkley ticket, now said that though he sympathized with Thurmond, he couldn't force other Texas Democrats to break with the national party. Texas was key to Dixiecrat hopes, but by the end of August Texas was beginning to appear out of reach, and the States' Righters looked for another strategy that would prod ordinary Texans to reject Truman and the Democrats.

Once again in Houston, the third parties clashed. The Texas Wallaceites organized an impressive demonstration outside the Sam Houston Coliseum during Thurmond's speech. While the Dixiecrats placed their hopes on grassroots support that had yet to materialize, the Wallace movement proved early on that its grassroots supporters would be impossible to ignore. In every state, local Wallace and Taylor clubs formed, and local Progressive Party committees organized public displays such as the protest against the Dixiecrats in Houston.[14] And to demonstrate that his campaign was truly national, Wallace scheduled appearances in North Carolina in August and in various other southern states in the fall. In time, the crowds would grow more hostile, but by August the tone of the fall was already set: Wallace would play the martyr.

Unlike Truman and his carefully crafted Ordinary Man, or Dewey and his carefully crafted Next President, or Thurmond and his rather sloppy Champion of Freedom, Wallace seems to have assumed the role of martyr without anyone advising him to do so. He had always been inclined toward self-righteousness, but after the Philadelphia meeting and the almost universal scorn of the press and the clear evidence of plummeting poll numbers, Wallace retreated to a universe in which he was right even if most of the country believed him wrong. He resigned from his position at *The New Republic* in order, he said, to be free to campaign. In fact, the liberal journal that once nurtured him no longer wished to be associated with him. In late July, he went on the warpath against Truman for cynically calling a special session of Congress when everyone knew that no good legislation would come from it. And rather than step back and take stock with Baldwin, Robeson, Davidson, Benson, and Tugwell, he plunged into a hectic travel schedule that allowed no time for reflection. As a result, Wallace and his party never really developed a coherent campaign plan. It was, instead, a campaign driven by the relentless energy of the candidate, by Wallace's need and desire to speak in every corner of the nation to whoever would pay to hear him.[15]

As August drew to a close, the two main parties prepared to join in the final battle, the two minor parties tried to generate enthusiasm in the face of resistance and apathy, and the public expressed no great excitement at the coming election. People would turn to politics when a candidate was in town, or when the summer gave way to cooler weather. They would make a choice about whom to vote for, and they would discuss it with friends and family. But if they listened to the radio or read the editorial pages of their local papers, they might have been even less inclined to pay attention, because according to the pundits, the outcome was already certain. The polls showed Dewey with a double-digit advantage, and though polls had not achieved the mystical lure they would acquire in subsequent decades, more than two-thirds of the editorial pages endorsed Dewey and nearly all predicted that the Republicans would glide to victory. So it was understandable that most people attended to local concerns, to the end of summer, to family and friends. And for Tom Dewey, comfortably in the lead, that was just swell.

CHAPTER SIXTEEN

The Victory Special

I AM BUSY as a one-armed paper hanger," Tom Dewey wrote his mother on September 14, "trying to write speeches and seeing too many people and as always, the speeches suffer and I will have to write considerably on the train I am afraid. We leave Sunday afternoon and will be gone just two weeks." Dewey may have lamented that he was falling behind in his work, and he may have had some trepidation about the upcoming weeks, but for the most part, he was quite pleased with the way things were going. In an article in the *New York Herald-Tribune,* Elmo Roper announced that on the basis of his latest survey, the election was essentially over. Dewey's 44 percent to 31 percent lead over Truman bore, said Roper, "an almost morbid resemblance to the Roosevelt-Landon figures of about this time in 1936." Only a "political convulsion," asserted Roper, could keep Dewey from the White House. Roper went on to characterize the election as a rather unspectacular horse race in which one horse was clearly superior and clearly destined for victory. Rather than continue to monitor this foregone conclusion, Roper stated that he preferred to devote his time and effort to other things.[1]

Roper was operating on a widely held assumption of voter behavior called "Farley's Law." According to New York State Democratic Chairman James A. Farley, voters made up their minds by early September at the latest. If a candidate hadn't swayed voters by Labor Day, then they weren't going to be swayed. Roper firmly believed that the man ahead early was almost certain to be the man ahead late, and that the outcome of an election was pretty much determined before a candidate "has uttered a word of campaign oratory." Roper may have made his case a bit more stridently than his colleagues, but George Gallup and Archibald Crossley and many hardened political journalists shared this view. Of course, voting behavior had only been subjected to systematic analysis since the ill-fated Roosevelt-Landon election of 1936. Roper and other professional predictors thus made sweeping generalizations based on three elections, each of which Franklin Roosevelt had won.

Dewey may have been a relatively unflappable man, but he was still comforted by the constant reports that he had nothing to worry about. Everyone said he would win; he wanted to win; and everything indicated that he would. He was also acutely sensitive to criticism, and he saw the 1948 election as a way to redeem himself for the 1944 campaign that he had lost to FDR. During 1944, the rap on Dewey was that he was too aggressive and too negative. At one point, he had even called Roosevelt a "traitor" who had knowingly allowed the bombing of Pearl Harbor. "Please don't make your campaign one of personal vilification, as you did in 1944," wrote a concerned supporter. "Attack the [Democratic] party and party politics all you want, but please don't attack persons." One of Dewey's chief image advisers, Bruce Barton, gave the same advice. Truman had honed a particular style that harkened back to an earlier era, what Barton called "horse-and-buggy campaigning—pre-newspapers, pre-radio, and pre-television." For Dewey, Barton preferred something different. "I'd rather have ten marvelous speeches by a rested and confident candidate, all carefully planned for the radio and the newsreels, than a thousand back platform chats any one of which could produce an embarrassing slip."[2]

Barton was an unusually astute observer of campaign trends. The counsel he gave Dewey was exactly the counsel campaign managers and image consultants would give their candidates in the decades ahead. As television came to dominate presidential elections and as network news evolved, the cost of making a slip during a speech rose exponentially. In 1948, such slips could be broadcast on the radio or reported in various journals and newspapers. But with the rise of television, a slip could be seen by everyone, over and over again. There is a vast and visceral difference between reading about what someone did or said and seeing for oneself. Television has an immediacy and an intimacy that registers in a way that reading an article does not. Dewey's men were sensitive to the changing dynamics of presidential elections. It was their misfortune to be slightly ahead of the curve. Advice that might well have helped Dewey four or eight years later, advice that became conventional wisdom during the television era, hurt him in 1948 when he ran against a candidate waging a pretelevision campaign.

Though Dewey avoided controversial topics, he still planned to travel extensively. Unlike McKinley in 1896, Dewey would bring himself to the people. He would, like Truman, campaign by train, and he would make stops at small towns as well as in large cities. Dewey was as much a whistle-stop candidate as Truman; he simply wasn't as effective or as comfortable with the format. His speeches were more canned, his rhetoric less homey, and his demeanor more stiff. Most of what he said and did was planned in advance in meetings with his secretary Paul Lockwood; with one of his primary writers, Elliott Bell; with press secretary James C. Hagerty; and with Brownell. Dewey believed that the same careful staff work that had served him well in the governor's office and that aided him at the 1948 convention would also propel him to the White House. By all accounts, meetings were freewheeling, and Dewey encouraged his advisers to speak openly. Different angles were considered, and various permutations were debated. Lockwood might disagree with Dewey, Bell might disagree with Lockwood, and Hagerty might disagree with all of them, but Dewey didn't mind. He didn't like yes-men, and he valued give and take.[3]

The first major tour began for Dewey on September 19. His fifteen-car train was confidently named the Victory Special. The itinerary called for a thirteen-state tour of the West, with the first major appearance in Des Moines, Iowa, on Monday evening, September 20. Dewey was scheduled to speak at the Drake University Stadium in front of 30,000, and the event was to be broadcast nationally on both CBS and Mutual. The speech was scheduled as a response to Truman's visit to Dexter, Iowa, two days earlier, and Dewey wanted to use the occasion to establish a contrast between his style and vision and that of his rival. But he wouldn't do so explicitly. In accordance with his strategy of adopting the role of "champ," he avoided mentioning Truman's name. He did not directly attack the Democrats nor did he go into any detail about what he would do as president. He left the hardball tactics to Harold Stassen, who had already delivered a blistering speech in response to Truman's Labor Day address in Detroit. Robert Taft also went on the warpath against the Democrats and Truman. While Taft and Stassen played the Republican bad cops, Dewey made a leisurely journey to Iowa and offered the calm crowd a bland buffet of platitudes.[4]

Dewey and his writers spent weeks working on the Dexter address. In fact, they took care with all of Dewey's homilies, yet for all the judicious crafting of the speeches, Dewey rarely gave a stirring one. As the campaign progressed, the reporters on the train began to notice an absence of substance. The vagueness of Dewey's campaign wasn't simply a product of his playing it safe. Just as he had assured the convention delegates that he accepted the nomination freighted with no prior obligations and promises, he wanted the electorate to know that as president, he would be beholden to no one faction. He had a philosophy of governing that dictated neutrality in the face of competing interest groups, and he refused to make campaign pledges that might come back to haunt him. Former prosecutor that he was, he intended to be a president with clean hands. He would not guarantee anyone a position in his administration, and he would not take specific stances that might limit his options once he became president.

The crowds who listened to Dewey were respectful and engaged, but they could hardly be called excited. "Dewey had good enough crowds," recalled Charles Greene of the New York Daily News, "good Republican crowds." Wherever the train stopped, Greene talked to bartenders and cops and firemen and local newspapermen and cab drivers. He canvassed as many people as he could and he bought a lot of drinks. "You spend a buck with a man over a bar and he'll talk to you," Greene liked to say. And after these conversations and sitting back and watching, Greene concluded that people "accepted Dewey, people thought, Well, he's going to be elected so we might as well show the flag." But there was no intensity, no sense of the importance of the moment. Only with Truman did Greene feel that something was happening.[5]

Iowa was a bastion of Republicanism, and in front of a docile audience in Des Moines, Dewey pledged that as president, he would be guided by one principle: "Is this good for our country?" He promised to staff his administration with people dedicated to the same thing. He said his White House would be governed by "team-work." He pledged an administration that would cooperate with Congress. He acknowledged that three years after the end of the war, many Americans still didn't have homes and many lacked a good education and many were troubled by the absence of peace abroad. He admitted that millions suffered from discrimination. But he didn't think that the problems were insurmountable. "I deeply believe that an administration which can unite our people will have taken the greatest single step toward solving these problems." He refused to place all the blame on "the current Administration," though he did fault "the Administration's lack of judgement." He believed in an America that stood as a beacon of freedom in the world, a nation of unity and idealism, "the hope of the world." He evoked the image of the martyrs to freedom such as Jan Masaryk, and he vowed that America would stand firm in the face of the tyranny sweeping the globe. "As I make specific proposals dealing with these problems of ours in the course of this campaign, they will not be the product of wishful thinking. I have no trick answers and no easy solutions. I will not offer one solution to one group and another solution to another group. . . . Let us go forward into the future as courageous, united Americans bound together by an invincible faith that liberty with justice under God is the most precious thing on earth."[6]

In the words of one columnist, Dewey delivered an eloquent, lofty speech—so lofty, in fact, "that it never touched ground at any specific point." This columnist, writing for the partisan and anti-Dewey paper the *New York Star,* noted the parallels between Dewey and Warren Gamaliel Harding, who had campaigned similarly. "Mr. Dewey asserts without equivocation or reservation that he is for unity, peace and prosperity. Although he did not specifically commit himself on this point, one may confidently assert that he is also against sin." Dewey's ethics may have been noble and his speech writing process may have been rigorous, but from them emerged a series of numbingly anodyne pronouncements.[7]

At the time, that seemed to be the wisest course, but some wondered if Dewey was playing it too safe. The ever-cantankerous Jaeckle, whose relations with J. Russel Sprague had deteriorated and whose interaction with the rest of the Dewey team had become strained, was troubled that Dewey never showed any emotion, and he had the uneasy sense that the campaign was taking too much for granted and placing too much faith in the polls. Earl Warren, who had met with Dewey in August to coordinate, toured on his own train during these weeks, visited thirty-eight states, and gave speeches about the impending demise of the Democratic Party. He was disturbed that Dewey was delivering talks that had been written weeks earlier and that he would not answer Truman's increasingly strident attacks. Warren also thought that Dewey needed to address the issue of farm prices and grain storage and that the campaign ought to do something to counteract the debilitating association between Dewey and the "do-nothing" Congress. Warren felt that the Dewey method was "lackadaisical," but he and the New Yorker had little contact, and when some of Warren's staff suggested changes, they were politely but firmly rebuffed by Dewey's managers.[8]

For the next two weeks, Dewey spoke in front of large audiences and in front of smaller crowds that gathered around the Victory Special. Some of the journalists on the train observed that Dewey was relaxed and at times even jocular. Someone would shout a greeting at the back of a throng, and Dewey would shout back, "Hi, there," and smile. At stops in the Midwest, he talked easily about his own farm in Pawling. He graciously accepted the various gifts he received, from the bushel of potatoes in Idaho to the grapes in California. But there was no escaping the "machine-like preciseness with which every detail is planned in advance." The press corps, wearing their bright orange badges, were given a detailed itinerary each day, and after a while, they began to notice that Dewey kept to the schedule. If it said that the train would arrive at Albuquerque at 7:50 a.m., the train arrived in Albuquerque at 7:50 a.m. If twenty minutes were allotted for a reception, the reception lasted twenty minutes. After several days, some reporters started to get an eerie feeling that it was all staged. Washington reporter Thomas Stokes felt that the Dewey campaign "was too mechanically perfect," down to "the china doll smile that never wears off." Stokes was particularly impressed by the speech Dewey gave in Los Angeles, expertly choreographed, meticulously delivered. "Hollywood never did it better," Stokes concluded. Observing the campaign from his perch in Washington, veteran journalist Joseph Alsop commented that "the Dewey show was opulent, organized down to the last noise-making device. . . . Dewey is able to raise a cheer with merely an endorsement of an early spring and a late fall or stern denunciation of the man-eating shark."[9]

Hundreds of thousands caught a glimpse of Dewey during this tour, but millions more heard the candidate on the radio or read about him in the papers or watched the professionally produced newsreels in movie theaters throughout the country. The newsreels emphasized Dewey's strength of character, complete with testimonials from distinguished Americans like Arthur Vandenberg. Playing in nearly 20,000 theaters, the newsreels were seen by as many as 65,000,000.[10]

As Dewey's staff worked out the inevitable first-week kinks, the train settled into a routine. The reporters and photographers drank in the club car, played cards, gossiped, smoked, joked, and stared at the passing landscape. They perused the schedule that the Dewey team had provided them and they marveled at the precision. Each time the train stopped, they mingled with the crowds and then listened to Dewey's remarks. Then they filed their stories, press releases from Lockwood or Bell tucked under their arms. They rushed to telephones and read their stories to the copy desk, or they gathered around the teletype machines and watched anxiously as their words were transmitted. Two minutes before the train was scheduled to pull out, Hagerty or Lockwood would blow a whistle to signal that it was time to board. Mrs. Dewey would make Tom's room ready, call their sons at school in Albany, and go over their social calendar for the next major stop, at Denver or San Francisco or Los Angeles or Seattle. The laundry would be sent out and the next stop would be told to have clean linens. And then Dewey would meet with his staff to go over the final draft of the next speech.[11]

The campaign also arranged logistics with the local Republican organizations. As with Democrats and to a lesser extent with the Progressives, the Republican presidential campaign represented the apex of a vast pyramid. On top were Dewey and Warren, but comprising successive layers were candidates for the Senate and the House of Representatives and state assemblies and governorships. These candidates pulled for Dewey and Warren, and Dewey and Warren often appeared with them on the campaign trail. Then there were the local committeemen, the state chairmen, the county chairmen, the precinct leaders, and the ward bosses in the cities. It was the opinion of several prominent Republicans that this election, like most elections, would be won not by Dewey or his advisers, not by good speaking or expert scheduling of the Victory Special, not by Warren on his train, and not by favorable national press or well-produced radio broadcasts. Rather, it would be won by thousands of local Republican activists contributing to their local party establishments. It would be won by urban bosses and county leaders and mayors and assemblymen, who hosted dinners and talked about Dewey and urged people to turn out and support him on election day. It would be won by the Dewey-Warren Clubs, those independent organizations set up by four or five friends who each gathered four or five friends, who then met and elected a chairman and a vice chair and a secretary, who then adopted a charter from the National Dewey-Warren Club Headquarters at the Republican National Committee in Washington, D.C.[12]

By the end of Dewey's first tour in early October, election observers believed that he had gained fourteen western and midwestern states to Truman's six. Counters had Dewey ahead in California, Colorado, Illinois, and Pennsylvania, while Truman was thought to be leading in Texas, Kentucky, Missouri, and Oklahoma. Correspondents gave Dewey high marks for his polished delivery and his mellifluous voice, and they found nothing in the first stage of the campaign to shake them from the belief that Dewey was cruising toward the inevitable victory that had been widely predicted for months.[13]

But lingering beneath the surface were two troubling trends. First, Dewey was still associated with the 80th Congress, and second, he was slowly losing the farm vote. The first trend was discernible in September. During the special session, the 80th Congress accomplished little other than the spy hearings. Though Brownell had tried to get Taft and other congressional leaders to pass some legislation along the lines of the party platform in order to help Dewey in the fall, the congressional Republicans allowed the session to expire without giving Dewey anything to brag about. Truman effectively tarred the 80th Congress with the "do-nothing" moniker, and some of that tar rubbed off on the Dewey campaign. Dewey couldn't distance himself too much from Congress or he would lose the support of his own party and perhaps jeopardize Republican chances in the congressional elections. Yet he needed to create some space between himself and the Congress in order to avoid being dragged down in their wake. It was a precarious position, and rather than risk addressing the problem, the Dewey team reasoned that the candidate could finesse the issue by avoiding any mention of Congress.

More ominous in the long run was the deteriorating relationship between Dewey and the farmers. Dewey frequently presented himself as a farmer and he liked to spice his remarks with homey mentions of life on his Pawling farm. On agricultural policy, he was advised by researchers from Cornell University, and though they opened offices in Des Moines, few farm leaders in the Midwest were fooled. They saw a bunch of eastern professors and didn't trust them. As Brownell observed, "It was very evident to the Middlewest farm leaders that the Governor's farm program was going to be run by a group of Easterners and many of the Middlewestern farm leaders considered them enemies. They thought that while technically they were farmers, they were farmers who were consumers or purchasers from Midwest farms." That tension was an old one, and the populist distrust of eastern elites had been a motif of national politics since the 1870s. But Dewey wasn't simply eastern. To the farmers of the Midwest, he just didn't look or sound like a farmer and when he tried to present himself as such, they recoiled in disgust.

It didn't help that, at the time, farm prices were falling and farmers were worried about the continuance of price supports under a Dewey administration. Dewey himself sent mixed signals, promising price parity on the one hand and on the other speaking about support levels being pegged to supply and demand. The notion of supply and demand was hard to reconcile with price supports, and though Dewey was trying to tread a path between free-marketers and New Dealers, he alienated farmers in the process. The Republican platform promised the maintenance of prices, but the House Republicans, in an act of portentous shortsightedness, failed to act decisively on an emergency grain storage bill. Without adequate grain storage facilities, grain would have to be sold or it would rot, and if it had to be sold, the price would plummet. Failing to provide for storage facilities was therefore tantamount to abandoning price supports.[14]

Unlike Dewey's, Truman's farm credentials were impeccable. Unlike Dewey, Truman sounded like a midwestern farmer. And unlike Dewey, Truman saw the farmers as the great unrepresented, unpolled voice in 1948. Eastern columnists might not have believed that the farmers would play a role in the upcoming election, but Truman wasn't about to make the same mistake.

CHAPTER SEVENTEEN

Whistle-Stops

G RAIN STORAGE facilities may not have been a stirring issue, but on it hinged the farm vote. The Truman fall campaign has been mythologized and debated and studied. It is remembered for "Give 'em Hell, Harry." It has been the source of endless fascination and anecdotes. It has assumed a place in our collective memory as a unique episode in American history. Underdogs in subsequent presidential elections have studied the Truman comeback for guidance. Truman's whistle-stop campaign is as ingrained on our consciousness as Lincoln's Gettysburg Address, Wilson's Fourteen Points, Roosevelt's New Deal, and Nixon's resignation.

Yet myth has obscured what actually transpired. Truman did not offer poetic rhetoric to the millions who heard one of his 280 speeches in the thirty states he passed through. He did not talk of grand philosophical themes along his 20,000-mile route, and he did not dwell on lofty ideas. Everywhere he went, he attacked the Republicans for the high cost of living and painted the Democrats as the party of the people. He also varied the message and tailored his remarks to fit the place. In Detroit, he focused on labor; in Denver, he mentioned mining; throughout the Midwest, he discussed farming; and in Texas, he talked about ranching. It was a campaign waged on small themes worked out in brief speeches. It was a campaign of plain speaking. And it was a campaign of us and them, of anger and bitterness, of the haves and have-nots. Truman fought to lead the country for another four years, and to achieve that victory he was willing to sow dissension, stir up fear, and slander his opponents.

For weeks, Truman hammered the Republican Congress for rewriting the charter of the Commodity Credit Corporation (CCC) and omitting the provision for providing substantial government subsidies for grain storage. Congress allocated no funding for wheat elevators, corn silos, soybeans, or any other crops. No storage facilities meant that farmers couldn't get bank loans on their crops because, unless bins were available, banks couldn't accurately predict what the crops would be worth. If the support price for corn was $1.47 a bushel, and if the farmer couldn't store the corn, then he'd have to sell the bushel for whatever he could get before the corn went bad. Though the Republican platform alleged a commitment to price supports, by stripping the CCC of its role in renting or constructing storage buildings, the Congress essentially drove down agricultural prices. At the same time, the cost of manufactured goods was rising. With less income from their farms, farmers were being pushed to the economic brink.

Setting out from Washington aboard the handsomely outfitted Ferdinand Magellan, Truman arrived at Dexter, Iowa, on September 18 to deliver a speech at the National Plowing Contest. It was a beautiful late summer day, and dressed like any other farmer in shirtsleeves, he sat down next to a group of farmers at a large picnic table covered with a red-and-white checked tablecloth to enjoy a country dinner of fried chicken, mashed potatoes, buttered corn, baked beans, tomatoes, cake, and coffee. Then he donned a pair of sunglasses and ascended the wooden platform draped with the presidential seal. Nearly 75,000 had gathered at Dexter, in the midst of rolling Iowa farmland. Some had driven their Cadillacs; others had arrived by private plane; and many had come in flatbed trucks or on tractors. Flanked by his daughter, Margaret, and his wife, Bess, Truman described the Republicans as "gluttons of privilege." He recalled how the farmer and the worker had suffered under Republican administrations in the 1920s, and he hinted darkly that Dewey would be no better than Coolidge or Hoover. "The Democratic Party represents the people," he said. "It is pledged to work for agriculture. It is pledged to work for labor. It is pledged to work for the small-businessman and the white-collar worker. . . . But the attitude of the Republican gluttons of privilege is very different. The big money Republican looks on agriculture and labor merely as expense items in a business venture. . . . And he looks upon the Government as a tool to accomplish this purpose. The Republican gluttons of privilege are cold men. They are cunning men. And it is their constant aim to put the Government of the United States under the control of men like themselves. They want a return of the Wall Street economic dictatorship."

For proof that the Republicans would despoil the people, Truman pointed to grain prices. "The big-business lobbyists and speculators persuaded the Congress not to provide storage bins for the farmers. They tied the hands of the administration. They are preventing us from setting up storage bins that you will need in order to get the support price for your grain." The Republicans, charged Truman, aimed at nothing less than extracting wealth from the farmers. "They believe in low prices for farmers, cheap wages for labor, and high profits for big corporations." That is the truth, Truman said, and he intended to keep saying it, over and over, across the country, until the whole nation knew it. "I'm not asking you to vote for me," he said in conclusion. "Vote for yourselves! Vote for your farms! Vote for the standard of living you have won under a Democratic administration. Get out there on election day and vote for your future!"[1]

The Dexter speech and dozens of others veered dangerously close to demagogy. Truman devotees then and since scoff that all is fair in campaigns, and that whatever rhetorical flourishes Truman may have indulged in, he was simply a better speaker than his Republican opponent. Yet the line between effective speech making and demagogy is not always so clear, and over the course of these weeks, Truman crossed it. He rarely said Dewey's name, and he almost never singled out particular Republicans. But he did make sweeping indictments that portrayed his opponents as a small elite who wished only harm to the majority of Americans. He presented an America divided between the forces of greed and rapaciousness on one side and the forces of democracy and good on the other. A vote for the Democrats was a vote for freedom and prosperity, and a vote for the Republicans was a vote for poverty and creeping tyranny. In championing the Marshall Plan and aid to countries like Greece and Turkey in the Cold War, Truman depicted the world as divided between those governed by the "will of the majority" and those who suffered from the oppression of a minority who forcibly imposed its will on the majority. The United States represented the former, while the Soviet Union stood for the latter. In running for president, Truman cast the Republicans in the guise of tyrants, and he cast himself as the defender of the people.

Of course, one person's demagogy may be another person's truth, but in the years since television arrived, there has been a noticeable shift in campaign rhetoric. Truman was only one in a long line of campaigners who went to extremes to excite the crowds, to rouse them to action, and to convince them to vote for him on election day. His rhetoric was less extreme than Strom Thurmond's and less messianic than Wallace's. He didn't embrace rabble-rousing the way Francis Townsend had in the 1930s, and he didn't drip with the same venom toward capitalists that Eugene Debs had at the turn of the century. But on the spectrum of political rhetoric, he was closer to these figures than he was to mainstream politicians in the second half of the twentieth century. And he was far more aggressive and far more substantive than almost any candidate has been during the age of television.

No matter what Truman or William Jennings Bryan or Huey Long or Teddy Roosevelt or dozens of others said in the course of a campaign, their remarks were primarily directed toward a small, specific audience of listeners and a slightly larger audience of readers. Candidates after the 1930s also had to consider radio listeners, but the overwhelming majority of Truman's speeches weren't broadcast. That was partly due to the shortage of funds that beset the Democratic Party. Truman simply couldn't afford to pay for many national radio addresses. The Labor Day speech in front of 100,000 in Detroit was cut off because the Democrats hadn't been able to pay for enough minutes. Truman had to rush through and drop passages in order to finish in the time allowed. Dewey and the Republicans had no such problem. They freely spent the $10,000 to $15,000 it required to broadcast a major address nationally, but members of the Democratic National Committee, including McGrath and publicity man Jack Redding, were reduced to the humbling state of last-minute fund-raising and personally carrying tens of thousands of dollars in cash to a radio network to pay for a broadcast. The labor organizations provided money and staff when they could, but radio was not as much of a priority for labor as getting bodies into seats at Truman's major speeches. Out of 337 speeches Truman gave in September and October, only about 70 were broadcast on the radio even locally, while but 20 were heard nationally. Often, while Truman was speaking at one whistle-stop or in one auditorium, the country was listening on the radio to Dewey or to Warren orating somewhere else.[2]

The fact that Truman knew he was speaking almost exclusively to the audience at hand gave him wide latitude in what he could say and how he could say it. If he went too far during a whistle-stop speech, if he played fast and loose with facts, or if he descended to flinging dirt at his opponents, he knew that at worst he would be ridiculed or criticized by the press corps. They might write negative articles, and columnists might invoke fair play and morality. But for most of the millions who would vote, the episode wouldn't exist. Some might read about the speech or peruse editorials against it; some might even hear it on the radio and recoil. But neither print nor radio had the same visceral effect that television would later have. In 1948, condemning big-businessmen as evil scoundrels could whip up the enthusiasm of crowds in Dexter without terminally dooming Truman in New York City. Television raised the stakes for each speech and made it prohibitively risky for candidates to go too far out on a rhetorical limb.

Because Truman was covered neither by television nor extensively by radio, he let himself say whatever he wanted: his rhetoric was effective in part because he was saying what he actually believed. He had never been a denizen of the Northeast, and he had spent many years of his life as a farmer and a small-businessman who distrusted the monied elites of Wall Street. When Truman spoke about the haves and have-nots, the crowds reacted to him as an honest man telling it like he saw and giving 'em hell.

If nothing else, the Truman campaign was fun. The reporters on the train fondly recalled how much they enjoyed accompanying Truman, how they reveled in the jocularity and the ease of playing cards and drinking, how they took guilty pleasure in believing that Truman was doomed even while they spent many pleasant hours talking with him and listening to him.[3] Where Dewey tended to be formal and politely distant, Truman was familiar and outgoing. Though no one ever forgot that he was president of the United States, he established a fluid rapport with the reporters, and he was equally adept with the local dignitaries who visited the train and occasionally rode for a few hours. One day, Senate contender Lyndon Johnson, sporting three days of stubble and exhausted from his recent Texas primary fight, staggered on board to wish the president luck.[4]

Truman also worked extraordinarily hard. He was up before dawn and he went well past midnight many days. The train was both campaign headquarters and a traveling White House for the last half of September and October. From the Ferdinand Magellan, Truman coordinated not just the whistle-stops and the speech writing, but national security and legislation. The Berlin crisis was again on the verge of a major meltdown, and the situation in Palestine was still tenuous and unstable. One minute Truman might be smiling at the back of the train, waving to the crowds, joking with his wife, or saying something about the hardy men of the Rockies or the sturdy farmers of Idaho. Ten minutes later he would be meeting with his advisers, or talking on the telephone to his secretary of state back in Washington trying to determine how to respond to the latest Russian demand over Berlin and how to end the stalemate between the Israelis and the neighboring Arab states. For the crowds and the reporters, however, Berlin and Jerusalem were in another world, far away and less important.

What was important were those grain facilities. "Pour it on those Commodity storage bins," Illinois's Senator Scott Lucas advised Truman. "It's having an effect, it's working." What was important was reminding people about all the accomplishments of the Democrats in the past sixteen years; about how Roosevelt ended the Depression; about how the Democrats created the New Deal and fought the war; of the prosperity America had enjoyed under Democratic administrations; and that Democrats embraced everyone, from businessmen to farmers, from workers to minorities. What was important was the endless stream of dignitaries whom Truman greeted, the county chairmen and the editors and the local union boards and the city managers and the police chiefs and the mayors and the county supervisors and Democratic committee members and the postmasters and court clerks and the district attorneys and the candidates for local and national offices. And what was most important of all was how Truman touched people and how they responded.

From Dexter to Denver to Salt Lake City and then across the Sierra Nevada to San Francisco and then Los Angeles, from California across the Southwest and into Texas. From El Paso to San Antonio and up to Dallas and then into Oklahoma, through Kentucky and back to Washington on October 2 for a brief rest before setting out again. At small towns, the local high-school bands turned out, the young men and women waiting for the train to pull in and then erupting into music and cheers. The head of a local women's group presented Truman with a bouquet of flowers and flashbulbs popped. In Provo, Utah, the Downy Quarterbacks' Club gave him an ashtray made of Geneva steel from the nearby Geneva Steel Company, whose president, Walter H. Mathesius, later came aboard to shake Truman's hand. At each stop, local leaders joined the president's entourage at the back of the train, and then, surrounded by a tight pack of family and supporters on the small rear platform, he would speak.

In Salida, Colorado, he said, "This is a wonderful city. You know my family used to take their vacations here at Buena Vista and they would come down to Salida for various reasons; my boss, Mrs. Truman, used to come down here to see the doctor." At Springville, Utah, he said, "I have been very much intrigued by the beauty of this valley as we came across it. They tell me that it is one of the most productive in the country, and for that reason you are interested in the policies of the Federal government towards such projects as makes the fertility of this valley possible." At the Mormon Tabernacle in Salt Lake City, he said, "Irrigation has given to the West a prosperous agriculture; it has brought thriving industries and enabled you to make use of your natural resources. With the aid of the Government, you have built the great dams that provide you with water and hydroelectric power." In Mojave, California, he said, "There are two theories of government in this country. One theory believes that the special interests—that is, the people who have control of everything—should get all the profits and all the welfare of the country and that whatever little trickles down the other people can get by chance. . . . The theory of the Democratic Party is that there should be an equal distribution of wealth." At Bells, Texas, he said, "I certainly appreciate that wonderful introduction from my good friend Sam Rayburn. . . . He is going to be Speaker Rayburn again next year, if I have anything to do with it." To thousands in Oklahoma City, he said, "I charge that the Republicans have impeded and made more difficult our efforts to cope with communism in this country. . . . I charge that the Republicans have attempted to usurp the constitutional functions of the Federal grand juries and of the courts." And to everyone, everywhere, he said, "Go out and vote!"[5]

While Truman spoke outside, his staff was busily preparing for the stops ahead. Every day, George Elsey received material from the Research Division about the next whistle-stops. Under the guidance of William Batt, the Research Division in Washington provided capsule digests of places like Salida and Bells, replete with demographics, local history, political leanings, and quirky characteristics. From these, Elsey prepared an outline that the president could use to shape his remarks. Longer speeches and more formal presentations went through a more arduous drafting process. Along with Elsey and David Noyes were senior staff such as Ross, Clifford, and Charles Murphy. David Niles and Phileo Nash worked on speeches concerning Israel and civil rights, respectively. And Truman himself met frequently with Elsey, Clifford, Murphy, Ross, and others to debate what he should say and how he should say it. The speeches were carefully coordinated so that Truman would not repeat himself on the same day in the same region. That meant that local papers would have more than one story to report, and it meant also that the national press corps riding the train would not be overcome with the boredom that comes from listening to the same thing over and over.[6]

In the days before television, journalists had an even more substantial impact on how a candidate was perceived. They provided the lens through which the public viewed the presidential contenders, and the photographers who accompanied them furnished the images. The fact that Truman had such good relations with the press corps was important, even if the exact way those relations translated is difficult to determine. Some reporters reacted negatively to Dewey. He set their teeth on edge, and they found him irritating. As a result, when it came time to file their stories, they probably didn't include certain adjectives that might have enhanced Dewey's image and they did insert other adjectives that cast him in a less favorable light. Reporters found it hard to resist Truman, however.

Southern governors meet with J. Howard McGrath (seated), chairman of
the Democratic Party. From left to right: Governor Ben Laney of Arkansas,
Gregg Cherry of North Carolina, William Lane of Maryland,
J. Strom Thurmond of South Carolina, Beauford Jester of Texas
(Stan Lewis/Thurmond Collection, Clemson University Libraries)

Harold Stassen of Minnesota and Governor Thomas Dewey of New York
enjoy a friendly meeting. *(Corbis/Bettmann-UPI)*

Dewey in Oregon, surrounded by "Cavemen" *(AP/Wide World Photos)*

Truman talks with reporters on his Western swing. *(Truman Library)*

Henry Wallace talks with schoolchildren and teachers, as Woody Guthrie sings.
(University of Iowa, Special Collections)

The repaired GOP elephant sits atop the marquee at Philadelphia's
Bellevue-Stratford Hotel. *(Corbis/Bettmann-UPI)*

Republican presidential nominee Dewey makes peace with former rival
Robert Taft of Ohio after the Republican convention. *(Corbis/Bettmann-UPI)*

The convention hall in Philadelphia is decked out for the Democrats.
(Corbis/ Bettmann-UPI)

Hubert Humphrey makes his speech on civil rights. *(Corbis/Bettmann-UPI)*

Happy delegates celebrate on the convention floor
as Truman is nominated. *(Corbis/Bettmann-UPI)*

Governor Fielding Wright of Mississippi addresses the
Dixiecrat convention in Birmingham.
(Corbis/Bettmann-UPI)

The Progressive leaders assemble in Philadelphia. Seated in front are Senator Glen Taylor of Idaho, Henry Wallace, and Paul Robeson. Behind them, from the left, are Rexford Tugwell, Clark Foreman, C.B. "Beanie" Baldwin, and Albert Fitzgerald. *(University of Iowa)*

The Democrat and Republican nominees meet at Idlewild Airport in New York City during the August lull. *(Corbis/Bettmann-UPI)*

Progressive vice-presidential candidate Glen Taylor poses proudly
in front of a picture of his running mate.
(University of Iowa)

The leaders of the Missouri Truman-Barkley club meet to plan strategy for the fall while a picture of the two candidates watches over them. *(Truman Library)*

Dewey and his running mate, Governor Earl Warren of California, discuss the upcoming campaign with Herbert Brownell (seated left) and Senator William Knowland of California (seated right). *(Corbis/Bettmann-UPI)*

The Dixiecrat campaign kicks off in Houston as Strom Thurmond and his wife, Jean, are greeted by regional chairman W.B. Bates and oilman H.R. Cullen (far right). *(Stan Lewis/Thurmond Collection, Clemson University Libraries)*

Dewey and his sons greet Joe DiMaggio at Yankee Stadium. *(Corbis/Bettmann-UPI)*

Truman and his wife, Bess, are sent on their way by Alben Barkley as the Ferdinand Magellan pulls out of Washington's Union Station in September. *(Corbis/Bettmann-UPI)*

Wallace talks about cotton with an Alabama farmer. *(Corbis/Bettmann-UPI)*

Governor and Mrs. Thomas Dewey are presented with good-luck flowers as the Victory Special pulls out of Albany. *(Corbis/Bettmann-UPI)*

During a speech, Wallace gets pelted with eggs. *(Corbis/Bettmann-UPI)*

Heavyweight champion Joe Louis wishes Dewey luck
as the campaign winds down. *(Corbis/Bettmann-UPI)*

Thurmond votes in Edgefield, South Carolina, accompanied by his sister, his mother, and
his wife. *(Stan Lewis/Thurmond Collection, Clemson University Libraries)*

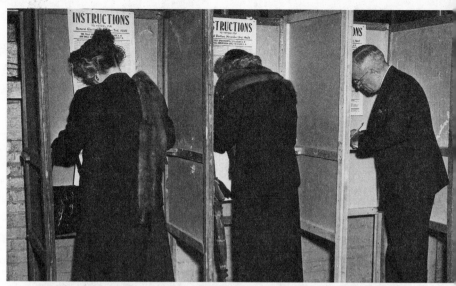

The Trumans vote in Independence, Missouri. *(Corbis/Bettmann-UPI)*

The famous photo *(Mercantile Library Association, St. Louis)*

One day, Chicago correspondent Carleton Kent was canvassing the crowd after one of Truman's talks, and in the midst of interviewing the locals, he didn't hear the whistle warning that the train was about to leave. He rushed over a bit too late and the train was beginning to pull away slowly. He asked a Secret Service man stationed on the train what he should do, and the man looked at him and said, "Well, I can't put you on board, but I'll turn my back, and it's up to the President, if he wants you to climb on board you can." Kent trotted along behind the train, and Truman was on the rear platform. Kent looked up pathetically and appealed to the president. Truman reached over the railing, grabbed him by the hand, and yanked him aboard. "Oh, you're all right," he said. "It's your editors that I have my problems with."[7]

Those editors and publishers, such as Colonel McCormick in Chicago, or the Hearst chain nationally or Henry Luce of the powerful *Time-Life* empire, did have it in for Truman. They were stung by his denunciations of big business because they were closely identified with it. The reporters, however, thought of themselves as working class, and they rarely had good things to say about management. They were inclined to be supportive of labor, farmers, and the little guy, and when the president of the United States hoisted one of them onto his train, they were going to sing his praises whether the Hearsts and the McCormicks and the Sulzbergers liked it or not.

While Truman meandered by train, his running mate Alben Barkley traveled the country by plane, and wherever he went, he too made a favorable impression with his homespun expressions, his gentle drawl, and his razor-sharp observations laced with humor and sarcasm. Though both Barkley and Truman avoided the Deep South, they made inroads in states that almost no one believed would vote Democrat, such as Iowa, Utah, and Colorado. Outside of Washington, Truman relished his role as underdog and he embraced the crowds and the journey. He was in many ways the perfect candidate. He loved the process. He loved meeting people and chatting with them. He loved freewheeling speeches, and he loved the feeling of connection to the land, to the people, to the issues that he cared about, to the crops soon to be harvested, and to the towns and cities and counties that he passed through. He loved the fight and he didn't care whether people thought he was fair. If they didn't, they'd let him know it on election day, and if they did, they'd send Thomas Dewey back to Albany.

As for the two other candidates, Truman made no mention of them. Having written off the Deep South, the Truman campaign had no reason to attack Thurmond, and though the president did speak about civil rights in some northern cities, that theme was not particularly prominent on the whistle-stops, where the audiences were primarily white. Wallace had already been diminished, but he was still strong enough in California and New York that he might deny those states to Truman. But rather than gracing the Progressives with the attention a frontal assault would bring them, Truman stuck to the overall strategy of veering left. The more he sounded like a Progressive and a Populist, the more he undercut Wallace. The only remaining issue was how to neutralize Wallace in New York, and that would have to wait until October, when Truman made his swing through the Northeast.

By the beginning of October, everyone still thought Truman would lose. A *Newsweek* survey of the fifty most prominent newspaper editors and columnists showed that all fifty believed that Dewey would triumph. Clifford handed Truman a copy of the article, and Truman looked it at for a few moments. "I know every one of these fifty fellows," Truman said, handing Clifford the article. "There isn't a single one of them has enough sense to pound sand in a rat hole."[8] The editors and columnists may have been more astute than that, but on this particular subject, Truman was listening to voices they weren't hearing.

CHAPTER EIGHTEEN

The Dark Night of Dixie

TRUMAN WASN'T paying any attention. Dewey couldn't have cared less. The national press corps was beginning to drift away. Radio stations offered increasingly limited airtime, and money was tight. But Strom Thurmond and Fielding Wright kept hoping, and they kept talking in front of large crowds and small gatherings. They had no doubt that they were fighting the good fight, and they trusted that they would produce some results.

By Labor Day, three states were committed to the States' Rights cause. The movement had control of the Democratic Party machinery in South Carolina, Alabama, and Mississippi. In those states, voters on November 2 would be presented with ballots listing electors pledged to the Thurmond-Wright ticket under the Democratic Party icon. In Mississippi, voters would not even have the option of voting for Truman and Barkley unless they wrote in those names. In the other two states, Truman and Barkley electors would appear, but not as the official Democratic nominees. As a result of these maneuvers, the Dixiecrats were all but assured victory in those three states, where voters were staunchly Democrat.

It was no coincidence that the three states to commit to the revolt were also three of the first four states to secede from the Union in 1861. The memory of humiliation by the North was woven into the fabric of the Deep South, and it took only minimal prodding to stir it up. The strong allegiance to the doctrine of states' rights had not been shaken by the outcome of the Civil War. This helps explain why the Dixiecrats began with the assumption that they were not a new party but that they were instead the legitimate representatives of the Southern wing of the Democratic Party. Throughout the South, the state Democratic organizations approached the national Democratic Party in much the same way that the southern states had dealt with the Union in 1861. The belief was that the national party could not compel the state parties to do anything. State parties could choose to adhere to the national platform, or they could opt out. And if the national party ignored the will of the state parties, then it was within the rights of the state parties to go their own way.

It was also no coincidence that those parts of the South with the highest concentration of blacks were also those with the highest percentage of whites who supported the Dixiecrats. Thurmond and Wright may have shied away from the race-baiting rhetoric that prevailed at the Birmingham convention, but the unavoidable truth was that race and fear of integration were the most potent forces fueling the States' Rights movement. Just as race had been the hair trigger of the Civil War, it was the bottom line of the Dixiecrat rebellion. Even though Thurmond and Wright couched their arguments in referrals to the Constitution, to tyranny, and to freedom, those who supported the movement most avidly were those who feared racial integration most intensely.

As of early September, the Dixiecrats were struggling to gain control of the state machinery elsewhere in the South. Focusing on the internal politics of state organizations made sense. However, wresting control of state parties was no simple task. Each state had its own arcane and labyrinthine rules for selecting electors and for placing names on the official ballot. The Dixiecrats had to master those rules, find local supporters, and then have those supporters undertake the laborious process of negotiating, back-slapping, wrangling, and persuading. A Dixiecrat representative in Arkansas, Georgia, or Florida had to be a man of standing in that state's Democratic Party. He had to have good relations with the state legislatures and the county chairperson and the informal network of businessmen, law enforcers, judges, and postmasters who governed the state. He had to meet with them at dinner, over drinks, on front porches in the late August summer, at fairs and festivals, in restaurants near the statehouse in Little Rock or Atlanta or Tallahassee, at estates and county meeting halls. He had to offer a convincing argument why the national party and Truman should be rejected. He had to assure them that the exclusion from the spoils doled out by the national party would not hurt them as much as signing on to the Dixiecrat cause would help them—electorally, financially, and perhaps even morally. He needed to intimate that the revolt could well catch fire and ignite the South and that those who lingered on the fence would be left out. And he had to do all that in the space of six weeks, because by mid-September, the ballots for November would be set.[1]

This effort in the political realm had to be complemented by constant effort in the public realm. Unlike Truman and Dewey, the Dixiecrats had to wage a two-fronted campaign. These two fronts were linked. The more popular support the Dixiecrats could demonstrate, the more strongly they could argue that state organizations would be flying in the face of public sentiment if they stayed with Truman and Barkley. If crowds turned out to cheer Thurmond, if Wright was greeted by enthusiastic throngs, if money poured into Dixiecrat coffers in Jackson, then the States' Rights advocate in Little Rock or Atlanta or Tallahassee could credibly assert that the tide was turning in their favor. Still, the public realm was distinct from the political, and it required a separate strategy, a large staff, and constant travel on the part of the candidates.

In addition to numerous informal addresses and brief remarks, Thurmond delivered three dozen major speeches between early August and late October; Wright was at least as active. "There are a lot of people in America today who have forgotten the meaning of the Constitution," Wright told an audience assembled for the Cotton Carnival in Tallulah, Louisiana, on September 17. "Harry Truman is on record as pledging himself and his administration to violate the Constitution of the United States. Henry Wallace is on record pledging himself to violate the Constitution of the United States. Tom Dewey is on record pledging himself to violate the Constitution of the United States." Each of them, charged Wright, supported civil rights proposals that infringed on the right of individual states to determine those aspects of law not specifically mentioned in the Constitution. Wright continued with a now-familiar litany of accusations. There was the reference to federal enforcement of hiring practices in the form of the FEPC. He attacked the three other candidates for advocating the creation of "a police state" of federal enforcers who would invade states on the dubious proposition that the lynching needed to be prevented. Everyone knew, Wright scoffed, that the southern states were perfectly capable of preventing lynching, and perfectly able to prosecute the rare episode. He said there were explicit parallels between Hitler's Nazi Germany and the America of Harry Truman and between the FEPC and a commission set up by Joseph Stalin in the Soviet Union. "Ladies and gentlemen . . . I appeal to you. Let's keep America free. We can keep her free by keeping intact the American Constitution which is the sole guarantee of all of our liberties."[2]

Thurmond's speeches were similar in content, though he tended to be more emotional and histrionic than his unprepossessing running mate. Wherever he went, Thurmond had one message. The only variation came with the introductory remarks, when he would say something pithy about the particular place he was visiting. "Coming back to Augusta and the Savannah Valley is like coming home to me," he told an audience of 3,000 at the Municipal Auditorium in Augusta on September 23. "The ties that bind Georgia and South Carolina are everlasting and they make us one people." He proceeded to praise the leadership of Georgia in the politics of the South, and he lauded Senator Russell as an exemplar of a southern leader. Then he launched into his tirade against "the forces at work in this country" who would lead America down the path of totalitarianism, forces that "have fashioned a powerful weapon of the machine-controlled blocs in the big city-states of this nation. Using that weapon, they have made a stooge out of Henry Wallace, a mouthpiece out of Harry Truman, and a puppet prince out of Tom Dewey." And to these pernicious forces, the South was the ultimate victim, and the prize. Having sacrificed and robbed the South, he said, these forces "will convert America into a Hitler state." He recalled the ordeal of Reconstruction and the legacy of high tariffs that he claimed had impoverished the South while enriching the North. For these forces, Thurmond continued, civil rights was simply a ruse. Using the wedge of the FEPC and a federal antilynching law, the so-called civil rights platform would be a Trojan horse placed in the heart of the South, and out would pour the carpetbaggers of old to plunder the South and leave it helpless.[3]

From their headquarters in Jackson, the Dixiecrats coordinated their two-track strategy. In early September, they received a sudden boost that temporarily gave credibility to Thurmond's claim that they would win enough electoral votes to throw the election into the House. On September 10, the Louisiana Democratic State Committee met in Baton Rouge. For months, Governor Earl Long, inheritor not just of his martyred brother's mantle but of his political machine, had wavered. As of late summer, Long evinced no interest in joining the rebellion. His competitors in Louisiana, however, had other ideas. Oil interests were a powerful force in Baton Rouge, and though Long was too strong to challenge directly, his enemies seized on his absence from the meeting to try to humiliate him and pursue their own agenda. They voted to replace Truman-Barkley with the Thurmond-Wright ticket, and that meant that Louisiana would land in the Dixiecrat column come November. The last time the Democrats had lost Louisiana was in 1908, and Roosevelt had carried the state by a margin of 281,000 to Dewey's 67,000 in 1944. The November ballots would have the Dixiecrat candidates listed next to the rooster icon, the traditional symbol of the Democrats. Many voters in Louisiana couldn't read, and they would vote for the symbol.[4]

From Jackson, the States' Righters issued a blizzard of press releases pointing to Louisiana as a harbinger. Giddy at the sudden windfall of Louisiana's 10 electoral votes, Thurmond predicted that in the end, his party would win at least 100 votes, enough to force the election into the House of Representatives. As of mid-September, the Dixiecrats were assured the 38 electoral votes of the four pledged states, and in Georgia and Tennessee, the States' Righters had a decent chance of emerging on top. The campaign still hadn't given up on Arkansas, Texas, Virginia, or North Carolina. In Tennessee, the Democratic Party was deadlocked: several electors announced for Thurmond; most pledged to remain with the national party; an entire slate of States' Rights electors were put on the ballot; and, in the end, Tennessee split its electoral vote, and one elector opted for the Dixiecrats. In Georgia, the Talmadge dynasty, in some respects similar to the Longs of Louisiana, gravitated toward the States' Rights camp. When Herman Talmadge won election as governor, the States' Righters thought that they had won Georgia. But though Talmadge himself wanted to lead Georgia into the Dixiecrat fold, he didn't control the state party and he wasn't able to challenge Senator Russell. The Talmadgeites were able to get a slate of States' Rights electors placed on the ballot, but Truman-Barkley remained the official candidates. By early October, the States' Rights Democrats, as they were called everywhere except for Mississippi, were on the ballot in thirteen states, twelve in the South, plus North Dakota, whose conditions for eligibility were easily met. In the month before the election, they would also meet requirements in Maryland and California.[5]

Perhaps taking the cue from Robert E. Lee, Thurmond decided to move his campaign into the heart of the North, to Washington, D.C., and Maryland and even into New York City and Boston. Stopping in Richmond to have breakfast with Governor Tuck, he went on to Washington and held a press conference. He softened his rhetoric considerably and spoke of the need to promote economic and educational advancement for "our Negro population." He claimed that, in the South, "We believe in racial integrity and are opposed to racial integration." In Baltimore, he was somewhat more strident and he snubbed Maryland's governor for not taking an aggressive stand against the federal civil rights program. In New York City, Thurmond spoke at the Overseas Press Club and tried to explain the rationale for the States' Rights movement to an audience that he knew to be hostile, albeit curious. He traced the evolution of the States' Rights movement and placed the onus on the other three parties for caving in to special interests. He drew an astute comparison between gangland murders in New York and lynchings in the South, saying that more people had been slain in New York in the past five years than had been lynched in the South during the last fifty. Yet no one called for a federal anti–gang murder law, and if someone did, Thurmond predicted that New Yorkers would be outraged. He observed that during Prohibition, New York violently opposed the law against liquor and New Yorkers flagrantly disregarded it.[6]

After New York, Thurmond retreated south of the Mason-Dixon line. He ventured north only one more time for a brief trip to Boston, where he gave a radio interview. He continued to traverse the South, and the States' Righters focused their energies on Florida (which in 1948 had only eight electoral votes), Virginia, Georgia, and Texas. If the Dixiecrats had any hope of achieving their objectives, it was essential that they capture Texas's twenty-three electoral votes. But though Governor Jester was sympathetic, the Texas Democratic Party stayed loyal to the national party, and Texas voters were at best tepid in their support of Thurmond and Wright. In mid-October, the States' Righters launched a Thurmond-Wright "ballot blitz" code-named "Operation Texas," which involved thirty different speakers visiting almost 400 towns and cities. The speakers included Governor Ben Laney of Arkansas, Senator Eastland, former Governor Sam Jones of Louisiana, and former Governor Frank Dixon of Alabama, as well as numerous congressmen. Laney was in the odd position of supporting the movement even though he had been passive in his own state and done little to help the Thurmond-Wright ticket in Little Rock. At the end of the week, Thurmond traveled by motorcade and gave several speeches. The contingent planned to assemble in Houston for a rally attended by 25,000 before they fanned out across the state. On a pleasant fall day, the crowds milled about and sampled barbequed beef. Surveying the scene, one person boasted that there was more beef being cooked "than at any time since the Chicago stockyards fire." "We are out to win Texas," campaign manager Merritt Gibson declared, "and we are confident that the campaign next week will do much to accomplish that objective."[7]

Thurmond enjoyed campaigning and he liked being in the limelight. The one-time county judge mingled with governors and senators who curried his favor. Win or lose, Thurmond had taken a great leap forward in his career. He relished the meeting and greeting. He consumed the attention and never gave indication that the process was anything but a delight. He attended dinner after dinner, surrounded by local bigwigs who treated him like visiting royalty, with his wife by his side. Whereas Truman showed off Bess and Margaret to demonstrate that he was just like any other man, Thurmond kept Jean at his side to remind people that he was a man who could keep a twenty-two-year-old there. He called her "Sugar" and encouraged her to talk to the press. When he was asked, as he inevitably was, why Jean was always with him, and if it was because she didn't trust him not to catch the eye of some other pretty young thing, he replied, with a grin, "Well, she says that it's just because I'm so ugly that she hates to kiss me goodbye." And the reporters laughed and elbowed each other and dutifully printed the answer.

To the end, Thurmond bragged that Georgia "was in the bag," that Texas would surprise everyone, that Virginia was about to make the leap, and that Maryland would wake up. He believed, along with Merritt Gibson, Fielding Wright, Frank Dixon, and thousands of others, that 1948 was only the first stage. "We've rolled up our sleeves," Gibson declared on the eve of the election. "We have laid the groundwork for a permanent organization on a national scale. The States' Rights fight is a long-range campaign, with the 1948 phase one battle in a total war."[8]

No matter how relaxed Thurmond was, or how much Gibson boasted, or how fervently Wright believed, or how many speakers made the pitch in Texas or Georgia, the plain fact was that by late October, the Dixiecrats had no money and little support outside of the four core states. In Tennessee and Georgia, the party commanded somewhere between 10 and 20 percent of the potential voters, according to the polls, and in Texas they had less than 10 percent. Some of the speaking was subsidized by local donors, and some of the speakers footed their own bills. Thurmond's trip north was listed as costing only $341.39, but the actual cost must have been far larger. The party headquarters in Jackson was never well organized, and though some money flowed in, the accounting procedures were sloppy to the point of incompetence. No one has ever been able to gauge how much the Dixiecrats spent, though estimates range from $150,000 to $250,000. But these figures only pertain to the national campaign, and as with the other parties, regional, local, and other expenditures augmented the total significantly. Aware of their accounting problems, the national headquarters actually included a list of what was permissible and what was not on their fund-raising mailings. "No contributions may be accepted from a corporation or a labor union; all contributions of $100.00 or more must be reported by amount, name of donor, and his address; quarterly reports of the above must be reported to the clerk of the House of Representatives by the national treasurer." In an age before campaign financing came under intensive public scrutiny, the Dixiecrats' fund-raising was so irregular that the party was concerned that it would be investigated and punished under the Federal Corrupt Practices Act.[9]

Wherever Thurmond went, the local press turned out in droves. But most editors of the major southern papers were cool toward the

States' Righters. It was partly a question of class bias. The editors—educated, upper-middle-class men—saw the Dixiecrats as the spearhead of poor, angry, illiterate whites. They thought the movement was a cynical attempt to manipulate old prejudices for political gain. The New Deal had been accompanied by the rise of southern liberalism and progressivism, and many of these new southern liberals rejected the segregationist, racist slant of the States' Righters. Granted, some of the leaders of the Dixiecrat movement were themselves southern progressives, but in the eyes of editors such as Mississippi's Hodding Carter, Ralph McGill of the *Atlanta Constitution,* Jonathan Daniels of the *Raleigh News & Observer,* and Virginius Dabney of the *Richmond Times-Dispatch,* Thurmond's progressivism was indelibly tainted by the white supremacist overtones of his rhetoric and antipathy to civil rights. Other editors disliked the scent of petroleum that clung to the States' Rights candidates. In general, newspapermen in the South had championed voting rights for blacks, and they had supported the New Deal. Even in South Carolina, many editors were uncomfortable with the racial aspects of the Dixiecrat movement. The result of the ambivalence or outright antipathy of the press was that even in the Deep South, the States' Rights movement was under assault. Granted, many of the supporters who would be inclined to vote for the States' Rights slate were illiterate and couldn't read whatever the newspaper editorials were saying. But the efforts of the Dixiecrats to convince local Democratic leaders to break with the national party were undermined by the consistent hum of criticism leveled by the local and regional press.[10]

As the campaign wound down, editors and pundits throughout the South were singing the same song as their brethren elsewhere in the country: Dewey would win in a landslide. The consensus of a poll of 150 daily newspapers in fifteen southern states taken the week before the election was that Dewey would win 343 electoral votes, Truman would obtain 150, and Thurmond would get the remaining 38. Forty-two percent of those papers endorsed Truman, while 16 percent supported Dewey and another 16 percent backed Thurmond. The support for Truman was often lukewarm, with one small paper in Arkansas declaring that it was endorsing Truman

because he was "the least objectionable of the four candidates." One
North Carolina editor wrote, "We consider President Truman honest, if dull. Mr. Dewey is not dull and may not be honest."

In the wake of the expected Democratic defeat nationally, the
editors predicted the South would regain its proper influence in the
party. Even if Dewey won, the southern bolters would have demonstrated that the Democratic Party could only survive if it was a
national party, and it could only be a national party if the wishes of
the South were respected. The most striking comment may have
come from the *Fort Worth Press:* "The real story in the South is not
that Truman will carry it, but that Democratic majorities will be
greatly reduced. Once a Southerner has bolted, he can do it again."
The States' Rights movement did in fact set a precedent, and after
1948, the firm allegiance of the South to the Democratic Party began
to soften and crumble. It would take the Great Society, the Civil
Rights Act of 1964, and the Voting Rights Act of 1965 to wean the
majority of the South away from the Democrats, and it would then
take another decade before they began voting Republican.[11]

Beneath all the stirring rhetoric, there was something fairly absurd about the States' Rights movement, and at times, an air of
desperation to it. Trying to convince an apathetic public to rally to
defend the South from the supposed threat of the federal government, the Dixiecrats resorted to wildly exaggerated warnings that
Truman was really Hitler in disguise, and they tried to relate abstract
threats such as the FEPC to the daily lives of average southerners.
"Southerners this week got a preview of what's in store for them in
the event Truman's Democrats, Dewey's Republicans or Wallace's
Progressives should ram the civil rights bill down the throats of the
American public," announced Judge Gibson on September 18. The
cause of his anger was the decision by the Federal Fish and Wildlife
Service to invalidate a Georgia law allowing for dove-hunting before
December 18. When Georgia's State Game and Fish director told
hunters to "open fire" on September 15, the federal agency alerted
thirty agents and furnished them with an airplane to aid them in the
arrest of any hunter who violated the federal regulations. "Just
imagine the bureaucratic invasion of states' rights," Judge Gibson
said, "if the federal government is given the authority proposed in

the so-called civil rights bills. If so much concern is evidenced over a few doves, it is conceivable that under the so-called civil rights program these bureaucrats might launch a full-scale invasion of a state."[12]

On Election Day, fewer than 20 percent of Georgia's voters supported the States' Rights slate. The States' Rights movement was the first shot in the next stage of a war between North and South that would be played out over the coming decades by Alabama's George Wallace and other governors. But in 1948, while one Wallace was cutting his teeth on Dixiecrat politics, the other Wallace was walking a solitary path into utter repudiation.

CHAPTER NINETEEN

Wallace Winds Down

From Kentucky to North Carolina to Tennessee and Alabama through Mississippi and Louisiana, Henry Wallace was showered with hate and pelted with vegetables and eggs. The former vice president of the United States, the leader of a major party and inheritor of the noble mantle of American progressivism, Wallace stood and tried to speak as boos and catcalls and rotten food rained down on his head.

In late August, he began a tour of the Deep South. He knew that he wouldn't win any votes, that he would encounter hostility, that he might even be in physical danger. Yet he went, and at the end of September, he went back. Instead of concentrating on those regions where he still had a chance, instead of focusing on New York or California or Illinois or Michigan, he traveled to Durham and Charlotte and Birmingham and Jackson and Shreveport and Houston. Commentators in the North assumed that it was all a desperate ploy. Sensing the change in the political climate, Wallace faced two more months of campaigning with diminishing returns. He needed some grand gesture to keep the Progressives in the public eye, and so he picked a fight. The southerners accommodated, and Wallace got his press.

Wallace was certainly not above political tricks. Because he traveled with an integrated retinue, refused to dine or rest anywhere that refused service to blacks, and insisted that all of his talks be open to all races, he knew that the South would not exactly greet him with warm smiles. But there was more to his journey than crass calculation. To begin with, the southern States' Righters were often progressives. They may have been racial separatist progressives, but they nonetheless shared the same animus toward the barons of Wall Street and distrust of the mainstream national parties. Wallace honestly thought that a significant minority in the South wanted to hear what he had to say. He correctly foresaw that the bold decision to campaign in enemy territory would be enough of an oddity to attract national attention and raise his profile in the North and West, where he still had a chance to win a substantial number of votes. Something else was at work, however. Wallace had for many years erected a fire wall between his mysticism and his politics, just as he had finessed the fact that he was a multimillionaire who benefited from Wall Street as much as the businessmen he reviled. Something happened to Wallace in 1948 that tore down that wall, and by late summer, he seems to have been acting out his own personal passion play. He was increasingly apt to compare himself to religious martyrs, and in order to justify that comparison, he needed to put himself in situations where he could be persecuted.

How else to explain his peculiar attitude toward Westbrook Pegler, a man who had done more than any single person to damage Wallace nationally? "I wouldn't do anything to interfere with Pegler's venom," Wallace told a reporter in Louisville, Kentucky. "It is a very great help. Attacks that are obviously purely venomous have always been a help to public figures." And with that, Wallace plunged into North Carolina prepared to interpret hostility as a blessing in disguise.

In fact, he courted hostility. He traveled with a black secretary, ate at black school cafeterias and restaurants, and invited black leaders to sit next to him or stand by him when he spoke. "What color is your father?" the good old boys asked. "Where's your black girlfriend?" They grinned and slapped each other on the back with each new insult. In Durham, two dozen hecklers threw eggs, set off firecrackers, and ignited stink bombs. A National Guardsman had to fire his rifle in the air to get the group to back off and let Wallace into the auditorium. A college boy acting as one his bodyguards was slashed eight times with a knife while Wallace tried to speak, and while his attackers jeered the police briefly detained the young man and threatened to arrest him for disturbing the peace. "What do you want for the South?" Wallace cried. "Thurmond," the hecklers shouted back.

In Hickory, he was showered with a cascade of garbage and eggs, and though most of the jetsam missed him and landed on the police escort, the stench and the boos and shouts made it impossible for him to deliver his prepared remarks. "Nigger lover," chanted one group of men. And when Wallace began to speak about the Cold War and American culpability, he was interrupted with derisive laughter. "Did Stalin tell you to say that?" yelled one. Standing stoically in the midst of the rising crescendo of hatred, Wallace finally yelled back, "As Jesus said to his disciples, if in any town they won't listen to you, then shake the dust from your feet and go elsewhere." Elsewhere was the resort town of Asheville, North Carolina, home of the novelist Thomas Wolfe and of Biltmore, the country estate of the Vanderbilts. The more genteel crowd was less violent but hardly more friendly as Wallace stumbled through his speech. Then his motorcade drove to Charlotte. The press corps, especially the northern reporters, succumbed to gallows humor and hummed, "Nothing could be finer than to be in Carolina in the morning," as the caravan made its way through the hills. The reporters tried to act casual, but some of them were shaken by the vehemence of the attacks and the intensity of the hatred. One Chicago reporter wrote that it was easy enough to wash off the smell of stinking garbage, but not "the memory of the horrid faces of middle-aged women, or red-necked, tobacco-spitting hillbillies who have hurled epithets all along the route." So disturbing were the reports coming out of North Carolina that Truman felt the need to condemn the attacks. In a statement read by press secretary Charlie Ross, the president declared that "he thought the throwing of eggs and other missiles at Mr. Wallace was certainly a highly un-American business and violated the American concept of fair play."

In Charlotte, Wallace tried to give a speech to 3,000 gathered in front of the Mecklenburg County Courthouse. The eggs hit a young girl near the front, as well as a heckler who was shouting, "Go back to Russia." Several signs were hoisted, including one with the slogan PEDDLE YOUR JUNK IN MOSCOW, HENRY. The troubadour Pete Seeger, who had accompanied Wallace on the pilgrimage, stood with his banjo and began to play the "Star Spangled Banner," but the crowd sullenly refused to join in and instead of lyrics offered only more heckles. Invoking the memory of the Mecklenburg patriots who had defied the British during the Revolutionary War, the Progressive leader declared, "I come from the same brood of man, and I tell you I won't be intimidated. My name is Wallace." That of course provoked more jeers, and Wallace tried to shout over the noise. "I come here in the sacred tradition of American liberty and in the sacred tradition of Christianity." He spoke for several more minutes, warning that shouting down speakers and threatening them with bodily harm was a step down the road to totalitarianism. American liberties, he yelled, "include, if they include anything, the right of even the most unpopular views. It should never be forgotten that the eggs are thrown not upon an insignificant and contemptible crew but upon the right of free speech in a free land."

The protests were repeated throughout Alabama and into Mississippi. Sometimes Wallace tried to dismiss the heckling as the "jovial pastime of misguided boys." At other times, he expressed sympathy. "The faces I have seen distorted by hatred are of people for whom I have in my heart profound compassion, because most of them have not had enough to eat." He kept going in spite of that hatred, speaking to mixed audiences and angry crowds while the police looked on stonily. Only in Mississippi did local law enforcement provide him with adequate protection and arrest demonstrators who tried to disrupt his remarks. Governor Wright wanted to make sure that any presidential candidate could get a fair hearing in his state. With or without police protection, Wallace was not deterred. "No one can intimidate me," he declared. And after wrapping up his tour after Labor Day, he returned north.[1]

He had certainly made an impression, and there was an element of pathos that touched even the most jaded observers. In the North, it was difficult to dismiss the images of Wallace, his eyes set, his teeth on edge, staring into crowds of men and women who were angry at him and enraged at the blacks who stood near him. Just as northerners confronted with images of Bull Connor hosing down demonstrators in Birmingham in 1963 redoubled their efforts to end segregation, so too the reports and the pictures of Wallace in 1948 in *Time* and *Life* and in daily newspapers cut through the disillusionment. In seeking attention, Wallace wasn't helping his cause. But by exposing the racial tensions in the South, he may have helped the cause of civil rights.

In New York City, Wallace basked in the warmth of 50,000

cheering, smiling supporters in Yankee Stadium. If he could claim strength anywhere, it was New York, and the Bronx in particular. They greeted him as a returning war hero, and he waved and expressed his gratitude that so many had turned out. For ten minutes, Wallace stood just near second base while the crowd gave him ovation after ovation. The usual cast of characters had warmed them up before Wallace appeared, with Gailmor raising $60,000, Vito Marcantonio castigating Mayor O'Dwyer, and Paul Robeson singing "Old Man River." Robeson offered a benediction lauding Wallace for "marching into the Southland and giving hope to Negroes all over the land." Once the crowd had settled, Wallace tried to explain what had gone on the weeks before. "The news reported last week was news of eggs and tomatoes. It was news of violence and threats of violence. And there were eggs. And there were tomatoes. And there was violence and threats of violence. Yes, and there were ugly spewings of hate and prejudice. . . . But the significance of our trip South was not the dramatic proof that there are seeds of violence and fascism and deep prejudice in the Southern states. . . . The significance of our Southern trip lies in the two dozen completely unsegregated, peaceful meetings which we were able to hold." The people of the South were not to blame, he continued. No, the fault lay with "the owners of the mines and mills and the great plantations . . . who incite the violence." The situation in the South, Wallace declared, proved how desperately the country needed progressive reform.[2]

After New York, Wallace went to Boston, traveled through New England, and then crossed the country via Pennsylvania, down to Texas and into California. The reception was cool. At Boston's Braves Field, he appeared at the end of a baseball game and was heartily booed. Hundreds yelled, "Give our regards to Stalin." On this tour, he tried to emphasize the dangers of inflation and how the high cost of living was enriching the "men of monopoly" who controlled the country. In 1933, he and Franklin Roosevelt "had driven the men of monopoly, the money changers, out of the temple." The war allowed those men to creep back in, and now, Wallace charged, they had lit on the excuse of a fake cold war in order to solidify their hold on the government and on the nation. In Pittsburgh, he came on stage during a matinee performance of *A Streetcar Named Desire* so that the actress and German refugee Uta Hagen could urge the audience to support him. The patrons listened politely, though some later confided that they felt imposed upon. In Houston, young men charged the crowd and grabbed signs and ripped them up; Wallace was then treated to another shower of abuse and eggs, though the police were somewhat more diligent in arresting or detaining protestors. In California, during the first weeks of October, the crowds were extremely small. He was the guest of honor at an expensive catered lunch at the home of a San Francisco socialite, and he dissected federal agricultural policies in front of small audiences in Fresno, Sacramento, and other towns and cities in California's Central Valley. Where Wallace's strength was once estimated at as many as 750,000 votes, the Progressives privately conceded that if they obtained 400,000, they would be fortunate.[3]

While Wallace whirled around, C.B. Baldwin confronted some harsh realities. First, he had to contain what would have been yet another public relations disaster. After the convention, Rex Tugwell was so distressed with the way Wallace had prevented the platform committee from presenting even the mildest criticism of Russian foreign policy that he contemplated quitting the party. On August 10, Tugwell admitted in a telephone interview that he was at that point "an uneasy member of the Progressive Party." He hinted that "the wrong people" had gotten control. At Baldwin's urging, Wallace hastened to issue a statement denying that the movement was controlled by Communists and that anyone who advocated the violent overthrow of the U.S. government was not welcome in the progressive tent. That seemed to mollify Tugwell, but other fires were erupting.

In Minnesota, the efforts of former governor Elmer Benson to make Wallace the official nominee of the Democratic Farmer-Labor Party came to nothing. Had Benson succeeded, Wallace would have been in the same position of strength in Minnesota that Thurmond was in Mississippi. Elsewhere, Baldwin was trying to secure ballot eligibility. The Progressive Party hoped to be on the ballot in every state, but it seemed unlikely that they would meet eligibility requirements in many southern states. The Progressives did receive an unexpected boost from the Dixiecrats, however. In order to get Thurmond's name on the ballot so late, states such as Florida and

Georgia changed the eligibility requirements. That allowed not just Thurmond's name to be entered, but Wallace's as well. Still, that gain was more than nullified by the blow suffered in Illinois. In a clever court maneuver, Illinois Democratic bosses invalidated Wallace's candidacy. With the concentration of immigrants and working-class voters in Chicago and its powerful labor unions, Illinois would have been one of Wallace's strongest backers.

After months of fielding candidates for the House and Senate, the Progressive Party decided at the end of September to withdraw from more than a dozen of these races and support the Democrats. Having tried and failed to compete with liberal Democrats in these races, the Progressives retrenched and decided that it was in the best interests of progressive politics to endorse liberal Democrats such as Helen Gahagan Douglas in California, Hubert Humphrey in Minnesota, Mike Mansfield in Montana, Adam Clayton Powell in New York, and gubernatorial candidate Chester Bowles in Connecticut. Wallace was furious at Baldwin for suggesting that the Progressives drop out, but faced with the numbers showing that they at best could ensure the election of the Republican in these races, he grudgingly agreed. The pain of this concession was not lessened by the response of Douglas and Bowles, both of whom refused the support of the Progressive Party on the grounds that it was hopelessly compromised by the taint of communism.[4]

Other liberals continued to distance themselves from the Progressives. A goodly portion of the staff of *The Nation* voted for Norman Thomas in a pre-election straw poll. They preferred the crusty anticommunist Socialist with his isolationist tendencies to Henry Wallace and his questionable bedfellows. Labor unions assembling for their fall meetings pointedly ignored the Progressives, even though Wallace had taken the most prolabor stance of any major candidate. The polls showed that the Progressive Party, which had begun losing support in the spring, was continuing to slip. In January, Gallup had estimated Wallace at 7 percent of the vote; on July 31, that had dropped to 5 percent; and in late September, the figure was just above 3 percent. Roper's numbers were almost identical.[5]

While the leadership of the party tried to stanch the bleeding, thousands of local members kept fighting. During the summer, Wallace went to Burlington, Vermont. He spoke to about fifty people at the Charles Pillsbury farm picnic, was entertained at a small private dinner, and then delivered an address to 400 in a hall meant to hold nearly 3,000. The poor attendance, said Helen MacMartin of Burlington, was terribly disappointing. But, she explained, people felt that the admission charge was too steep and they were, frankly, scared of being seen at a Wallace rally. They worried about the repercussions if their names or faces were publicized in the local papers.

The visit was a brief moment for Wallace, and it barely registered. But for MacMartin it was the high point of the campaign. In her letters instructing the various volunteers on what to do to prepare for Wallace's arrival, she referred to it as "The Big Day." As the secretary and director of Vermont's Independent Progressive Party, she had spent months coordinating the visit and drumming up support in Burlington and throughout the state. Throughout the summer and fall of 1948, she wrote to everyone she could think of to ask them to give money, time, and energy to the Wallace campaign. "Even though Vermont has only three electoral votes and is not important in the election of a presidential candidate, it has a reputation for independence, clear thinking and acting. It is heartbreaking to see Vermonters duped and deluded. I believe that Mr. Wallace and all of us who support him are primarily concerned with telling the truth so that earnest, honest people will have some chance of forming right judgements."

MacMartin, a widow, held meetings in her home. She served cookies and Vermont milk, and talked strategy and politics with friends and acquaintances. She urged her friends to talk to their friends and relatives about the Progressive movement. "I wonder," she wrote to all the chapter heads in Vermont at the end of August, "if those of us in the Northern Counties could get together to map out how we can combine a campaign of publicity to inform voters about the value to them of the Progressive Party, to get out the vote (see that all are registered), at the same time get more membership and set up county organizations. As a last resort, let's correspond: exchange ideas and information." She divided up the northern part of Vermont into wards and assigned various people to each ward. She provided them with the Progressive Party pamphlet on how to canvass, complete with the "Canvasser's Credo," which stated, "I am a Wallace canvasser. I walk up steep stairways and down crooked hallways. I knock on doors and ring bells. I seek out people wherever they are. I bring answers to their questions, clarity, hope, encouragement. I bring information, facts. I help mobilize America for peace and security at home and abroad. I am a Wallace canvasser." The pamphlet included a message from Wallace praising the canvassers as the vital ingredient for victory in November, and it detailed helpful suggestions such as "Look voters in the eye," and "Try to get past the doorway." MacMartin also circulated a small brochure issued by Elinor Gimbel and the Women-for-Wallace committee. Entitled "I've Got the Jitters," the brochure featured a housewife sitting at a kitchen table, frowning. The caption read, "I woke up feeling depressed. I dreamt my husband was overseas again. I glanced at the headlines and began thinking about another war. I had a wild desire to go out and buy a new bonnet to cheer me up." Then she notices that prices are too high to afford a bonnet. "Something is wrong when corporation profits are the highest in history and each day my dollar buys less."

By late October, MacMartin's spirits were sagging. She confessed her exhaustion in her letters, and she felt that it was such a shame that Tom Dewey was going to win. Truman and Dewey, she said, were "hell-bent for war and destruction of all human values." She kept at it right up until November 2, and after. For years, she tried to keep the Progressive Party alive in Vermont. People eventually stopped giving money, stopped listening to Helen, stopped answering her letters. She told a friend in 1951 after a meeting, "I did not feel a bit sorry for myself at your house for the meeting. . . . I can't seem to get things done. . . . My courage is at a low ebb. Can't seem to get organized and do anything worth while. Even tho' not employed, I should be very busy. Hope I can snap out of it soon." MacMartin died a few months later. But for those weeks in 1948, she felt her life was meaningful because of the campaign, because of Wallace.[6]

The Progressive Party consisted of hundreds of Helen MacMartins throughout the country, and thousands who volunteered and arranged meetings and rented spaces and stuffed envelopes. Each time Henry Wallace ascended a platform or sat down to dinner or met with a group in a hospitality suite, he was converging with people who had dreamed about meeting with him, who had spent days arranging his visit and working out the logistics. They carried a mental picture of him wherever they went, a picture derived from photographs and campaign posters, from a radio speech or an interview, from Progressive Party mailings or his columns in *The New Republic,* and from their own dreams, their own hopes, from what they wanted him to be and what they needed him to be and what they hoped and prayed that he would do for them and for the country.

AND AT THE END of October, Wallace returned again to New York City, his refuge. He appeared in front of a capacity crowd in Madison Square Garden, and for the last time, he slipped into the fantasy that his message was being heard and that he was at the head of a Gideon's army that would transform America. Tonight, he proclaimed, it was time to look forward. November 2 represented only "one battle in a long war." Though the national press corps and the established parties had expended considerable energy to silence, distort, and destroy the Progressive movement, he said, the party had succeeded in exposing the hypocrisy of the Cold War. It had made sure that the fragile state of Israel was not sacrificed on the altar of international relations. And in spite of all the obstacles, Gideon's army had grown.

The speech came at the end of an intensive two-week radio campaign during which the party spent tens of thousands of dollars to get Wallace on the airwaves. Between October 26 and November 2, Wallace gave thirty-three speeches in New York City in order to defray the cost of the airtime. He and Paul Robeson were heard on the Mutual Broadcasting Network on October 29, when Robeson again praised Wallace as a man of genuine courage and the only real defender of freedom in national politics. And on the eve of the election, Wallace took to the radio one final time. "Tomorrow, when you go to the polls," he said, "you will be voting for one world at peace or two worlds in conflict. Because the Progressive Party exists, voters in forty-five states will have a choice between these two ideas of what our lives should be. Without the Progressive Party, there would be no real choice." The two major parties were in truth the same, both committed to war, both governed by "bankers and generals. . . . Tomorrow," he said, his voice heavy with emotion, "the Progressive Party comes of age. Together, we shall march boldly into the future, holding in our hands the promise of a better life."[7]

Wallace offered the voters a choice, but the voters had turned their attention elsewhere, to the contest between two men whom he claimed were two sides of the same coin. If Wallace had taken the time to listen to the man from Independence, he might have been surprised and dismayed—surprised at the vigor and the message, and dismayed because, far from sounding like a pawn of big business, Truman was beginning to sound like he was running for president on the Progressive Party ticket. Henry Wallace had spent months attacking Truman as the antithesis of everything the Progressive movement represented. Like the martyr he aspired to be, Wallace ended up being crucified for the same message that carried Truman to victory.

CHAPTER TWENTY

Going Through the Motions

THERE WAS A FULL month left, and every informed observer believed that it was already over. Not even bookies would take bets on Dewey. But the candidates couldn't just quit. Dewey couldn't simply retreat to his Pawling farm and wait for the inevitable, and Truman wasn't about to get off his train and concede defeat. They may have been going through the motions, but the motions were important. It was imperative that each of them play his part, if not to perfection, then at least convincingly. Because for all the prognostications, the election lay weeks in the future and the future might hold surprises. If Dewey wanted to ensure his victory, he couldn't act as if he knew he would win, because such unambiguous arrogance could turn voters against him, and Truman couldn't comport himself like a loser or he would almost certainly become one. Given their respective scripts, Dewey had a more difficult task because he didn't believe he could lose and he wasn't adept at behaving as if he might. Truman believed that the election was in doubt, and so it was easy for him to campaign as if it was.

Having called the election in September, the press were left with an entire month to write about a race devoid of surprise or excitement. At least, that was the attitude of the reporters on the two trains, and of the columnists and pundits in Washington and New York. Local reporters could still muster some enthusiasm describing a visit by one of the presidential aspirants or their running mates, but for editors at *Time, Newsweek,* and *U.S. News & World Report;*

for writers like Arthur Krock, James Reston, or Cabell Phillips of the *New York Times;* Edward Folliard of the *Washington Post;* Freda Kirchwey of *The Nation;* or for syndicated columnists like Marquis Childs, Walter Lippmann, the Alsop brothers, Drew Pearson, and Lowell Mellett, the month of October was an exercise in trying to find innovative ways to say the same thing over and over.

Because they had already decided that the outcome was sealed, reporters and commentators ignored signs that might have pointed in a different direction. Even the most jaded observer noted that the crowds that came out to greet Truman were larger and more enthusiastic than those that gathered around Dewey. Different explanations were offered for this phenomenon. The president's advisers bravely told reporters that the size of Truman's crowds reflected a shift in momentum and demonstrated that voters were still undecided and still prepared to reelect Truman. But the journalists and commentators didn't take that explanation seriously because polling data flatly contradicted it. The president's own retinue touted the turnout as a good sign during formal interviews, but privately over drinks in the club car, they were just as likely to muse about what was in store for them and the country when Dewey won. There were several other possible causes that seemed more plausible. For instance, if nothing else, Truman was proving to be good entertainment. For the small towns he visited, his whistle-stop appearances were the single most exciting event of the fall. Even in Albany, Tom Dewey's stronghold, thousands waited by the train tracks and stood rows deep to listen to the president speak. According to Bert Andrews of the *New York Herald-Tribune*, reporters had the following explanation: "The voters are turning out to see the President of the United States; turning out in larger numbers than they will to see candidate Dewey." Under this reasoning, people naturally wanted to get a glimpse of the most powerful man in the country, even if he was soon to be the ex–most powerful man in the country.[1]

As the campaign evolved, it also became clear that most Americans were not passionately interested in the election, nor were they closely following developments. In part, the lack of excitement was a symptom of the widespread belief that Dewey would coast to victory. It was also an offshoot of good economic times. Relative to the Depression or war years, Americans were generally enjoying prosperity. Though both Truman and Wallace dramatized how much more prosperous and secure people could be, the previous sixteen years had seen periods of far greater struggle. Having been forced to confront politics and the world outside since 1932, many Americans didn't want to be bothered. For the first time in a long while, they didn't have to pay attention, and as a result, many of them didn't. Crossley's polls predicted that 52,000,000 people, or 56 percent of adult citizens, would vote. Radio ratings of candidates' speeches lagged well behind entertainment programs. In a nationally broadcast talk on October 2, Truman had an 8.2 rating and drew 25 percent of the audience, but Groucho Marx had an 11.6 rating and 33 percent of the listeners. Later that evening, Governor Warren's radio address came in last of the four programs being aired. A few days earlier, Dewey was soundly beaten by Al Jolson. Even on television, the election was not a big draw. The candidates hardly made use of the new medium, and when Truman made the first-ever television broadcast from the White House in early October, only a few newspapers bothered to report on it, and then only in short items buried on the back pages.[2]

For those who did pay attention, October offered more of Truman's whistle-stops and more of his hard-hitting oratory. There was also more of Dewey's leisurely jaunt through the country and more of his airy rhetoric. On October 11, he set off on a seven-day tour of the Midwest just after Truman had trundled through upstate New York and Albany. Arriving in Kansas City, Dewey came as close as he ever would to attacking Truman directly. Stressing the need for integrity in government, he promised the 12,000 people in the audience that in his administration, no one would be appointed simply because "they tell funny stories or because they are somebody's old friends. . . . It seems particularly appropriate," he continued, "to talk about good government in Kansas City. You have known how bad a bad government can be. You rose up and threw it out and you know how good a government can be." Local leaders and reporters listening to the speech immediately identified these words as a barb at Truman, his known tendency to appoint "cronies," and his former association with Kansas City boss Tom Pendergast.[3]

This jab notwithstanding, the reluctance of Dewey to criticize Truman did not go over well with all of his advisers. Some of them wished that the candidate would show some of the hard-edged vehemence that he brought to his job as a prosecutor, and they proposed that he use the visit to Kansas City to underscore the sordid side of the New Deal. Dewey refused, saying that it wouldn't be dignified to make such a speech in Truman's home state. As one columnist observed, the one-time choir singer in Owosso was "proud of the fact that he has gone through the whole 1948 campaign without saying a bad word." Dewey was pleased with the efficiency of his staff and pleased when he read someone like Marquis Childs stating that the Victory Special "might have been called the Destiny Special. For over it hangs a large air of destiny and great events to come." By not stooping to attack his opponents, Dewey hoped to weave an image of a man whose destiny was so certain that he didn't need to do what ordinary candidates did. Granted, that did lead to the problem of what to say. He gave an address defending the Taft-Hartley Act during the Midwest tour, but otherwise he displayed an increasing tendency to talk about the weather. Asked in Kansas City what he thought the country really needed, Dewey paused for a moment and replied, "We need a rudder to our ship of state." Pressed to elaborate, he continued, "and a firm hand on the rudder." By the last weeks of the campaign, his talks were notable only for taking place, not for any specific message.[4]

Becoming desperate for good copy, newspapers and magazines that would normally have devoted space to debating who was ahead and why turned instead to prognostications of what a Dewey presidency would look like. The most egregious examples of this journalistic leap could be found in *Life* and *Kiplinger's*. For its last issue before the election, *Life* featured a full-page photograph of Dewey and his wife in San Francisco, with the caption "The Next President Travels by Ferry Over the Broad Waters of San Francisco Bay." *Kiplinger's* ran nearly thirty pages of articles under the general rubric "What Dewey Will Do," including pieces about Dewey the man; President Dewey and his relationship with the Republican 81st Congress; Dewey and labor, agriculture, foreign policy; and Dewey and his advisers and appointees. Trying to come up with new angles, Samuel Grafton of the *Chicago Sun* confessed that after months of following the Republican nominee, he didn't "really know Mr. Dewey very well," nor did the country. "If there is any time when a man should not be a puzzle, it is two weeks before he is named president." Grafton concluded that the people would still probably turn to Dewey on election day, but they wouldn't take any pleasure in doing so.[5]

Dewey did make one major gaffe just before the election, and it was gleefully reported by a hungry press corps. During his swing through Illinois in mid-October, the Victory Special encountered some hecklers who pelted the train with debris. As they rushed toward the train, the engineer mistakenly backed up instead of speeding away, and Dewey was overheard saying, "That's the first lunatic I've had for an engineer. He probably should be shot at sunrise." Word spread through the press car and the engineer was interviewed. "I think just as much of Dewey as I did before," said the railroad man, "and that's not very much." The story went out on the wires that evening, and for the next week, Truman took full advantage of the episode and used it to prove his allegations that Dewey lacked compassion for or connection to ordinary Americans and that the Republicans were the party of privilege.[6]

No one noticed it at the time, but Truman was moving closer to the progressive Left, drawing crowds on Wallace's message, and igniting people with a combination of populist rhetoric and escalating attacks. At a public address in Buffalo, he declared that "Republican policies are depriving millions of families of the housing they need. Republican policies are keeping up prices of much of the food you eat." In Ohio, he took the fairly moderate Earl Warren to task for being unrepresentative of his own party. "I think you know that my opponents in this campaign are not speaking plainly or honestly," he told a group in Hamilton. In Wisconsin, he again lambasted the 80th Congress for passing "a rich man's tax bill, so the rich could get relief from taxes, at the expense of the workingman. . . . That Congress knocked the props out from under farm prosperity. They tried their best to strangle cooperatives." He told a large gathering in St. Paul, "Andrew Jackson did not seek unity with the moneymakers in Philadelphia. He made the issues so clear that the people decided to place the control of money in the Government of the United States, and not in a few private banks. . . . Franklin D. Roosevelt in 1933 did not seek unity with the economic royalists. He proposed the New Deal." At a whistle-stop in Clarksburg, West

Virginia, he said, "We're on a crusade, a crusade of right against Republican money might."

In Miami, where 200,000 lined the roads and strained to catch a glimpse of the motorcade, he briefly halted his assault and offered a sober defense of his conduct of foreign policy. When Wallace had sent an open letter to Stalin to discuss peace, he was denounced as a Soviet pawn. Several days before appearing in Miami, Truman floated the idea of sending Chief Justice Fred Vinson on a mission to Moscow, but in the face of intense public criticism and questions in his own cabinet, he backed away from the idea. He spoke of this episode in Miami. "My purpose was to ask Premier Stalin's cooperation in dispelling the present poisonous atmosphere of distrust that now surrounds the negotiations between the Western powers and the Soviet Union." Having made this Wallace-esque plea for peace, he flew to Raleigh, North Carolina, for his only foray into the South and there resumed his attacks. "Republicanism means that the Federal Government is controlled by the powerful men and greedy Wall Street interests that want cheap labor and cheap farm products. Republicanism puts the almighty dollar first and is not above using a little tidelands oil money to grease the way to power. Today, big-money Republicanism is on the march."

In Pittsburgh on October 23, Truman made fun of Dewey's refusal to talk particulars. "Now the people know where I stand. But the Republican candidate refuses to tell where he stands. My opponent is conducting a very peculiar campaign. He has set himself up as some kind of doctor with a magic cure for all the ills of mankind." Truman continued by portraying Dewey as a doctor who says his patient (the American people) is fine. Some minor ailments of course, but overall, just fine. "You shouldn't think about issues," the doctor tells the patient. "What you need is my brand of soothing syrup—I call it unity." The patient is confused. He feels fine, and he asks the doctor what's wrong.

"I never discuss issues with a patient," the doctor replies. "But what you need is a major operation."

"Will it be serious?" the patient asks.

"Not so very serious," he says. "It will just mean taking out the complete works and putting in a Republican administration."

The crowd laughed heartily at this scathing depiction of the

Dewey campaign, and they listened attentively as Truman listed the litany of complaints he had been touting over the past weeks. He also laced into Dewey for saying "Me, too" about many of Truman's initiatives. Whatever Dewey might say, Truman concluded, "the Republican record still says, 'we're against it.' "

While Dewey all but ceased campaigning outside of New York in late October, Truman kept going. He issued statements supportive of peace between Israel and the Arab states, and he vowed that the United States would stand by its commitment to Israel's territorial integrity in accord with United Nations agreements. He broke form and mentioned the Wallace movement during a speech in Indiana criticizing Dewey for hinting that the Truman administration was soft on communism. "The Communists are doing everything in their power to beat me," Truman asserted. "They have taken over the Third Party and are using it in a vain attempt to split the Democratic Party. The Republicans have joined up with this Communist-inspired Third Party to beat the Democrats. They finance the situation right here. The Republicans financed the Third Party to get on the ballot right here in Indiana."

In Chicago on October 25, Truman made one of the most vicious speeches of the campaign. After receiving a five-minute ovation from the crowd of 23,000, he was left with less time to deliver his remarks within the fixed radio schedule. Energized by the cheering, Truman lit into the Republicans with something approaching hatred. He recalled the heroic efforts of Franklin Roosevelt in leading the country during the war, and he praised those who had the foresight to see the threat to the American way of life represented by the Nazis. Now, Truman continued, the threat did not lie abroad, or with communism. "The real danger to our democracy does not come . . . from those extremes. It comes mainly from the powerful reactionary forces which are silently undermining our democratic institutions. . . . If the antidemocratic forces in this country continue to work unchecked, this Nation could awake a few years from now to find that the Bill of Rights had become a scrap of paper." Truman then identified these forces. They were groups "working through the Republican Party," groups that wanted to see inflation continue unchecked and that wanted to concentrate economic power in their hands alone. "When a few men get control of the economy of a nation, they find a front man to run the country for them. Before Hitler came to power, control over the German economy had passed into the hands of a small group of rich manufacturers, bankers, and landowners. These men decided that Germany had to have a tough, ruthless dictator who would play their game and crush the strong German labor unions. So they put money and influence behind Adolf Hitler. We know the rest of the story. We also know that in Italy, in the 1920s, powerful Italian businessmen backed Mussolini, and that in the 1930s, Japanese financiers helped Tojo's military clique take over Japan." The situation was now similar in the United States, and Truman warned that "great corporations have been expending their power steadily. . . . The lobbies which work for big business found that they could get what their bosses wanted from the Republican leaders of the 80th Congress." He listed the ways in which the Republicans had become the tool of big business and then said ominously, "That's what the Republican candidate calls delivering for the future. Is that the kind of future you want?"

In the words of one reporter who was present, "You could go beyond saying the speech was hard-hitting; you could say it was demagogic." The Chicago address was part of an overall strategy in these waning days to stir up religious groups such as Catholics and Jews (who were especially sensitive to the recent memory of fascism) and to alert minority groups to the risks in not voting and thereby allowing the Republicans to capture the Oval Office. Truman didn't say anything that Strom Thurmond had not said, and he didn't make any claims that Wallace hadn't already made. But unlike them, Harry Truman was president of the United States. What he said carried far greater weight and had more significant ramifications. He had likened a major presidential candidate to Adolf Hitler and made a not-so-veiled comparison between the Republican Party and Fascists. It was one thing to champion the cause of farmers and workers; it was another to critique his opponents as wealthy men who wished primarily to line their own pockets at the expense of tens of millions of hardworking Americans. But in Chicago, Truman crossed a line that few major candidates had ever crossed, and it would come back to haunt him when the Republicans, furious at what they felt was a dirty campaign, unleashed their own demagogs during Truman's second term.[7]

Unperturbed and unapologetic, Truman continued on to Boston, where thousands of working-class Irish Catholics lined the streets and thousands more came to Mechanics Hall to listen to him explain why the Communists were supporting the Republicans. In New York, where more than a million came out to cheer, he spoke at Madison Square Garden, at the Brooklyn Academy of Music, and in Harlem, where he gave a rare address on civil rights. Meanwhile, Dewey spoke in Chicago and Cleveland, where he charged the Democrats with a desultory policy toward communist expansion in Europe but refused to answer Truman's attacks in kind. Even after Truman had broken all the unwritten protocols of personal attacks, Dewey would not respond. He had drafted a speech in response to Truman's Chicago tirade, but after consultation with his inner circle, he chose not to use it. Instead, he endured Truman's ridicule and even the ridicule of actress Tallulah Bankhead, an Alabama native whose father and uncles had served in Congress. "What is Mr. Dewey for? Again and again he has said that he is for unity. Will all the candidates who are for disunity please stand? The next thing we know he'll be endorsing matrimony, the metal zipper, and the dial telephone." But Dewey saw no reason to descend and respond to these gibes. For every actress who teased him, Dewey could point to others who endorsed him with gratitude and respect. Soon after Bankhead taunted him, Joe Louis, heavyweight boxing champion and a hero to African Americans, made a public display of deserting Wallace and seeking out Dewey at the governor's Manhattan headquarters. He just missed the candidate at the Roosevelt Hotel but caught up with him in Grand Central Station, where he gently shook Dewey's hand, wished him luck, and smiled for photographers.[8]

Some of Dewey's advisers, including his campaign manager, Herbert Brownell, and Ed Jaeckle, were beginning to wonder. Mid-October polls indicated that Truman was gaining, not enough to jeopardize Dewey's considerable edge, but enough to sound some precautionary bells. In surveys in *Time* and the *New York Times,* Dewey was believed to be comfortably ahead, with approximately 350 electoral votes in his column. It also appeared that the Republicans might lose control of the Senate, and many House races were so close that it was impossible to predict the results. Though that was hardly good news for Dewey, it wasn't nearly bad enough to force a change in strategy. It wasn't simply his inner circle that advised Dewey to stay the course. Even the reporters on the train believed that the choice to preserve a noble mien was the right one, and a Roper poll from early October showed that voters liked the fact that the Dewey campaign was "dignified, sincere, and clean." Only 5 percent of those surveyed found it "dull," whereas 25 percent were uncomfortable with Truman's "mudslinging" and less than 10 percent thought that the president's whistle-stops were "inspiring." As of late October, both Lockwood and Bell acknowledged that the race had tightened, but they believed that any dramatic shift in tone and tactics entailed unnecessary risk, and Dewey concurred.

One of the most prescient pieces of advice came from a Wall Street supporter, Edward Hutton of the firm E. F. Hutton. From late September to late October, Hutton fired off a series of letters to campaign headquarters, urging Dewey to descend from "the high level of constructive platitudes and reach the people in language and words which bounce along the sidewalks. It is the man on the street who holds in the palm of his hands the future destiny of America. That is the man who should be reached. . . . The abuse of democracy marks the steps to despotism. It should be pointed out that Mr. Truman is creating hatred between citizens and citizens and class against class. . . . It is my opinion that to combat this, Governor Dewey must answer in kind, take off the kid gloves and start to slug. That is what people like and that is where the votes are. . . . Against a man armed with brass knuckles, well schooled in the art of eye-gouging, biting and kicking, it is poor judgement to defend oneself with a powder-puff. The time has come to nail the lies, refute the slander and hit back." Hutton reiterated his advice in a telegram to Dewey on October 25 warning that contrary to all the polls and pundits, defeat was in the air unless Dewey showed some hints of the toughness he once exuded as a prosecutor. E.F. Hutton spoke, but no one listened.[9]

SUDDENLY it was quiet. Tuesday, November 2, had arrived, and at last the candidates had no more to say. After years of effort, months of preparation, weeks of intensive campaigning, after conventions in the heat of summer, after sleepless nights of arguing over platforms and running mates, after tens of thousands of miles of train tracks, thousands of newspaper articles, and hundreds of speeches, after breakfasts and picnics and cookouts and lavish dinners, after millions of dollars raised and spent, the end had come.

Campaigns halt abruptly. One minute, hundreds of staff and reporters and supporters are rushing to and fro, and the next minute, all anyone can do is go to the nearest polling station, sit back near a radio or a television, and wait. There is something humbling about an electoral democracy, and something awesome about being a candidate. No matter how many miles Truman or Dewey or Thurmond or Wallace covered, no matter how many millions cheered them on or argued about them over dinner or thought about what they said in the quiet of their own minds, on Election Day, each candidate represented only one vote: his own. Truman in Independence, Barkley in Kentucky, Dewey and Wallace in New York, Warren in California, Taylor in Idaho, Thurmond in Edgefield, and Fielding Wright in Jackson. They were eight votes out of nearly fifty million. The only thing any of them controlled on November 2 was his own hands in his own voting booth.

The weather throughout the country was generally fair. Even so, more people were expected to stay home than to vote. Estimates of how many would participate had gone steadily downward with each passing week, and it was beginning to look as if the 1948 election would have one of the lowest turnouts of the century. Having been told that the result was preordained, millions decided that there wasn't any reason to take the trouble. If Dewey was so far ahead, then no individual vote really mattered, and for many, voting was an unpleasant duty that entailed getting to a polling station, waiting in line, deciphering the ballot, and making decisions. The final Gallup Poll in October actually showed evidence of a statistically tight race, with Dewey at 49.5 percent and Truman at 44.5 percent, Wallace at 4 percent, and Thurmond rounding out the field at 2 percent. Assuming that the outcome was already certain, election handicappers paid no attention to the poll. Had these numbers penetrated the conventional wisdom, Americans might have realized with a start that what had seemed only weeks ago a runaway for the Republicans was now a close contest.[10]

Truman arrived in Independence having delivered almost 300

speeches and traveled nearly 22,000 miles in thirty-three days stretched over more than six weeks. Covering 16,000 miles, Dewey had maintained a less punishing pace, but he had hardly been indolent. Wallace also ranged over vast amounts of territory, and though his crowds dwindled by the end, he had remained in the public eye. Thurmond had by some calculations rolled up more mileage than Truman in order to establish himself as a visceral presence south of the Mason-Dixon line.[11] On Election Day, each of them had private hopes and personal demons. Truman appeared cool and confident, as did Dewey, but who knows what went through their minds as they pulled the lever or marked the box next to their name? Wallace had the air of a man who could not deny the grim truth of what was about to happen yet could not admit it either. Thurmond had shown no sign during the campaign that he was prone to deep thought, and he went about his affairs with a carefree attitude that was only occasionally offset by the stinging fury of his rhetoric. He knew that victory was impossible, but when he voted that day in Edgefield with his wife, he looked more relaxed than any of his competitors.

Voters across the country were presented with a total of eleven candidates for president. Most of these were only on the ballot in a few states. Besides the four major contenders, Norman Thomas represented the Socialists and Claude Watson represented the Prohibition Party. Farrell Dobbs was the nominee of the Socialist Workers, and Edward Teichert rounded out the Left as the standard-bearer for Socialist-Labor. John Scott stood for the populist Greenback Party, while the grizzled Dr. John Maxwell led the Vegetarian Party ticket. Also on the ballot was Gerald K. Smith of the white supremacist Christian National Crusade. Though these other men had received scant press attention and though none of them had any illusion of victory, they had campaigned and given speeches. They had volunteers handling their correspondence and coordinating mailings. They had platforms and policies, and each represented a distinct perspective. Whites who believed in the hierarchy and separation of races could vote for Smith; farmers and agricultural workers who did not hear a sufficiently stringent critique of Wall Street could vote Greenback; and those who regretted the end of the Volstead Act and the passage of the Twenty-first Amendment could vote to turn back the clock by endorsing Watson.

In addition to these presidential candidates, thousands of names appeared on the state ballots for national and local office. People voted then as they do now for their congressional representatives, for their governors and assemblymen and county supervisors and mayors. They voted on ballot initiatives and on local ordinances. They often voted for the entire party slate. A Democrat would pick the Democrat in every race that he or she could vote for; a Republican would do the same. They might not know the names or have any sense of the individuals for whom they were voting, but they believed in the party, and trusted its leaders to select honorable, competent candidates who would fairly represent their constituents.

Truman hoped that Republican voters would feel less compelled to vote and that Democrats would be sufficiently riled to turn out in force. Dewey hoped that Democrats would be so demoralized that they wouldn't bother. But on Tuesday there was nothing more that either of them could do. Dewey strolled between the Roosevelt Hotel and the polling station, and took the genial smiles and waves of the people as a positive sign. "Good luck, Mr. President," they shouted. Truman ducked out to avoid the people in Independence, knowing full well that their smiles would be forced and their shouts of "Good luck" would be despondent. Wallace was surrounded by his family and advisers, and that gave him some comfort. Thurmond was greeted by adoring crowds in his hometown, and he knew that, win or lose, he was their hero.

Truman took his bath, ate his sandwich, and went to sleep. Dewey stayed up late into the night and sat passively as his career took an unexpected turn. It was rumored that when Dewey took leave of his inner circle at about 11:00 that night, he turned to his wife and said, "Frances, how would you like to go to bed with the President of the United States?" And Mrs. Dewey turned to him and replied, "Sure, why not?"[12] Downstairs in the main ballroom of the Roosevelt, the cream of the New York Republicans, attired in formal wear, waited for the victory speech. By midnight, they were beginning to doubt. By dawn, the unthinkable had happened.

CHAPTER TWENTY-ONE

The Aftermath

TRUMAN HAD done it. He had won. It was the most dramatic and surprising result of any presidential election in the history of the United States. It was the greatest upset ever.

Truman won 24,105,812 to Dewey's 21,970,065. He captured 49.5 percent of the popular vote, along with 303 electoral votes, while Dewey won 45.1 percent and 189 electoral votes. In Congress, Democrats retook control of both houses by a substantial margin. They went from a 6-seat deficit in the Senate to a 12-seat majority, and in the House, they went from a 246-to-188-seat disadvantage to a 263-to-171-seat edge. Fifty-six percent of the electorate voted Democratic in Senate races, and 60 percent in House elections. In gubernatorial contests, the Democrats broke the former 24-to-24 statehouse deadlock and emerged with victories in 29 states, leaving the GOP in control of 19 .[1]

One of the only correct forecasts the press and pollsters and pundits made was that the turnout would be low. Barely forty-nine million voted, just over 51 percent of eligible adults compared with 55 percent in 1944. Though a far larger portion of the electorate showed up on November 2, 1948, than had voted in the midterm elections of 1946, the 1948 presidential election had the lowest participation rate of any national race until the 1980s. Explanations for the paucity of voters ranged from Dewey's postmortem claim that the polls had lulled his supporters into a false sense of security to the observation made by Arthur Krock that many Americans were sufficiently complacent and content that they didn't see the need to vote.[2] It was not the last time the argument would be made that low voter turnout in the United States is a sign of the strength of American democracy, not of its weakness. In 1948, given the range of options, a credible case can be made that voters simply chose not to choose. Subsequent elections, however, have offered fewer options, and the absence of diverse views has become a factor in voter apathy.

The only other non-surprise was the showing of the third parties. As expected, Wallace received considerably fewer votes than had once been forecast. Though the polls showed him with more support than the 1,157,172 votes he eventually received, nearly half of those votes came from New York City and its environs, and he won no electoral votes. Strom Thurmond carried four states—Louisiana, South Carolina, Alabama, and Mississippi—for a total of 1,169,021 votes. The other seven presidential candidates collected 279,080 votes, slightly more than half to Norman Thomas and the Socialists, and most of the rest to the Prohibitionists.

The other forecasts were so completely wrong that, at first, the professionals who made a living knowing exactly what to say were speechless. The reporters who covered the election were dumbfounded that they could have been so blind to what was going on. The pollsters who had touted the arrival of scientific sampling had their faith tested. The pundits whose reputations depended on at least the image of sagacity wondered how they had misread the public mood so completely. As for the party leaders, they were also astonished. The Democrats had not expected such a windfall, and the Republicans certainly hadn't anticipated such a defeat. Colonel Robert R. McCormick's *Chicago Tribune* made the campaign's most memorable gaffe with its early morning edition on November 3, but while the picture of Truman laughing with a copy of the paper in his hand is the most indelible image of the campaign, McCormick wasn't the only publisher to get it wrong. Not only did *Life* print the picture of Dewey "the next president," but *Billboard*'s November 6 cover also featured a portrait of Dewey, with the headline "Our Next President."

Many magazines and newspapers had the good grace to admit their mistake without excuses. Arthur Krock stated that "the principal item on our menu will not be beefsteak, not terrapin, but crow." Elmo Roper, who was deeply shaken, would say only, "I could not have been more wrong." Gallup vowed to take another survey "to find out just what happened." The editors of *Life* were particularly gracious and humble in the aftermath: "In common with 90% of the U.S. press we were wrong in doping the presidential election. We make no apology for having supported Thomas E. Dewey. . . . But we do feel badly about falling victim to a mass illusion. . . . Instead of eating crow we insist on our own cliche: we are wearing sackcloth and ashes." The editors then tried to answer the question of the moment: "Just how did we, in common with most publications, manage to muff the job of prognostication? The plain fact of the matter is that editors, reporters, columnists, and pundits were fundamentally bored with the candidates and the seeming lack of issues as far back as last summer. The boredom affected the pollsters; they went through the motions of scientific sampling of public opinion . . . but they weren't sufficiently suspicious or sufficiently interested to try to penetrate the great mystery of the undecided vote." The polls in turn reinforced the boredom of the press, who succumbed to natural human laziness, stopped looking for new angles, and simply saw what they expected to see. Reporters spent too much time on the trains talking to each other and too little energy going out and talking to ordinary voters. The pundits, the editors continued, were guilty of looking down on Truman. He wasn't as widely read or as deeply versed in diplomacy, economics, or history as most editors at *Time* or *Life*, and he certainly couldn't conduct an erudite conversation with Walter Lippmann, Marquis Childs, or the Alsop brothers. But he knew America, he knew Americans, and most of all, he knew the Midwest better than any of those denizens of Georgetown or Park Avenue. Though *Life* hadn't supported his candidacy, "in his coming adventure as a president in his own right, we wish him well."[3]

The shame of the pollsters was unsurpassed. When Wilfred Funk of *The Literary Digest* mispredicted the 1936 election, he was ridiculed and driven out of business. Gallup and Roper had touted scientific polling as a guarantee that Funk's mistake would never be repeated. Yet, if anything, the errors of 1948 were even worse, if only because the press and the politicians placed far more faith in the three main polling organizations. Funk was sought out for his reaction. "I do not want to seem malicious," he replied, "but I couldn't help but get a good chuckle out of this." The scientific polling organizations, which spent tens of thousands of dollars and were courted by the powerful, had been bested by the Staley Milling Company's informal Pullet Feed Poll in Kansas City, and that alone was enough to cast aspersions on the whole enterprise of modern polling.[4]

The main problem was how the undecided votes had been calculated. The pollsters tended to distribute those answering "don't know" proportionally to those who stated a specific choice. So, if 15 percent were undecided, Crossley would distribute those 15 percent in a manner that reinforced the impression of a Dewey lead, because Dewey did lead among those who said they had already decided. Combined with the presumption that voters made up their minds early, this method of calculating undecided votes created a false impression that Dewey held a substantial lead. Crossley and his colleagues didn't believe that many people would change their minds, yet as later surveys demonstrated, substantial numbers of voters did switch allegiances late in the game. For that reason, the Gallup polls taken near Election Day were more accurate. Late in the campaign, the number of "don't knows" decreased, and Gallup polls from mid-October showed that Truman had narrowed the gap nearly to the point of a statistical dead heat once the margin of error was factored in. But with Dewey still in the lead, people were inclined not to make much of the fact that the lead had shrunk. The only good to come from the polling error was that Gallup and Roper spent the following years scrutinizing their methodology and, in time, they were able to solve the problem of how to factor undecided voters. There were many close elections in the following years, as well as several landslides, and the major polling organizations called each of them fairly accurately.

Then there was the question of how Truman had won. To this day, that issue has not been adequately resolved and it likely never will be. Truman claimed that his victory was due to the support of organized labor, and indeed, in the last weeks of the campaign the AFL and the CIO each spent over $1 million funding radio spots and distributing literature. Much of labor's energies went not into assisting Truman but toward defeating congressional Republicans. Taft-Hartley was labor's red flag, and unions were resolved to defeat the representatives who had passed the bill over Truman's veto. Their support was vital to the success of senatorial candidates like Hubert Humphrey in Minnesota, Paul Douglas in Illinois, and Lester Hunt in Wyoming. Labor unions had also been at the forefront of the opposition to Wallace, and their assiduous efforts to prevent the union rank and file from voting for him both weakened the Progressive Party and aided the Democrats. But for all the assistance that organized labor provided, Truman did not fare that well in the industrial centers. In states such as Michigan and Pennsylvania, which Truman lost, he attracted less support than the congressional Democrats. In big cities, where unions were still strong in the late 1940s, Truman polled nearly a third fewer voters than Roosevelt had in 1944. Truman also barely carried Ohio, another strong labor state as well as an agricultural one, though Roosevelt had lost it in 1944. However, in some areas, Truman probably benefited from a reverse coattails effect and picked up votes from popular Democratic congressional candidates.

It was in the farm states that Truman made substantial gains. With Iowa, Wisconsin, and Ohio, he obtained 101 electoral votes in the Midwest, 26 more than Roosevelt had. He also defeated Dewey in agriculture-rich California. In preelection surveys, Dewey was picked to win California, Idaho, Washington, Oregon, Montana, Wyoming, Ohio, Iowa, Indiana, and Minnesota, as well as the Republican belt of North Dakota, South Dakota, Nebraska, and Kansas. Of these fourteen states, he won only six. All of these states had large numbers of farmers, agricultural workers, or people who lived in cities but were connected in some way to the business of farming. Here Truman did far better than anyone had predicted.

In that respect, Truman's populist, anti–Wall Street rhetoric was vindicated. He understood better than his advisers or adversaries the deep currents of distrust and fear of big business than ran through the areas of the United States that were defined by farming. He knew how potent these people could be if aroused. In many respects he was like them, and though he had learned how to maneuver in the East Coast worlds of money and power, he never modified his personality to fit in. Even as president, he continued to view politics through the lens of a farmer from Missouri. When Truman left the White House in 1953, he returned to Independence and spent the rest of his life puttering around his library.

Truman was also aided by good times and superb staff work. Over the years, political scientists would discover that incumbent presidents almost never lose when the economy is strong, and in 1948, the country was prosperous and becoming more so. Rising prices may have been a fraught political issue, but in overall economic terms, they were a sign of a robust economy in which demand was outpacing the ability of businesses to generate products. Only in the agricultural sector were prices depressed, and even here, the reason was good harvests combined with highly efficient farming, not lack of demand.

As he made his way across the country, Truman was surrounded by one of the most impressive teams of campaign managers ever assembled. Beginning with the Clifford-Rowe memorandum and continuing with the creation of the Research Division and the refined technique of speech writing that developed during the June tour and reached its apex during the fall whistle-stops, Truman's staff gave him a decided edge over his opponents. Though his campaign appeared haphazard and loose when compared to Dewey's, that was a reflection of Truman's demeanor, not an indication of lax organization. At every stage, he was carefully briefed and skillfully counseled, and his acute political instincts enabled him to utilize advice that would be helpful and to discard suggestions that would not work for him.

Finally, Truman benefited from two developments that at first threatened to doom him. The presence of the Dixiecrats to his right and the Progressives to his left gave him the freedom to speak forcefully on civil rights and to make a populist, anti–big business plea without running the risk of being called a Communist. He could fruitfully campaign on the Left because Wallace insulated him. Of course, the only reason he could be a man of the Left and garner votes was because in 1948, a majority of Americans believed in the New Deal. They wanted an active government that protected ordinary citizens from threats overseas and from the rapaciousness of large corporations. In 1948, Americans remembered the 1920s, when Republican administrations had been inclined to give free rein to those "captains of industry" who cared not a whit for farmers or laborers. Dewey understood this, and he carefully excised hints of isolationism or of Coolidge Republicanism from the party platform and from his own speeches. But the 80th Congress did not play along, and the obvious divide between Dewey and the Congress allowed Truman to paint the Republicans as the party of privilege and to undercut Dewey's efforts to portray himself as a moderate who would preserve the New Deal while halting its growth.[5]

Overall, Truman did significantly less well in traditional labor strongholds than Roosevelt had. He did manage to maintain substantial support in cities, and Catholics and urban blacks overwhelmingly voted Democrat. His strategy of tarring Dewey with the brush of fascism was effective, at least insofar as it scared a significant portion of urban voters into continuing to vote Democratic. But Truman and the party could look at the results in those areas as a mixed sign. While the president hadn't slipped enough to give the election to Dewey, he had indeed slipped, and the Republicans had gained. Perhaps they had gained because Dewey was so moderate and so centrist, perhaps because the country truly was ready to have less government and the Republicans were perceived as a party that would be less activist. Though Truman had performed strongly in agricultural regions, demographic developments pointed to the cities and their suburbs as the real future. Truman's success in the short term thus masked several warning signs. One of the unintended consequences of his victory was that the leaders of the Democratic Party didn't pay as much attention to these signs as they should have, and that in turn helped pave the way for Democratic setbacks in the 1950s and beyond.

AFTER THE ELECTION, the candidates went their separate ways. Truman boarded his train for Washington, and when he arrived at Union Station, some 750,000 lined the route to the White House. He was humble in victory, saying he was more overwhelmed by what lay ahead than relieved by what had just happened. He did rib the pollsters and reporters, but he now had only kind words about his Republican opponent. Dewey, in turn, slipped away from New York after his postelection press conference. Though he was dazed by the outcome, he never talked about it in public and none of his colleagues or family ever hinted that he had discussed it with them in private. Dewey reluctantly ran for and was elected to another term as governor. In 1956, he retired from public office and spent the remaining years of his life as a lawyer in private practice. He stayed active in

Republican politics and used his influence to help steer the party away from Robert Taft in 1952 and toward the moderate centrism that would characterize Republicanism under Dwight Eisenhower.

Henry Wallace retreated from public life, resigned from the Progressive Party in 1950, and retired to his farm in Connecticut, where he died in 1965. The Progressives tried to survive the McCarthy years without him under the leadership of C.B. Baldwin, but by the end of 1952, the party had all but disappeared.

Strom Thurmond was rather publicly snubbed by Truman during the inaugural ceremonies in January 1949, and if he hadn't realized that his days in the Democratic Party were numbered, he soon did. He tried to run for the Senate as the Democratic nominee in 1950 but he lost in the primary in the face of strong opposition from the party establishment. Undeterred, Thurmond ran again in 1954, still as a Democrat but without seeking the aid of the party. In a stunning race, he became the first and last person ever to be elected to the United States Senate as a write-in candidate. At the end of the century, Thurmond was still in the Senate, though he had long since switched parties and found a comfortable home with the Republicans.

TRUMAN'S SECOND term began with the upset of the century, but it quickly turned sour. Nineteen forty-nine was a year of revolution in China punctuated by the detonation of the first Soviet atomic bomb. Nineteen fifty was worse. Between Korea, labor unrest, and the efflorescence of McCarthyism, Truman spent the remaining years of his term embroiled in constant crisis. The standing of the Democratic Party was so low in 1952 that Eisenhower coasted to an easy victory over Adlai Stevenson, and the Republicans retook the House of Representatives.

Yet the unraveling of the presidency during the second term was directly related to the way Truman won. That point was lost on people at the time, and it has rarely been adequately emphasized. Truman made a devil's choice in order to stage his comeback. By unleashing his rhetoric, Truman stoked class resentment and agrarian fear. He successfully marginalized Dewey by caricaturing him. Dewey assisted in his own demise by refusing to defend himself. For the most part, candidates will avoid character assassination and unbridled assaults not because they respect each other but out of self-interest. It is easy to call your opponent vile names and accuse him of sordid behavior, but it is difficult to defend yourself when your opponent does the same. Certain types of words in a campaign constitute the rhetorical equivalent of nuclear weapons. Each side has them and each side knows the other side has them, so both tend to shy away lest they embark on a path of mutual destruction.

Frequently, that reluctance dissipates when one side believes that it is on the verge of defeat. Then the possible benefits outweigh the costs. Because Truman seemed to be losing so early, he was less restrained from the outset. He was fortunate that Dewey refrained from heeding the advice of E.F. Hutton and chose not to meet Truman's tactics with an equivalent response. But other Republicans were not so forgiving or forbearing. They were enraged at how Truman campaigned. They believed that he had stolen an election that was rightfully theirs and that he had broken the unwritten compact between the parties. Since he had played foul, they intended to play foul in return, and when a senator from Wisconsin decided to make wild and unsubstantiated claims about communist penetration of the Truman administration, party elders such as Robert Taft made no effort to stop him. Joseph McCarthy could never have pursued his destructive vendetta against the Democrats had the leaders of the Republican Party not supported him. And the GOP leaders would have been less inclined to support McCarthy if Truman had fought fairly during the fall of 1948. Truman did not cause McCarthyism, but to a far greater degree than is usually cited, he helped provoke it.

The election of 1948 was notable not just for the severity of Truman's oratory, but for the substantive debate that the candidates waged. Though Dewey's fall speeches were pallid, during the primary fight with Stassen he articulated a complex, nuanced vision of government in explaining why he didn't believe in outlawing the Communist Party. Wallace presented a series of critiques of the international system and contemporary capitalism, and Thurmond offered a perspective on the Constitution, on the balance of power between the states and the federal government, and on the proper role of the federal government that may have been deeply tainted by bigotry but was nonetheless representative of a long tradition of American political thought. At no point since 1948 has such a range of views been represented in a presidential election, and been presented with such cogency, depth, and sophistication.

Television was clearly the proximate cause of the change. The television era saw a decline in the number of options and a descent into the kind of platitudes that characterized the latter stages of the Dewey campaign. The rise of the networks as for-profit entities meant that if candidates wanted access to television, they would have to pay for it, and as television became a major medium in the 1950s, candidates needed its exposure if they wanted to win. The prohibitive costs of access combined with the absence of any legislative provision for public airtime on the networks meant that only those presidential aspirants with substantial financial backing could hope to wage a national campaign. But as the financial struggles of the parties in 1948 demonstrate, it wasn't cheap to run for office during the age of radio, and though television costs more, the differential alone was not substantial enough to explain why the television era has seen less choice.

As a result of the Cold War, American politicians closed ranks on foreign policy, and as a result of the protests of the 1960s, both politicians and the public became concerned that too much political debate could lead to chaos. The amalgamation of these two forces and television narrowed the spectrum of choice and debate in national elections. Nineteen forty-eight provides a window onto what presidential politics in America might have been like had not television, the Cold War, and the sixties interacted the way they did.

It is tempting to romanticize the 1948 election as an example of what our politics can be. In many ways, that temptation is justified. The contest offered people a range of different visions of what America should be, and for the most part, it was waged on the issues. For those who idealize pretelevision elections as more civil and more genteel, however, the reality of 1948 is a reminder of how rough American politics can be. The campaign witnessed starkly defined philosophies that weren't prettified or softened. Candidates strove to articulate their positions effectively; they tried to gain as much support as possible. They did not try to avoid alienating groups that disagreed with them, and they did not recoil from making enemies. They did not subject their remarks to test groups, but to the test of coherence. If a speech conveyed the message, it was effective.

But it is also true that 1948 helped create our modern campaign system. Perhaps the greatest irony is that while Dewey lost, he set the tone for television candidates of the future. In the immediate aftermath, many voters and commentators said that Dewey never seemed real to them. He appeared packaged and people didn't trust someone who looked to have been molded by professional managers into the perfect facsimile of a candidate. Whereas Dewey was presented to voters as the future president who would bring unity, Truman was offered as a common man who happened to be president. In 1948, that gave Truman a huge edge. The Dewey campaign was designed not to offend and not to alienate; the Truman campaign was designed to allow Truman to be Truman. After the election was over, no one was certain who Dewey was, or what he stood for. He may have had a governing philosophy to maintain clean hands, but he never communicated that effectively. He may have been a serious thinker who would have made a superior president, but his campaign never allowed people to see the man behind the candidate. The difference, then, was that Truman campaigned as a real person, who joked with crowds and reporters and who was often carried away by his passion and his pugnaciousness. It took a large support staff to enable him to run this way, but in the end, the man people listened to on the back of the train was Harry Truman, speaking his mind in his own words.

In subsequent years, however, public taste shifted. People began to prefer the safe, smooth, photogenic candidate over the tell-it-like-it-is common man. Perhaps in reaction to the sixties, they started to support candidates who didn't harshly attack their adversaries. For all of the complaints about negative campaigning in the television age, no subsequent major candidate compares with Truman for sheer demagogy and character assassination. Television campaign ads often unfairly malign candidates, but usually by hinting rather than stating. They are sometimes laced with innuendo and false claims, but rarely do they enunciate unambiguous positions on divisive issues. Attack ads have been successful, but the public has recoiled even from these. The platitudes that characterized Dewey's campaign have become standard fare. Even in our most contentious recent elections, major candidates have refrained from speaking like Truman did, and they rarely pit class against class. Decrying that one party is out of sync with the country is not the same as saying that one party has betrayed, robbed, and defrauded the American people. That is how Truman campaigned, and it was how candidates had conducted themselves in most elections before 1948. Before the era of television, candidates attacked their opponents' character, their opponents' platform, and their opponents' competency, and the public often rewarded the candidate who most forcefully articulated his positions and most devastatingly deconstructed his adversary's. Not so since.

After Truman, the public tended to select candidates who trumpeted unity and to ignore aspirants who overtly emphasized divisions. By the end of the twentieth century, ideological fervor had all but disappeared from presidential politics. Elections became more civil than in the days before television, but also more bland and less substantive. Fewer issues were debated; fewer options were presented; and the choices became less dramatic. Style became ever more important, and images were more subtly crafted. Nowhere is this transformation more evident than in the career of Richard Nixon, who, in the course of the 1950s, remade himself for television. He established himself in the 1940s and early 1950s as an attack dog who spoke bluntly. But that manner didn't suit television, and beginning with his maudlin "Checkers speech" in the 1952 campaign, Nixon learned to present himself in a softer manner. Though he was never comfortable on television, he learned to modulate his rhetoric and to steer clear of direct assaults on his opponents' character. Of course, like many others, he perfected the art of indirect and even covert attacks, but the change in his public image demonstrated how substantially presidential politics shifted during his career.

As a result of the new ethos, a candidate who spoke too specifically on too many issues would fare poorly, because in a representative democracy, taking an unequivocal stand generates both support and animosity. That meant that since 1948 controversial views have often been pushed out of mainstream politics. If people are alarmed at the prospect of division, if they don't much care for attack campaigns, then ideological third parties have no place at the electoral table. The Dixiecrats and the Progressives can only exist if the public is willing to support freewheeling campaigns that offer choices some people find abhorrent. There have been a number of major third parties in subsequent elections but, for the most part, they have fielded protest candidates who react against the main parties and serve as a channel for voter frustration about the lack of issues, substance, and choice. Other than George Wallace in 1968, who in many respects was the second coming of Strom Thurmond and the Dixiecrats, and Ross Perot in 1992, third parties since 1948 haven't presented coherent alternatives so much as they have rejected the alternatives offered by the two main parties.

Of the four men who ran for president in 1948, Dewey was the harbinger of the future, while Truman was the last of his kind. For the final time, a pretelevision candidate, one who cultivated an unpolished image, who gave 'em hell and told it like it was, triumphed. For all of his rough edges, Truman captured the hearts of voters in 1948, and he has since become an icon of honesty, integrity, and grit. After the election, Dewey mostly sat on the sidelines, watching events that he had expected to shape. But forces larger than both of them were writing a different script than the one they played out in 1948. The cool, detached Dewey, the packaged candidate who ran so as not to lose, who steered clear of controversy, and who made a good show of appearing presidential—that was the model that Americans chose after 1948. "Dewey Defeats Truman," the famous headline, so memorable for being so wrong, had it right after all.

Notes

INTRODUCTION

1. Details come from *Life* (November 15, 1948); Charles Ross, "How Truman Did It," *National Weekly* (December 25, 1948); Irwin Ross, *The Loneliest Campaign: The Truman Victory of 1948* (New American Library, 1968); Robert Ferrell, *Harry S. Truman: A Life* (University of Missouri Press, 1994), pp. 280–285; David McCullough, *Truman* (Simon & Schuster, 1992), pp. 703–710; Alonzo Hamby, *Man of the People* (Oxford University Press, 1996); Jonathan Daniels Oral History, Harry S. Truman Library [hereafter HST], Independence, Missouri, pp. 146–150.

2. "The Election," *Newsweek* (November 8, 1948); Richard Norton Smith, *Thomas E. Dewey and His Times* (Simon & Schuster, 1982); Ross, *The Loneliest Campaign.*

3. Reuven Frank, *Out of Thin Air: The Brief Wonderful Life of Network News* (Simon & Schuster, 1991), pp. 8–10; Saul Carson, "A Look at Television," *The New Republic* (June 7, 1948).

4. Taken from an interview with Theresa McGlinchey Zammiello conducted by the staff at the HST. Election Vertical File, "Election Night, 1948." No date for the interview is given. HST.

5. "Summary of Remarks by George Elsey in Politics 203, Princeton University, January 11, 1949," Box 32, Elsey Papers, HST.

6. Curtis Macdougall, *Gideon's Army* (Marzani & Munsell, 1965); Graham White and John Maze, *Henry A. Wallace: His Search for a New World Order* (University of North Carolina Press, 1995), pp. 274–285; Henry Wallace, "America Is Freedom," Text of Radio Address, October 18, 1948. Henry Wallace Papers [hereafter HWP], University of Iowa Library, Iowa City, Iowa.

7. Information on Strom Thurmond comes from author interview with Senator Thurmond, Washington, D.C., January 1998. Photo archives of the Strom Thurmond Papers [hereafter STP], Special Collections, Clemson University.

Blanche Gibbs, "Thurmond Votes Amid Friends at Edgefield," *Columbia Record* (November 2, 1948).

8. Krock quotation from *Life* (November 15, 1948), p. 43.

CHAPTER ONE: Prelude to the Year That Was

1. Spencer Weart, *Nuclear Fear* (Harvard University Press, 1988); Richard Rhodes, *The Making of the Atomic Bomb* (Simon & Schuster, 1986); Fred Inglis, *The Cruel Peace: Everyday Life and the Cold War* (Basic Books, 1991); Gerhard Weinberg, *A World at Arms: A Global History of World War II* (Cambridge University Press, 1994).

2. Sara Evans, *Born for Liberty: A History of Women in America* (The Free Press, 1989), pp. 234–243.

3. Kenneth Jackson, *Crabgrass Frontier: The Suburbanization of America* (Oxford University Press, 1985), pp. 234–241.

4. Nicholas Lemann, *The Promised Land: The Great Black Migration and How It Changed America* (Alfred A. Knopf, 1991).

5. Quoted in William Chafe, *The Unfinished Journey: America Since World War II* (Oxford University Press, 1995), p. 88. On civil rights, see Steve Lawson, *Black Ballots: Voting Rights in the South* (Columbia University Press, 1976).

6. Truman made this speech on the advice of Dean Acheson. See Dean Acheson, *Present at the Creation: My Years in the State Department* (W. W. Norton, 1969); James Chace, *Acheson* (Simon & Schuster, 1998); Howard Jonas, *A New Kind of War: America's Global Strategy and the Truman Doctrine in Greece* (Oxford University Press, 1989).

7. See Kai Bird, *The Chairman: John J. McCloy the Making of the American Establishment* (Simon & Schuster, 1992); Bird, *The Color of Truth: McGeorge Bundy and William Bundy* (Simon & Schuster, 1999); Walter Isaacson and Evan Thomas, *The Wise Men: Six Friends and the World They Made* (Simon & Schuster, 1986); David Fromkin, *In the Time of the Americans* (Alfred A. Knopf, 1995).

8. On Germany, see Frank Ninkovich, *Germany and the United States: The Transformation of the German Question Since 1945* (Twayne, 1995); Melvyn Leffler, *A Preponderance of Power* (Stanford University Press, 1992).

9. The Wallace-Truman split is recounted in White and Maze, *Henry Wallace,* op. cit., pp. 220ff; Norman Markowitz, *The Rise and Fall of the People's Century: Henry Wallace and American Liberalism, 1941–1948* (The Free Press, 1973), pp. 182–186; Robert Ferrell, *Harry S. Truman: A Life* (University of Missouri Press, 1994), pp. 224–226; Richard Walton, *Henry Wallace, Harry Truman, and the Cold War* (Viking, 1976), pp. 33ff. Text of Truman dismissal of Wallace, September 20, 1946, President's Secretary's Files, in B

File (1948 Election material), HST. Harry Truman, *Memoirs: Year of Decisions* (Doubleday, 1955).

10. Quoted in White and Maze, p. 257.

11. Allan Chandler Young, *A Modern Isaiah: Henry A. Wallace and the 1948 Presidential Campaign* (University of North Dakota Ph.D. dissertation, 1992), pp. 70–76.

12. Henry Wallace, "Third Parties and the American Tradition," *The New Republic* (January 19, 1948), pp. 12–14.

13. Arthur Krock, "Again It Will Be the Smoke-Filled Room," *New York Times Magazine* (February 1, 1948).

CHAPTER TWO: Truman Plans Ahead

1. For Clifford's own reminiscences, see Clark Clifford, *Counsel to the President* (Random House, 1991); also, Clifford Oral History interviews, HST. On the Clifford memo, see Allen Yarnell, *Democrats and Progressives: The 1948 Presidential Election as a Test of Postwar Liberalism* (University of California Press, 1974), pp. 30–46; Gary Donaldson, "The Wardman Park Group and Campaign Strategy in the Truman Administration, 1946–1948," *Missouri Historical Review* (April 1992); Donaldson, *Truman Defeats Dewey* (University Press of Kentucky, 1998), pp. 20–28.

2. Clark Clifford et al., "Memorandum for the President," November 1948. Student Research File, "B File," HST.

3. As reported in the *New York Times* (May 27, 1946).

4. For a superb account of populism in the United States, see Michael Kazin, *The Populist Persuasion* (Basic Books, 1995); also Richard Hofstadter, *The Age of Reform* (Vintage, 1955).

5. Oral History Interview with William Batt Jr., July 26, 1966, HST; Jack Redding, *Inside the Democratic Party* (Bobbs-Merrill, 1958), pp. 119–124; Ross, *The Loneliest Campaign,* p. 79.

6. Richard Rovere, "President Harry," *Harper's Magazine* (July 1948), pp. 27–34; Alonzo Hamby, "The Mind and Character of Harry S. Truman," in Michael Lacey, ed., *The Truman Presidency* (Cambridge University Press, 1989), pp. 19–52.

7. Lawrence Davis, "California Party Unites on Truman," *New York Times* (February 1, 1948), p. 4. The truce between Roosevelt and the other factions reported on by Davis was short-lived.

8. Robert Donovan, *Conflict and Crisis: The Presidency of Harry Truman, 1945–1948* (W. W. Norton, 1977), pp. 332–337; Anthony Leviero, "35 Moves Set Out," *New York Times* (October 30, 1947), p. 1; "Formula for Civil Rights," *Washington Post* (October 30, 1947); "Scars on the American Conscience," *PM* (October 30, 1947), p. 14.

9. Text of Truman's Message on Civil Rights, *New York Times* (February 3, 1948).

10. *Washington Post* (February 4, 1948); Eastland quoted in William Leuchtenberg, "The Conversion of Harry Truman," *American Heritage* (November 1991), p. 62.

11. Arthur Krock, "Democrats Try Hard for a Show of Unity," *New York Times* (February 15, 1948); Clayton Knowles, "Truman Charts Campaign of Progressive Liberalism," *New York Times* (February 20, 1948); "Splinters in the South," *New York Herald-Tribune* (February 27, 1948); Walter Lippman, "The Jefferson-Jackson Speech," syndicated column (February 23, 1948); "Democrats: Bleak Week," *Time* (March 1, 1948), pp. 11–12; Harvard Sitkoff, "Harry Truman and the Election of 1948: The Coming of Age of Civil Rights in American Politics," *The Journal of Southern History* (November 1971), pp. 602–603.

CHAPTER THREE: Dixie Reacts

1. Fielding Wright biography, Fielding Wright biographical file, Mississippi State Archives, Jackson, Mississippi; Richard Etheridge, *Mississippi's Role in the Dixiecrat Movement* (Unpublished Ph.D. dissertation, Mississippi State University, 1971), pp. 30–33; V.O. Key, *Southern Politics in State and Nation: A New Edition* (University of Tennessee Press, 1949), pp. 236–238, 330–333.

2. Text of Folsom speech, January 27, 1948, Official File, Box 947, HST; William Barnard, *Dixiecrats and Democrats: Alabama Politics, 1942–1950* (University of Alabama Press, 1974), pp. 100–105; Robert Garson, *The Democratic Party and the Politics of Sectionalism, 1941–1948* (Louisiana State University Press, 1974), p. 189.

3. W.J. Cash, *The Mind of the South* (Alfred A. Knopf, 1941); C. Vann Woodward, *Origins of the New South, 1877–1913* (Louisiana State University Press, 1951); Edward Ayers, *The Promise of the New South: Life After Reconstruction* (Oxford University Press, 1992).

4. Arthur Krock, "The South Is Incensed," *New York Times* (February 4, 1948); John Popham, "Southern Governors Delay Civil Rights Action 40 Days," *New York Times* (February 8, 1948), p. A1; Robert Bendiner, "Dixie's Fourth Party," *The Nation* (February 14, 1948).

5. Quoted in Ann Mathison McLaurin, *The Role of the Dixiecrats in the 1948 Election* (Unpublished Ph.D. dissertation, University of Oklahoma, 1972), p. 66.

6. Richard Chesteen, "Mississippi Is Gone Home: A Study of the 1948 Mississippi States Rights Bolt," *Journal of Mississippi History* (February 1970), pp. 50–54; Jack Bass and Marilyn Thompson, *Ol' Strom: An Unauthorized Biography of Strom Thurmond* (Longstreet, 1998), pp. 100–104; "4000 in

Mississippi Want Truman Out," *New York Times* (February 13, 1948), p. 1; "Top Secret Plans Adopted by White Democrats Here; Drive Opens Headquarters," *Jackson Daily News* (February 23, 1948).

7. Hodding Carter, "The Civil Rights Issue as Seen in the South," *New York Times Magazine* (March 21, 1948); picture in Ralph McGill, "Will the South Ditch Truman?" *Saturday Evening Post* (May 22, 1948).

8. Senator Richard Russell to Governor J. Strom Thurmond, February 17, 1948; Beauford Jester to Thurmond, April 26, 1948; Digest of replies received from Southern Governors, Senators, and Congressmen, late February 1948. Folder 3230, STP.

9. "Independents Crown Lucas Sweetheart," *Clemson Gamecock* (February 20, 1948), STP clippings.

10. Biographical details about Thurmond come from Nadine Cohodas, *Strom Thurmond and the Politics of Southern Change* (Simon & Schuster, 1993); Bass and Thompson, *Ol' Strom;* "Southern Revolt," *Time* (October 11, 1948), pp. 24–26; John Lofton, "Dixie's Paradox for President," [no date; late August or September 1948], Folder 3239, STP.

11. Letters from February and early March found in Folders 3188 and 3189, STP.

12. "Little Southern Pats," *Time* (March 22, 1948), p. 23; "Revolt in the South," *The New Republic* (March 8, 1948), pp. 14–21; Committee Report Adopted by Southern Governors Conference, Washington, D.C., March 13, 1948, Folder 3273, STP.

13. "Pepper Against Taking Truman Off the Ballot," *Charlotte Observer* (February 28, 1948); Etheridge thesis, op. cit., pp. 50–51.

14. "Committee for Statewide Drive Selected Monday," *Jackson Clarion Ledger* (March 2, 1948); "Southern Democrats Call May Meeting in Civil Rights War," *Memphis Commercial Appeal* (March 21, 1948).

15. Edward Folliard, "South Defied by President in Stand on Civil Rights," *Washington Post* (March 9, 1948).

CHAPTER FOUR: Wallace Gets Going

1. The "chosen man" staging described by Jack Redding, *Inside the Democratic Party,* p. 144.

2. "Voice of the People?" *Time* (January 12, 1948), pp. 11–13; Max Lerner, "Henry Wallace: A Political Portrait," *PM* (February 1, 1948); Lerner, "On Building a People's Party," *PM* (February 8, 1948); Freda Kirchwey, "Wallace: Prophet or Politician?" *The Nation* (January 10, 1948); Karl Schmidt, *Henry A. Wallace: Quixotic Crusade 1948* (Syracuse University Press, 1960), pp. 51–53. On Lerner and *PM,* see David Margolick, "*PM*'s Impossible Dream," *Vanity Fair* (January 1999).

3. Dwight Macdonald, *Henry Wallace: The Man and the Myth* (Vanguard Press, 1948); Arthur Schlesinger review, *New York Times Book Review* (February 22, 1948); Russell Lord, "Macdonald's Wallace and the One I Know," *The New Republic* (March 1, 1948).

4. James Wechsler, *The Age of Suspicion* (Random House, 1953), p. 227. Quoted in Edward and Frederick Schapsmeier, *Prophet in Politics: Henry A. Wallace and the War Years, 1940–1965* (Iowa State University Press, 1970), p. 185; Cabell Phillips, "That Baffling Personality, Mr. Wallace," *New York Times Magazine* (February 8, 1948); Cabell Phillips, *The Truman Presidency: The History of a Triumphant Succession* (Macmillan, 1966), pp. 200–206; Allen Yarnell, *Democrats and Progressives: The 1948 Election as a Test of Postwar Liberalism* (University of California Press, 1974), pp. 46–70, 88–107.

5. "Wallace Proposes Campaign Promise," *New York Times* (February 2, 1948); Henry Wallace, "Stand Up and Be Counted," *The New Republic* (January 5, 1948), pp. 8–10; Steven Gillon, *Politics and Vision: The ADA and American Liberalism, 1947–1985* (Oxford University Press, 1987), pp. 33–45; Eugene Dennis, *The Third Party and the 1948 Elections* (New Century, 1948). Dennis was the secretary-general of the American Communist Party.

6. For various debates on communism and American life, see Richard Gid Powers, *Not Without Honor: The History of American Anticommunism* (Free Press, 1996); Harvey Klehr, et al., *The Secret World of American Communism* (Yale University Press, 1995); Ellen Schrecker, *Many Are the Crimes: McCarthyism in America* (Little Brown, 1998); Sam Tanenhaus, *Whittaker Chambers: A Biography* (Random House, 1997).

7. "Henry Wallace: The First Three Months," Report prepared by the Americans for Democratic Action [no date, probably April 1948], Clark Clifford Papers, Student Research File, Folder 2, HST.

8. A.H. Raskin, "A.F.L. Bars Support of Wallace; Calls Him Front for Communists," *New York Times* (February 3, 1948), p. 1.

9. Baldwin obituary, *Washington Post* (May 14, 1975); William Henry Hale, "What Makes Wallace Run?" *Harper's Magazine* (March 1948). After Wallace resigned from the Progressive Party leadership, Baldwin remained secretary of the remnants of the organization until 1952.

10. Helen Fuller, "Third Party Prospects," *The New Republic* (March 22, 1948), pp. 10–11; James Hagerty, "Wallace Will Test Strength Tuesday," *New York Times* (February 15, 1948); "Wallace Man Wins Bronx Election," *New York Times* (February 18, 1948); "Isaacson's Victory Is Aid to Wallace," *New York Times* (February 23, 1948); "They Voted Against Us," *Time* (March 1, 1948); "Leo Isaacson," FBI Report, February 23, 1948, President's Secretary File, in Student Research File, Folder 10, HST.

11. Felix Belair, "Wallace Accuses Truman of Leading to Russian War," *New York Times* (February 25, 1948); "No Need to Arm, Wallace Asserts," *New York Times* (March 19, 1948); Norman Markowitz, *Rise and Fall of the People's Century* (Free Press, 1973), pp. 272–274.

12. William Shelton, "The ADA's Dilemma: HST or GOP," *The New Republic* (March 1, 1948); Gillon, *Politics and Vision,* p. 39; Truman, St. Patrick's Day Address, March 17, 1948, *Public Papers of the Presidents of the United States: Harry S. Truman: 1948* (U.S. Government Printing Office, 1964), pp. 187–189.

13. "Four Major Radio Networks Offer Time to Wallace for His Answer to Truman," *New York Times* (March 19, 1948); "Wallace Accuses Truman of Terror," *New York Times* (March 27, 1948).

14. Figures for radio costs and Anita McCormick Blaine's campaign contributions come from: Letter of Henry Wallace to Anita McCormick Blaine, July 15, 1948; memorandum from Ralph Shikes to C.B. Baldwin and Lew Frank [undated]; memorandum from C.B. Baldwin to Jack Kamaike, Progressive Party Headquarters, October 26, 1948. Details about the Federal Communications Commission from Memorandum to Ken Dyke, NBC, from Edward Frisbie, Director of Radio, PCA, April 22, 1948, in papers of C.B. Baldwin and Progressive Party Papers [hereafter CBB and PPP, respectively], University of Iowa Library, Iowa City. Neal Gabler, *Winchell: Gossip, Power, and the Culture of Celebrity* (Alfred A. Knopf, 1994), pp. 375–377; Richard Neuberger, "It Costs Too Much to Run for Office," *New York Times Magazine* (April 11, 1948).

CHAPTER FIVE: Dewey and His Rivals

1. Letter of Thomas Dewey to Anne Dewey, January 20, 1948. Thomas Dewey Papers [hereafter TDP], University of Rochester Library, Rochester, New York.

2. "Who's Who in the G.O.P.: Dewey," *Time* (April 5, 1948); Stanley High, "The Case for Dewey," *Life* (March 22, 1948); Herbert Brownell with John Burke, *Advising Ike: The Memoirs of Attorney General Herbert Brownell* (University Press of Kansas, 1993), pp. 79ff; Richard Norton Smith, *Thomas E. Dewey and His Times,* op. cit., passim.

3. James Patterson, *Mr. Republican: A Biography of Robert A. Taft* (Houghton Mifflin, 1972); "Who's Who in the Republican Party: Taft," *Time* (April 19, 1948); Felix Morley, "The Case for Taft," *Life* (February 9, 1948); "My Political Credo . . . Senator Robert Taft," National Taft-for-President Committee, Spring 1948, Series 2, TDP.

4. Harold Stassen, *Where I Stand* (Doubleday, 1947); Roscoe Drummond,

"The Case for Stassen," *Life* (March 1, 1948); "Who's Who in the GOP: Stassen," *Time* (April 26, 1948); Alec Kirby, "A Major Contender: Harold Stassen and the Politics of American Presidential Nominations," *Minnesota History* (Winter 1996–97), pp. 150–165.

5. Arthur Krock, "Friction in GOP Grows as Convention Prelude," *New York Times* (February 1, 1948); "The News of the Week," *New York Times* (February 22); Joseph Goulden, *The Best Years, 1945–1950* (Atheneum, 1976), pp. 374–380.

6. Oral History with Edwin Jaeckle, conducted by William Diez on May 11, 1981. Edwin Jaeckle Papers, Box 6, University of Rochester Library, Rochester, New York.

7. Bruce Barton to Thomas Dewey, February 20, 1948; Dewey to Barton, February 25, 1948; Series 10, Box 3, TDP; Minutes of publicity meeting in Tom Stephens's office, February 3 and February 10, 1948, Series 2, Box 47, TDP; Raymond Carroll, "Harry Truman's 1948 Election: The Inadvertent Broadcast Campaign," *Journal of Broadcasting and Electronic Media* (Spring 1987), pp. 119–132.

8. Albert Frank-Guenther Law to Thomas Stephens, September 2, 1947, Series 2, Box 38, TDP.

9. Minutes of Meeting in Stephens's office, "Wisconsin," February 16, 1948; Robert Bendiner, "Campaign Notes," *The Nation* (April 24, 1948).

10. Lindesay Parrot, "M'Arthur's Censor Filters Comment," *New York Times* (March 11, 1948); James Hagerty, "Republican Aspirants Face Tests in 7 April Primaries," and Cabell Phillips, "New Elements Emerge in the Republican Race," *New York Times* (March 14, 1948); Clayton Knowles, "As of Today, the GOP Seems Certain Winner," *New York Times* (March 21, 1948); Leo Egan, "Dewey Off to Tilt in Wisconsin Lists," *New York Times* (April 1, 1948); Clayton Knowles, "Wisconsin Sweep By M'Arthur Seen," (April 2, 1948); Miles McMillan, "Wisconsin—Anybody's Guess," *The Nation* (April 3, 1948); Dewey to Anne Dewey, April 4, 1948, TDP.

11. Dewey to Anne Dewey, April 13, 1948, TDP; Leo Egan, "Dewey in Albany Cheered by Gains," *New York Times* (April 4, 1948); Ross, *The Loneliest Campaign*, p. 45; "Political Notes," *Time* (April 12, 1948).

CHAPTER SIX: The Cruelest Month

1. Humphrey to Loeb, March 24, 1948. ADA Papers, quoted in Yarnell, *Democrats and Progressives*, p. 96; William Shelton, "ADA Puzzle: How to Square Truman with the Liberals?" *PM* (February 23, 1948).

2. Michael Straight, "Truman Should Quit," *New Republic* (April 5, 1948); Dale Kramer, "Must It Be Truman?" *The Nation* (March 13, 1948).

3. Donovan, *Crisis and Conflict,* pp. 388–391; Redding, *Inside the Democratic Party,* p. 147; "Revolt Against Truman," *The Nation* (April 3, 1948).

4. "Revolt Against Truman," *The Nation* (April 3, 1948).

5. Harold McGrath Oral History, HST, pp. 12–17.

6. Quoted in Stephen Ambrose, *Eisenhower: Volume One* (Simon & Schuster, 1983), pp. 477–478.

7. "Arvey Picks Ike," *New Republic* (April 12, 1948).

8. Lippmann quoted in Ronald Steel, *Walter Lippmann and the American Century* (Little, Brown, 1980), pp. 514–515. Other studies of journalists in this period include Neal Gabler, *Winchell,* op. cit.; Stanley Cloud and Lynn Olson, *The Murrow Boys* (Houghton Mifflin, 1996); Richard Norton Smith, *The Colonel: The Life and Legend of Robert R. McCormick, 1880–1955* (Houghton Mifflin, 1997); Edwin Yoder Jr., *Joe Alsop's Cold War* (University of North Carolina Press, 1995); Sara Alpern, *Freda Kirchwey: Woman of the Nation* (Harvard University Press, 1987); Walter Cronkite, *A Reporter's Life* (Alfred A. Knopf, 1997).

9. "The Black and White Beans," *Time* (May 3, 1948); Redding, *Inside the Democratic Party,* pp. 145–147; Morris L. Ernst and David Loth, *The People Know Best: The Ballots vs. The Polls* (Public Affairs Press, 1949), pp. 114–118.

10. Milton MacKaye, "He'll Sink or Swim with Harry," *Saturday Evening Post* (May 29, 1948).

11. "Remarks at Young Democrats Dinner," May 14, 1948, *Public Papers of the President,* pp. 259–261; Anthony Leviero, "Truman Sees His Election," *New York Times* (May 15, 1948).

12. Truman's mood as of April described in McCullough, *Truman,* pp. 612–613.

13. Cabell Phillips, "Nomination of Truman Now Seen as Certain," *New York Times* (May 9, 1948).

CHAPTER SEVEN: Dewey Versus Stassen

1. Dewey to Ann Dewey, April 27, 1948; "Statement by Governor Thomas Dewey from Hood River, Oregon," May 14, 1948, Box 19, Series 2, TDP; Clayton Knowles, "Dewey Tells Why He Fights Red Ban," *New York Times* (May 4, 1948).

2. Cabell Phillips, "With Stassen on the Hustings," *New York Times Magazine* (April 4, 1948); Dale Kramer, "Progress of a Prodigy," *The New Republic* (April 19, 1948); Michael Straight, "Battle for Ohio," *The New Republic* (May 3, 1948).

3. James Patterson, *Mr. Republican,* pp. 405–407; Arthur Krock, "Stassen's Rising Sun Is Changing the Scene," *New York Times* (April 18, 1948); Walter

Ruch, "Taft Says Stassen Seems a New Dealer," *New York Times* (April 23, 1948); Warren Moscow, "Stassen Discounts Taft as GOP Chief," *New York Times* (April 25, 1948); James Reston, "Stump Indignities Make Taft Uneasy," *New York Times* (May 1, 1948); "Candidate's Humor Eased Ohio Battle," *New York Times* (May 5, 1948); Robert Bendiner, "Campaign Notes," *The Nation* (April 24, 1948).

4. Clayton Knowles, "Dewey in Oregon Lashes at Stassen," *New York Times* (May 2, 1948).

5. Robert Spivack, "Tactics of a Scared Candidate," *The Nation* (May 8, 1948).

6. Stanley Allyn to Dewey, April 23, 1948, Series 2, Box 19, Folder 1; letter from employee of Portland power station, May 3, 1948, Box 19, Folder 4, TDP.

7. "Local Dewey Programs," May 12 through May 17, 1948; "Oregon Students-for-Dewey;" Statement of the Anti-Vivisection Association of Oregon, Series 2, Box 19, TDP; Memo for Mr. Brownell, June 1, 1948, plus attachments such as Ray Gill, "Oregon Farmers for Dewey," May 11, 1948, and pamphlet "Oregon Farmers Swing to Dewey," Dewey to C.C. Cogswell, April 27, 1948, plus "Wisconsin Farmers for Dewey," April 6, 1948, Series 2, Box 38, TDP.

8. "Out West, Podner," *Time* (May 17, 1948); Richard Neuberger, "Stassen vs. Dewey—Second Round," *The Nation* (May 22, 1948); Ross, *The Loneliest Campaign*, pp. 46–48. Ford Bond letter to Lockwood, May 11, 1948, Series 2, Box 19, TDP. Photo caption from Associated Press Archive.

9. "Stassen-Dewey Debate Transcript," *New York Times* (May 18, 1948).

10. Richard Norton Smith, *Thomas Dewey*, pp. 491–494; Jules Abels, *Out of the Jaws of Victory* (Henry Holt, 1959), pp. 55–57; Ross, pp. 50–53; Arthur Krock, "Oregon Confirms Idea GOP Race Is Wide Open," *New York Times* (May 23, 1948); "As the Dust Cleared," *Time* (May 31, 1948); letter from Linda Checkam to Dewey, May 17, 1948, Series 2, Box 17, TDP.

CHAPTER EIGHT: Dixie Gets Serious

1. A.G. Kennedy to Thurmond, April 8, 1948, Gubernatorial Series, Folder 3202; Branscomb to Thurmond, May 18, 1948, Folder 3190; Chambers to Thurmond, April 12, 1948, Folder 3192; Cottingham to Thurmond, May 25, 1948, Folder 3192; letter from Beaumont Hotel, March 29, 1948, Folder 3201; "Jim Crow Rides at Midnight," April 28, 1948, Folder 3187, STP.

2. Barnard, *Dixiecrats and Democrats*, pp. 109–111; Willard Shelton, "Bi-Partisan Dump Truman Plan Offered as Bait to Dixie Rebels," *PM* (April 25, 1948).

3. "States' Rights Jeffersonian Democrats Hold Meeting," *Jackson Clarion Ledger* (March 25, 1948); "Button Sale Planned to Help Beat Truman," *Memphis Commercial Appeal* (March 28, 1948); pamphlets found in States' Rights Subject File, 1948, Mississippi State Archives, Jackson, Mississippi.

4. Speech of Fielding Wright at Walthall County Music Festival (Spring 1948), RG 27, Fielding Wright Speeches, Mississippi State Archives.

5. Radio Address delivered by Donald Richberg and Raymond Moley, Mutual Broadcasting System, March 30, 1948, Folder 3218, STP.

6. "Conversation Between Governor J. Strom Thurmond—a Gentleman from Meet the Press and Miss Martha Rountree on April 23, 1948 (Telephone)," Box 3220, STP.

7. Etheridge, *Mississippi's Role in the Dixiecrat Movement,* pp. 96–98; "Place Trust in White Friends, Mississippi Negroes Are Told," *Memphis Commercial Appeal* (May 10, 1948).

8. Etheridge, p. 107; Willard Shelton, "Dixie Dem Moderates May Join Northern Liberals to Back Ike," *PM* (May 9, 1948); Kenneth Toler, "South's Rebels Pour into Jackson to Map Battle with Truman," *Memphis Commercial Appeal* (May 9, 1948); "States' Rights Keynoter Sounds Southern Meeting Call for Action," *Jackson Daily News* (May 10, 1948); James Ewing, "States' Righters to Meet in Birmingham if National Platform Is Anti-Southern," *Jackson Daily News* (May 11, 1948); John Lofton, "Dixie's Paradox for President" [publication unknown, probably August 1948], Folder 3239, STP.

9. Photo and caption, *Charleston Evening Post* (May 20, 1948).

10. "Cooling of South's Anti-Truman Revolt," *U.S. News & World Report* (May 21, 1948); John Henry, "Revolt Effort Doomed, Jackson Leaders Admit," *Atlanta Constitution* (June 10, 1948); Kenneth Toler, "Mississippi Walkout Is Slated if Truman Receives Nomination," *Memphis Commercial Appeal* (June 23, 1948).

CHAPTER NINE: Wallace Hits His Stride

1. Cabell Phillips, "Why They Join the Wallace Crusade," *New York Times Magazine* (May 23, 1948); George Eckel, "Wallace Charges War Profit Scare," *New York Times* (April 11, 1948); Address by Henry Wallace, Chicago Stadium, April 10, 1948, Speech File, PPP; Karl Schmidt, *Henry Wallace: Quixotic Crusade 1948* (Syracuse University Press, 1960), pp. 166–169. The amount raised by Gailmor at Chicago was variously reported at anywhere from $18,000 to a high of $39,000, according to *Time* (April 19, 1948).

2. Senator Glen Taylor, "I Take My Stand with Henry Wallace," (Text of February 23 speech), published by National Wallace for President Committee,

Box 55, PPP; "The Story of Glen Taylor," published by the Progressive Party, PPP; William Pratt, "Glen Taylor: Public Image and Reality," *Pacific Northwest Quarterly* (January 1969), pp. 10–16; "Hi-Yo Taylor," *Time* (March 1, 1948), pp. 13–14.

3. *Shreveport Journal* (May 14, 1948); "Taylor, Under Bail in Alabama in Racial Case, Will Make Test," *New York Times* (May 3, 1948); "With Publicity for All," *Time* (May 17, 1948); *Newsweek* (May 10, 1948); "Taylor, Arrested in Birmingham, to Fight City's Jim Crow Laws," *PM* (May 3, 1948).

4. "Wallace Plants Manhattan Plot" [with photo], *Baltimore Sun* (April 21, 1948); Elmo Roper, "Rumor, Not Roper, Took Wallace Poll," *Chicago Sun-Times* (April 8, 1948).

5. Most of this account comes from the superb research done by others, particularly Graham White and John Maze, *Henry Wallace*, op. cit., pp. 60–125; Jules Abels, *Out of the Jaws of Victory*, pp. 112–114; also Henry Wallace Oral History, Columbia Oral History Collection; *Newsweek* (March 22, 1948).

6. For the pamphlet, see footnote 6, chapter 5. Eleanor Roosevelt's columns were reprinted by the ADA and mailed out along with other material denouncing Wallace. Copies can be found in the HST. Also see Allen Yarnell, "Liberals in Action: The ADA, Henry Wallace, and the 1948 Election," *Research Studies* (December 1972), pp. 260–267; Abels, pp. 22–23; Transcript of Town Meeting, George Denny, Moderator, April 27, 1948, Box 35, PPP.

7. Henry Wallace, "An Open Letter to Premier Stalin," May 11, 1948; text of Stalin's response, May 18, 1948, PPP, also reprinted in *New York Times*, May 12 and May 18, 1948, address by Henry Wallace, Madison Square Garden, May 11, 1948, National Wallace for President Committee, Speech File, PPP; "As We See It," *Detroit Free Press* (May 13, 1948).

8. Wallace itinerary and description and photographs of speeches and events drawn from the following sources: Jim Dix, "Moline Rally Is Orderly," *Moline Daily Dispatch* (April 28, 1948); address by Wallace to Founding Conference New York State Women for Wallace, Commodore Hotel, May 8, 1948; address by Wallace, Portland Oregon, May 24, Speech File, PPP; Frank Morris, "Wallace Rallies Chrysler Strikers," *Detroit Times* (May 13, 1948); "Wallace Hits Idea Russia Perils U.S.," *Los Angeles Times* (May 17, 1948); Mary Ellen Leary, "Wallace in Bay Area Speech Hails Stalin's Reply," *San Francisco News* (May 18, 1948); "Dewey and Wallace—Their Trails Crossed Here," *Seattle Post-Intelligencer* (May 22, 1948); Ashley Holden, "Wallace Rally Had Strange Air," *Spokane Review* (May 24, 1948); John Weiss, "Wallace Sees Truman About-Face on Bias," *PM* (May 25, 1948); Wallace Interview by Edward R. Murrow, June 3, CBS, Speech File, PPP. "Henry Wallace Being Fooled, Mrs. Roosevelt Says," *Baltimore Sun* (June 13, 1948); *The*

Man on the Merry-Go-Round, June 21, 1948, pamphlet prepared by William Batt, Subject File, Box 20, Clifford Papers, HST.

9. From Wallace's acceptance speech, Philadelphia, July 24, 1948. Quoted in the introduction, see page 15.

CHAPTER TEN: Truman Goes West

1. John Bourke, "The Institutional Presidency," in Michael Nelson, ed., *The Presidency and the Political System* (Congressional Quarterly Press, 1990), pp. 383–405; Samuel Kernell, "The Evolution of the White House Staff," in James Pfiffner, *The Managerial Presidency* (Brooks/Cole Publishing, 1991), pp. 43–60.

2. *Memoirs, Vol. II,* p. 178; Ross, *The Loneliest Campaign,* pp. 76–80.

3. Raymond Carroll, "Harry S. Truman's 1948 Election: The Inadvertent Broadcast Campaign," *Journal of Broadcasting & Electronic Media* (Spring 1987), pp. 119–132.

4. Eben Ayers Oral History, HST, pp. 102–106; Arthur Krock, "Truman Pins Big Hopes on Pulse-Taking Trip," *New York Times* (May 30, 1948); "Truman Travels," *New York Times* (May 30, 1948); Ross, *The Loneliest Campaign,* pp. 80–82; McCullough, *Truman,* pp. 623–626.

5. Richard Strout (Reporter, *Christian Science Monitor*) Oral History, pp. 24–26, HST; "President Quips Nonpolitical Trip," *New York Times* (June 5, 1948).

6. Robert Nixon Oral History, pp. 546–548, HST; Edward Folliard (correspondent, *Washington Post*) Oral History, pp. 7–10, HST; Ayers Oral History, p. 109, HST; Ross, pp. 76–80; McCullough, pp. 623–626.

7. Anthony Leviero, "Truman Calls This Congress Worst; Taft Will Answer," *New York Times* (June 10, 1948); Norman Grieser, "Presidential Sales Trip," *The New Republic* (June 21, 1948), pp. 19–22.

8. Redding, *Inside the Democratic Party,* pp. 177–179.

9. Truman Address before the Greater Los Angeles Press Club, June 14, 1948, in *Public Papers of the Presidents, Harry S. Truman 1948,* pp. 348–353; Donovan, *Conflict and Crisis,* pp. 400–402; McCullough, pp. 628–629; Howard McGrath (Director, Democratic State Central Committee of California) Oral History, pp. 12–14, HST.

10. John McEnery (Member, California State Democratic Central Committee) Oral History, pp. 132–137, HST; Robert Nixon Oral History, pp. 565–567, HST; Allen Matusow, *Farm Policies and Politics in the Truman Administration* (Harvard University Press, 1967).

11. "Home to Cheers," *Kansas City Star* (June 17, 1948); "Turn Congress Out, Truman Demands," *Washington Post* (June 17, 1948).

12. Thomas Reynolds, "The West Sees a New Truman," *PM* (June 13, 1948); Bert Andrews, "Truman Has Made 6 Boners on Trip," *New York Herald Tribune* (June 13, 1948); Joseph Driscoll, "The Real Truman Is Revealed as Folksy, Hearty, and Humorous," *St. Louis Post-Dispatch* (June 14, 1948); Max Lerner, "How True Is Truman Now?" *PM* (June 15, 1948); Thomas Reynolds, "Truman Still Slugging as He Ends Coast Trip," *PM* (June 20, 1948).
13. "Suggestions and Comments on Western Trip," June 23, 1948, SRC, Folder 6, HST.

CHAPTER ELEVEN: The Republicans Decide

1. "The Boys in the Smoke-Filled Room," *The New Republic* (June 21, 1948); James Hagerty, "Dewey Aides Press Philadelphia Tack," *New York Times* (June 16, 1948); Arthur Krock, "Question of Deadlock Overhangs Convention," *New York Times* (June 20, 1948); "The Crucial Third Ballot," *Time* (June 14, 1948); "The Big Show," *Time* (June 28, 1948).
2. "Agenda for Publicity Meeting, May 17, 1948," Series 2, Box 47, TDP.
3. Brownell, *Advising Ike*, pp. 74–78.
4. There is a considerable literature on the changing nature of the convention in light of television. See Byron Shafer, *Bifurcated Politics: Evolution and Reform in the National Party Convention* (Harvard University Press, 1988); Clifford Ness and Byron Reeves, "Technology and Roles: A Tale of Two TVs," *Journal of Communication* (Spring 1996), pp. 120–125; Martin Linsky, ed., *Television and the Presidential Elections: Self-Interest and the Public Interest* (DC Heath, 1983); Erik Barnouw, *Tube of Plenty: The Evolution of American Television* (Oxford University Press, 1982); Gary Paul Gates, *Air Time: The Inside Story of CBS News* (Harper & Row, 1978); Robert MacNeil, *The Influence of Television on American Politics* (Harper & Row, 1968); Shanto Iyengar, *Is Anyone Responsible? How Television Frames Political Issues* (University of Chicago Press, 1991); Martin Plissner, *The Control Room: How Television Calls the Shots in Presidential Elections* (The Free Press, 1999).
5. J. Leonard Reinsch, *Getting Elected: From Radio and Roosevelt to Television and Reagan* (Hippocrene, 1988), p. 48.
6. Meyer Berger, "GOP Women Create Coke-Filled Room," *New York Times* (June 20, 1948); Doris Greenberg, "Women Enlarge Convention Role," *New York Times* (June 20, 1948); Meyer Berger, "Men Were Men in the Convention of 1900, Says One Who Was There," *New York Times* (June 24, 1948).
7. Cabell Phillips, "The Stage Is Set for the GOP Jamboree," *New York Times Magazine* (June 20, 1948); Meyer Berger, "Philadelphia Din Rises Steadily," *New York Times* (June 20, 1948); "Sunshine Campaign," *Time* (June 21, 1948).

8. James Hagerty, "New Yorker Leads," *New York Times* (June 21, 1948); Joseph Loftus, "Warren Puts Hope in Wide Open Race," *New York Times* (June 21, 1948); Meyer Berger, "Republican Exuberance Reaches New High Since Days of '32," *New York Times* (June 22, 1948); "How He Did It," *Time* (July 5, 1948); Richard Norton Smith, *Thomas Dewey*, pp. 496–500; Patterson, *Mr. Republican*, pp. 409–418.

9. "Text of Platform Proposed for Adoption by the Republican Party," *New York Times* (June 23, 1948).

10. "Dewey Notes for Autobiography," Series 13, Box 1, TDP. Brownell, pp. 78–79; "How He Did It," *Time* (July 5, 1948); William White, "Opposition Falls," *New York Times* (June 25, 1948).

11. "Text of Dewey's Speech to GOP," *New York Times* (June 25, 1948).

12. Ed Cray, *Chief Justice: A Biography of Earl Warren* (Simon & Schuster, 1997), pp. 186–189; John Gerrity, "The GOP's Choice," *Pathfinder* (July 14, 1948); [Mississippi] *Meridian Star* (June 26, 1948).

13. Meyer Berger, "Convention Hall Is Rechristened," *New York Times* (June 25, 1948); Robert Bendiner, "The Nominee Nobody Loves," *The Nation* (July 3, 1948); *Time* (July 5, 1948); Helen Fuller, "Dewey's Brisk Young Men Move In," *The New Republic* (July 5, 1948); Richard Norton Smith, *Dewey*, p. 502.

CHAPTER TWELVE: The Democrats Assemble

1. Reinsch, *Getting Elected*, pp. 50–51; Reuven Frank, *Out of Thin Air*, pp. 9–27; "Emma and the Birds," *Time* (July 26, 1948); Redding, p. 196; Neale Roach Oral History, p. 41, HST.

2. Clayton Knowles, "Truman Insists He Will Run," *New York Times* (July 2, 1948); "Eisenhower Boom Presses Truman," *New York Times* (July 5, 1948); Warren Moscow, "Convention to Get Name," *New York Times* (July 7, 1948); "Wake & Awakening," *Time* (July 12, 1948); "Back to Truman, by Default," *Newsweek* (July 19, 1948); Frank Gervasi, "Truman's Troubles," *Collier's* (July 3, 1948).

3. William White, "Southern Leaders Abandon Drive to Make Truman Quit," *New York Times* (July 10, 1948); James Weschler, "Douglas: The Best Hope," *The Nation* (July 10, 1948); "A Rebellion, an Army, but No Chief," *New Republic* (July 19, 1948); Arthur Krock, *Memoirs: Sixty Years on the Firing Line* (Funk & Wagnalls, 1968), pp. 242–244; J.R. Wiggins, "Last Opposition to Truman Collapses; 1944 Civil Rights Plank Backed in Principle," *Washington Post* (July 11, 1948); Ross, *The Loneliest Campaign*, pp. 120–122.

4. Carroll, "The 1948 Truman Campaign," pp. 175–177; Arthur Krock, "The Democrats Could Learn from Television," *The New York Times* (July 4, 1948).

5. Reinsch, pp. 48–49; picture of India Edwards, "Woman Democrat Says Women Will Decide the Election," *St. Louis Post-Dispatch* (July 8, 1948).

6. "Convention Gives Barkley a Big Hand," *New York Times* (July 13, 1948); "Lucky Star," *Time* (July 19, 1948).

7. Meyer Berger, "Democrats Match Quaker Sabbath," *New York Times* (July 12, 1948); Meyer Berger, "Democrats' Gifts Keyed to Utility," *New York Times* (July 13, 1948); Fern Marja, "Women and the GOP Get Distaff Scoldings," *New York Post* (July 15, 1948).

8. Harvard Sitkoff, "Harry Truman and the Election of 1948: The Coming of Age of Civil Rights in American Politics," *The Journal of Southern History* (November 1971), pp. 612–613; Gillon, *Politics and Vision*, pp. 48–49; Helen Fuller, "The Funeral is Called Off," *New Republic* (July 26, 1948); "Civil Rights Row Clarified," *Philadelphia Inquirer* (July 16, 1948); The 1948 Platform of the Democratic Party, Student Research Collection [hereafter SRC], HST; "Democrats," in *National Party Conventions, 1831–1948* (Congressional Quarterly Press, 1991); Speech by Hubert Humphrey in Behalf of the Minority Report on the Civil Rights Plank, July 14, 1948, Minnesota State Historical Society, St. Paul.

9. "The Line Squall," *Time* (July 26, 1948); "Walkout Squad Treads Calmly Through Howls of Convention," *Memphis Commercial Appeal* (July 15, 1948).

10. "Truman, in a Gay Mood, Receives Acclaim of Big Convention Crowd," *New York Times* (July 15, 1948); Robert Bendiner, "Rout of the Bourbons," *The Nation* (July 24, 1948).

11. Charles Murphy, "Some Aspects of the Preparation of President Truman's Speeches for the 1948 Campaign," December 6, 1948, Papers of Charles Murphy, Folder 4, SRC, HST; memorandum, "Should the President Call Congress Back," June 29, 1948, Papers of Samuel Rosenman, Folder 13, SRC, HST; Alton Lee, "The Turnip Session of the Do-Nothing Congress: Presidential Campaign Strategy," *Southwestern Social Science Quarterly* (December 1963), pp. 256–265.

12. Oliver Crawford, "Extent of Federal Control Is Nation's Prime Issue," *Philadelphia Inquirer* (July 9, 1948); Charles A. Fecher, *The Diary of H. L. Mencken* (Alfred A. Knopf, 1989), p. 453.

13. John Danner, "John Cameron Swayze Remembers: TV a Stepchild at '48 Conventions," *Kansas City Times* (August 28, 1968).

14. Bernard Smith, "Television: There Ought to Be a Law," *Harper's Magazine* (September 1948), pp. 34–41.

CHAPTER THIRTEEN: Dixie Rises

1. John Hancock, "Truman Has It in Bag with Nobody Holding, Dix-iecrats Bamabound," *Jackson Daily News* (July 13, 1948); Hancock, "Vacant Galleries Prove Democratic Convention Dead," *Jackson Daily News* (July 15, 1948); Purser Hewitt, "Dixie to Fight for Electors," *Jackson Clarion Ledger* (July 15, 1948); Henry Cauthen, "Convention Sidelights," *Columbia Record* (July 12, 1948); A.G. Weems, "Mississippi Wakes Up Angry after Long Night at Radios," *Memphis Commercial Appeal* (July 16, 1948).

2. "It's on to Birmingham," *Memphis Commercial Appeal* (July 15, 1948); J.R. Wiggins, "Dixie-Crats Jammed the Lock Going Out," *Washington Post* (July 18, 1948).

3. Gary Clifford Ness, *The States' Rights Democratic Movement of 1948* (unpublished Ph.D. thesis, Duke University History Department, 1972), pp. 157–159; Etheridge, *Mississippi's Role in the Dixiecrat Movement*, pp. 166–174; Barnard, *Dixiecrats and Democrats*, pp. 113–116; Garson, *The Democratic Party*, pp. 281–285; Ben Price, "An Issue Since 1787," *Charlotte News* (July 18, 1948); John Popham, "Southerners Name Thurmond to Lead Anti-Truman Fight," *New York Times* (July 18, 1948); *Birmingham News* (July 19, 1948).

4. Leroy Simms, "Gov. Thurmond Heads the States' Rights Plank," *Savannah Morning News* (July 18, 1948); John Popham, "Southerners Map Border Campaign," *New York Times* (July 19, 1948).

5. Summary of press reaction, Folder 3273, STP. David McConnell, "Wright Sees No Chance for Bolters' Return," *New York Herald-Tribune* (July 22, 1948); "It's Not New Party, Wright Points Out," *Memphis Commercial Appeal* (July 22, 1948); "Revolters' Prospects," *Charlotte Observer* (July 22, 1948); John Popham, "Thurmond, Candidate of Rebels, Decries White Supremacy Idea," *New York Times* (July 20, 1948).

6. "Where Will the South Go?" *Charlotte News* (July 24, 1948); "No Time for Fourth Party," *Memphis Commercial Appeal* (July 19, 1948) "A Fourth Party Is Illogical," *Savannah Morning News* (July 19, 1948).

7. Author interview with Senator Thurmond, January 1998.

8. Information about tidelands oil comes from author interview with William Minor, former reporter for various Mississippi newspapers, Jackson, Mississippi, February 7, 1998; Ann Mathison McLaurin, *The Role of the Dixiecrats in the 1948 Election* (unpublished Ph.D. dissertation, University of Oklahoma, 1972), pp. 80–89; Ernest Bartley, *The Tidelands Oil Controversy: A Legal and Historical Analysis* (University of Texas Press, 1953); Richard Chesteen, "Mississippi Is Gone Home," *Journal of Mississippi History*, p. 53,

statement by R.B. Creager, Republican National Committeeman from Texas, October 1947, enclosed with a note from Herbert Brownell to Dewey, November 4, 1947, Series 10, Box 6, TDP; statement by Strom Thurmond, July 26, 1948, Folder 3273, STP; "Wright Denies Oil Link," *Memphis Commercial Appeal* (July 21, 1948); Edward Harris, "Tidelands Oil," *St. Louis Post-Dispatch* (August 18, 1948); "Oil and the Dixiecrats," *St. Louis Post-Dispatch* (August 19, 1948); Stewart Alsop, "The Oligarchs and the Dixiecrats," *Washington Post* (October 20, 1948).

9. Sims, "Gov. Thurmond Heads States' Rights Plank," op. cit.; "Thurmond to Be Speaker at Mullins Leaf Opening," *Charlotte Observer* (July 22, 1948); address of J. Strom Thurmond, Watermelon Festival, Cherryville, North Carolina, July 31, Folder 3273, STP.

CHAPTER FOURTEEN: The Progressives Congregate

1. Schuman's perspective comes from his notes on the convention. Box 4, Folder 21, PPP. Other details come from Mary Van Rensselaer Thayer, "Wallace Her Man Mrs. Gimbel Says at Convention," *Baltimore Sun* (July 25, 1948); H.L. Mencken, "Sudden Flapping of Wings Would Prove No Surprise," *Baltimore Sun* (July 24, 1948); Alistair Cooke, "New Party Youthful, Folksy," *Baltimore Sun* (July 24, 1948); Howard Smith, "The Wallace Party," *The Nation* (August 7); "The Pink Facade," *Time* (August 2, 1948); "Supporters of Wallace Will Strive to Sing Him into the Presidency," *New York Times* (July 23, 1948); James Hagerty, "Revival Fervor Hails Nominees," *New York Times* (July 25, 1948); Joseph and Stewart Alsop, "Wallace Must Wonder Sometimes," *Washington Post* (July 25, 1948); William Miles, *Songs, Odes, Glees, and Ballads* (Greenwood, 1990); Markowitz, *The Rise and Fall of the People's Century,* pp. 284–289; White and Maze, *Henry A. Wallace,* pp. 274–277; schedule of proceedings, Public Relations Department Press Release, July 22, 1948, PPP.

2. Dewey Fleming, "Wallace Bars Guru Question," *Baltimore Sun* (July 24, 1948); "Question! Question!" *Time* (August 2, 1948).

3. Marquis Childs, "The State of the Nation," syndicated column (July 23, 1948); H.L. Mencken, "Finds a Few Raisins in Paranoic Confection," *Baltimore Sun* (July 26, 1948); cartoons from the *Indianapolis Star* (July 23, 1948), *Chicago Herald-American* (July 24, 1948), and *New York Sun* (July 23, 1948).

4. Curtis Macdougall, *Gideon's Army* (Marzani and Munsell, 1965).

5. J.A. Ruccio to Josiah Gitt, June 17, 1948, Box 14, Folder 18, PPP.

6. Transcript, opening session, July 23, Box 25, CBB.

CHAPTER FIFTEEN: The Calm Before the Storm

1. George Gallup, "High Cost of Living Looms as Hottest Campaign Issue," *Washington Post* (July 16, 1948); George Gallup, "Only 14 Percent of Voters in South to Back Dixiecrats," *Philadelphia Evening Bulletin* (August 20, 1948); Elmo Roper, "Dewey Still Leading Truman in Popularity, Survey Shows," *Atlanta Journal* (August 12, 1948); Elmo Roper, "Dewey Weakest in Midwest, Truman in Dixie," *Atlanta Journal* (August 26, 1948); David Kaiser, *Epic Season: The 1948 American League Pennant Race* (University of Massachusetts, 1998).

2. The quote is from Martin Agronsky, July 12; Morris Ernst and David Loth, *The People Know Best: The Ballots vs. The Polls* (Public Affairs Press, 1949), p. 103; excerpts from Editorial Comment on the President's Nomination, *New York Times* (July 16, 1948).

3. Marquis Childs, "Republican Strategy in Congress," *Washington Post* (July 28, 1948); William White, "Southerners Win in Poll Tax Fight," *New York Times* (August 5, 1948); Carl Levin, "Stumping on Capitol Hill," *The Nation* (August 14, 1948); "The Do-Nothing Congress," *The New Republic* (August 14, 1948); "Barkley Doubts Spies as a Vote Issue," *New York Times* (August 18, 1948); A.J. Liebling, "The Wayward Press," *The New Yorker* (August 28, 1948); Tanenhaus, *Whittaker Chambers,* pp. 206–229; Donovan, *Conflict & Crisis,* pp. 413–415.

4. Letters from Thomas Dewey to Anne Dewey, July 12 and August 9, TDP.

5. Leo Egan, "Dewey Declares Democrats Turn to Quack Remedies," *New York Times* (August 12, 1948); for insights on Dewey's governing philosophy, I thank Richard Neustadt (author interview, June 6, 1999).

6. Leo Egan, "How a Candidate Plans a Campaign," *New York Times* (August 8, 1948); Gladwin Hill, "Warren Outlines Campaign Policy," *New York Times* (August 9, 1948); Holmes Alexander, "Dewey's Courtship of the Dixiecrats," *St. Louis Star Times* (August 9, 1948); Leo Egan, "Dewey Arranging Trans-U.S. Drive," *New York Times* (August 13, 1948); Leo Egan, "Big Campaign Role Set Up for Warren at Dewey Meeting," *New York Times* (August 17, 1948).

7. Memorandum to Clifford from Batt, "How the President Can Reach the People," July 22, 1948, Clifford Papers, Political File, Box 22, HST; pamphlet, "Remember in November the Congress That Forgot You," Elsey Papers, Box 32, HST.

8. Biffle's mission is described in Abels, *Out of the Jaws of Victory,* pp. 163–164.

9. Memorandum for the President, "The 1948 Campaign," August 17, 1948, Clifford Papers, SRC, HST.

10. Clayton Knowles, "Truman Clubs Plan 48-State Campaign," *New York Times* (August 12, 1948).

11. "Dixiecrats to Enter Presidential Ticket in All 48 States," *Memphis Commercial Appeal* (July 25, 1948); "Thurmond Launches Dixiecrat Campaign," *Memphis Commercial Appeal* (August 1, 1948); Charles Hill, "Pledge Vote Gov. Thurmond," *Jackson Clarion Ledger* (August 4, 1948); Hunt Clement, "Own Election Machinery Enmeshes Democrats," *Washington Post* (August 8, 1948); George Gallup, "Thurmond Strength in South Gauged at 14 Percent in Poll," *Memphis Commercial Appeal* (August 20, 1948); "States' Righters Aim at 35 State Ballots," *Memphis Commercial Appeal* (August 20, 1948).

12. "Dixiecrat Box Lunches to Aid Campaign," *Jackson Clarion Ledger* (August 14, 1948); "Support These Courageous Men," [no date], STP.

13. "Special Train to Be Run to Houston," *Jackson Clarion Ledger* (August 5, 1948); Brian Spinks, "Dixiecrats Open Campaign with Barrage from Big Guns," *Houston Post* (August 11, 1948); Address of J. Strom Thurmond, Houston, August 11, STP.

14. "Wallaceites to Picket Rebels," *Houston Post* (August 12, 1948).

15. Henry Wallace, "Farewell and Hail!" *The New Republic* (July 19, 1948); text of radio address, NBC, July 29, PPP; "Henry Wallace: A Liberal or a Lollipop," *Time* (August 9, 1948).

CHAPTER SIXTEEN: The Victory Special

1. Thomas Dewey to Anne Dewey, September 14, 1948. TDP. "Ordinary Horse Race," *Time* (September 13, 1948); "Mr. Dewey's Chances: Why Republicans Are Confident," *U.S. News & World Report* (September 17, 1948).

2. Barton and constituent quotations from Stuart Little, *Vital Citizens: Individual Opinion and Postwar Politics, 1948* (Unpublished Ph.D. dissertation, Department of History, Indiana University, 1995), pp. 64–66, 107; Richard Norton Smith, *Thomas E. Dewey,* p. 429.

3. Adam Hatch, "The Men Around Dewey," *Harper's Magazine* (October 1948), pp. 38–47; Stanley High, "The Case for Dewey," *Life* (March 22, 1948).

4. Milburn Akers, "Dewey Confident, Adopts Champ Role," *Chicago Sun* (September 12, 1948); "Dewey Opens Drive on Sept. 20 in Iowa," *New York Times* (September 9, 1948); Leo Egan, "All-Out Campaign Charted by Dewey," *New York Times* (September 16, 1948); Robert Albright, "Dewey Goes West to Open Drive Today," *Washington Post* (September 20, 1948).

5. Charles Greene Oral History, pp. 22–27, HST.

6. "The Challenge of Tomorrow," text of Des Moines Address, published by Republican National Committee, in Elsey Papers, Box 33, HST.

7. Gerald Johnson, "Dewey May Be No Harding, But. . . ." *New York Star* (September 29, 1948); "Pitched High," *Time* (September 27, 1948).

8. Earl Warren Oral History, HST, pp. 14–23; text of Warren Speech in Manhattan, *New York Times* (October 1, 1948); Jaeckle Papers, Box 6, TDP.

9. Charles Van Devander, "Dewey Campaign Trip Planned Carefully—Nothing Left to Chance," *New York Post* (September 20, 1948); Milburn Akers, "The Men Around Dewey," *Chicago Sun* (September 21, 1948); Thomas Stokes, "Co-Starring the Deweys," *Washington News* (September 27, 1948); Dewey Fleming, "Dewey's New Warmth Born in Primary Fight," *Baltimore Sun* (September 30, 1948); Alsop quoted in *Trainman News* (October 2, 1948); J.A. O'Leary, "The People Seem to Like Gov. Dewey's Human Touch," *New York Star* (October 3, 1948); "Dogi Cligin & the West," *Time* (October 4, 1948).

10. Kathleen Hall Jamieson, *Packaging the Presidency: A History and Criticism of Presidential Campaign Advertising* (Oxford University Press, 1996), pp. 32–33.

11. Samuel Brightman Oral History, pp. 27–32, HST; Robert Albright, "Fling at Statesmanship Didn't Sidetrack Dewey," *Washington Post* (October 3, 1948); Abels, *Out of the Jaws of Victory*, p. 196.

12. See material from various local Republicans sent to the Dewey campaign, Dewey Papers, Series 2, Box 19, TDP; also "Dewey-Warren Clubs" brochure in Elsey Papers, Box 32, HST.

13. James A. Hagerty, "Dewey Held to Net 14 States, Truman 6 by Western Tours," *New York Times* (October 4, 1948); Raymond Brandt, "Dewey's Trip Has Helped Him and Hurt Democratic Chances of Getting Control of the Senate," *St. Louis Post-Dispatch* (September 27, 1948).

14. Robert Albright, "Dewey Gives Lie to Critics of Farm Policy," *Washington Post* (September 18, 1948); C.P. Ives, "Mr. Dewey's Bid for the Farmer's Vote," *Baltimore Sun* (September 20, 1948); "Farm Prices: Campaign Dilemma," *U.S. News & World Report* (September 10, 1948); Harlan Phillips interview with Brownell, Series 13, Box 1, TDP.

CHAPTER SEVENTEEN: Whistle-Stops

1. Address at Dexter, Iowa, September 18, *Public Papers of the President,* pp. 503–508; "Summary of Remarks by George Elsey in Politics 203, Princeton University, January 11, 1949," Box 32, Elsey Papers, HST; Robert Nixon Oral History, pp. 622–626, HST; Carleton Kent Oral History, pp. 55–57, HST; William Bray, "Recollections of the 1948 Campaign" (written for the

Truman Library, August 1964), SRC, HST; Willard Shelton, "Truman Calls GOP Party of Privilege," *New York Star* (September 21, 1948); Edward Segal, "The Whistle-Stop Campaigns," *Washington Journalism Review* (July/August 1988), pp. 38–41.

2. Carroll, "Harry Truman's 1948 Election," p. 126; Redding, *Inside the Democratic Party,* pp. 229–238; Thomas Reynolds, "Lack of Funds Keeps Truman Off Radio," *Chicago Sun* (September 22, 1948).

3. See the oral histories in the Truman Library of reporters such as Carleton Kent, Robert Nixon, Edward Folliard, Raymond Brandt, Charles Greene, and Jonathan Daniels, among others.

4. The details of the Johnson visit taken from Jonathan Daniels Oral History, pp. 162–163, HST.

5. List of visitors at Toledo, Ohio. President's Secretary's Files, SRC, Folder 10, HST; "Utah" President's Secretary's Files, Folder 12; speech excerpts from *Public Papers of the President;* W.H. Lawrence, "Truman Thinks His Trip Will Make a Difference," *New York Times* (September 19, 1948); Milburn Akers, "Whistle-Stop Race Gets Going," *Chicago Sun* (September 19, 1948); Walter Lippmann, "Mr. Truman on Tour," *Washington Post* (September 27, 1948); Joseph Driscoll, "Briefs from His Whistle-Stop Talks Reveal the Real Truman," *St. Louis Post-Dispatch* (September 27, 1948); "They'll Tear You Apart," *Time* (October 4, 1948).

6. George Elsey Oral History, pp. 60–71, HST; William Batt Oral History, pp. 9–10, HST; Kenneth Birkhead Oral History, pp. 50–54, HST.

7. Kent Oral History, p. 63, HST.

8. Attitudes about Thurmond and Wright, from Kenneth Birkhead Oral History, pp. 44ff, HST; John Barriere Oral History, pp. 15–20, HST; Clifford interview with David McCullough, quoted in McCullough, *Truman,* p. 695.

CHAPTER EIGHTEEN: The Dark Night of Dixie

1. V.O. Key, *Southern Politics in State and Nation,* pp. 330–344; James A. Hagerty, "Southern Revolt Gaining Strength, Aids Republicans," *New York Times* (September 13, 1948); Hodding Carter, "A Southern Liberal Looks at Civil Rights," *New York Times Magazine* (August 8, 1948); Emile Adler, *The Dixiecrat Movement: Its Role in Third Party Politics* (Public Affairs Press, 1955); "Democratic Party Rules Out Bolters," *New York Times* (September 3, 1948).

2. Address of Governor Fielding Wright, September 17, Fielding Wright Speeches, RG 27, Mississippi State Archives.

3. Address of J. Strom Thurmond, Augusta, September 23. Also see Thurmond speech at Fairfield, Alabama, September 3, Box 3274, STP.

4. Key, p. 341; "Anti-Truman Drive Mounting in South Nets 45 Electors," *New York Times* (September 12, 1948); "Democrats to Fight Louisiana Action," *Washington Post* (September 12, 1948); W.H. Lawrence, "Solid South Is Broken by Dixiecrat Inroads," *New York Times* (September 12, 1948); Gould Lincoln, "Southern Revolt Grows to Major Proportions," *Washington Star* (September 14, 1948); "The Cracking South," *Time* (September 20, 1948); Clayton Knowles, "2 States in South Balk on President," *New York Times* (September 21, 1948); Joseph Miller, "Louisiana Voters Favor Dixiecrat Candidates," *Philadelphia Inquirer* (October 16, 1948).

5. "Open Breach in Tennessee Party Crystalizes During Week," *Memphis Commercial Appeal* (September 19, 1948); "Thurmond Says He Will Poll 100 Electoral Votes," *Augusta Herald* (October 1, 1948); "142 Electoral Votes Is Dixiecrat Aim," *Memphis Commercial Appeal* (October 3, 1948); John Horner, "Dixiecrats Expect to Rule Party," *Washington Star* (October 10, 1948); "Democracy in the South: An Editorial," *New Republic* (October 12, 1948); "Dixiecrats Joined by Talmadgeites," *Baltimore Sun* (October 14, 1948); Robert Louis Pritchard, *Southern Politics and the Truman Administration: Georgia as a Test Case* (unpublished Ph.D. dissertation, Department of History, UCLA, 1970), pp. 130–140.

6. Gary Clifford Ness, pp. 215–218.

7. George Gallup, "Dixiecrats Ahead in Four Southern States, Make Virginia and Florida Battlegrounds," *Washington Post* (October 15, 1948); "Top Rights Leaders Launch Ballot Blitz," *Jackson Daily News* (October 17, 1948).

8. "Thurmond Briefs," *Lynchburg News* (October 12, 1948); "South Prefers to Go Down Fighting, Senator Brown Writes," *Columbia* [S.C.] *Record* (October 14, 1948); "Dixiecrat Plan Studied," *Baltimore Sun* (October 17, 1948); "Dixiecrats Urging Maryland Write-In," *Washington Post* (October 18, 1948); David Snell, "States' Rights Democrats See Their Field Broadening," *New York Sun* (October 22, 1948); Barnard, *Dixiecrats and Democrats,* pp. 117–121.

9. "SR Contributions Are $158,975; State Gives $82,060.25," *Jackson Daily News;* financial material in Box 3251, STP.

10. Emile Ader, "Why the Dixiecrats Failed," *The Journal of Politics,* Vol. XV, No. 3 (1955), pp. 356–369; Frank Ashley, *Selected Southern Liberal Editors and the States' Rights Movement of 1948* (unpublished Ph.D. dissertation, Department of History, University of South Carolina, 1959); "Press Plays Important Role," *Christian Science Monitor* (September 2, 1948).

11. Peter Edson, "Dixie Editors See Dewey Landslide," *New York World Telegram* (October 26, 1948); Peter Edson, "Dixie Editors Offer Cure for Split," *New York World Telegram* (October 28, 1948); Helen Fuller, "The New Confederacy," *New Republic* (November 1, 1948).

12. "Anti-Dove Ban Called Example of Federal Meddling," *Jackson Daily News* (September 19, 1948).

CHAPTER NINETEEN: Wallace Winds Down

1. John Newman, "Wallace, Here for Speech, Asserts Pegler's Venom Is Helping Him," *Louisville Courier-Journal* (August 25, 1948); John Popham, "Wallace Pelted With Eggs, Fists Bang His Car in South," *New York Times* (August 31, 1948); Newbold Noyes, "Egg and Tomato Barrage Strikes Wallace," *Washington Star* (August 31, 1948); "It's Un-American to Egg Hank, Says HST," *Washington News* (September 1, 1948); Edward Folliard, "Roar of Hecklers Again Marks Final North Carolina Talk," *Washington Post* (September 1, 1948); Howard Norton, "Wallace Endures New Egg, Tomato Assault," *Baltimore Sun* (September 1, 1948); "With Wallace in North Alabama," *Birmingham News* (September 2, 1948); Edwin Leary, "Hatred of Wallace Sears Reporters Too," *Chicago Daily News* (September 3, 1948); "Am I in America?" *Time* (September 6, 1948); Tarleton Collier, "The Dixiecrats Have Their Youth, Too," *Louisville Courier-Journal* (September 9, 1948); "Wallace in the South," *The Nation* (September 11, 1948); "The South Gets Rough with Wallace," *Life* (September 13, 1948).
2. Speech by Henry Wallace at Yankee Stadium, September 9, 1948, PPP; "Love That Man," *Time* (September 20, 1948).
3. "Two Actresses Back Wallace," *Pittsburgh Gazette* (September 15, 1948); Grace Davidson, "Wallace Booed at Braves Field," *Boston Post* (September 19, 1948); text of Wallace radio address, NBC, delivered from Dallas, September 27, PPP; Jim Carroll, "Eggs and Tomatoes Hurled at Wallace," *Houston Press* (September 30, 1948); Stanton Delaplane, "Wallace in S.F.," *San Francisco Chronicle* (October 6, 1948); Karl Schmidt, *Wallace,* pp. 204–211.
4. "New Party's New Policy," *The Nation* (October 2, 1948); "Progressive Policy Change," *New Republic* (October 11, 1948); "Henry Wallace: The Last Seven Months of His Presidential Campaign," report prepared by the Americans for Democratic Action, Oscar Chapman Papers, SRC, Folder 5, HST.
5. "Henry Wallace: The Last Seven Months," p. 30; Freda Kirchwey, "How Are You Going to Vote?" *The Nation* (October 30, 1948).
6. Helen MacMartin letters and clippings, Box 3, Folders 11 and 13, PPP.
7. Howard Norton, "Peace Campaign Success, Wallace Tells New Yorkers," *Baltimore Sun* (October 27, 1948); Henry Wallace pre-election broadcast, ABC, November 1, PPP.

CHAPTER TWENTY: Going Through the Motions

1. "Surest Bet He Ever Saw, Says Carroll," *St. Louis Globe-Democrat* (October 3, 1948); Bert Andrews, "Will Truman Campaign Catch Fire?" *New York Herald Tribune* (October 16, 1948); "Why They Came Out," *Time* (October 18, 1948).

2. Ratings for speeches of October, Warwick and Legler Office Memorandum, October 14, SRC, HST; "President's Gestures Feature of Telecast," *New York Star* (October 12, 1948); John Crosby, "Radio in Review," *New York Herald Tribune* (October 15, 1948); Archibald Crossley, "Voters Apathetic Toward Nominees," *Charlotte Observer* (October 19, 1948); John Crosby, "Bad Radio Timing Can Foul Up Election Candidates," *Los Angeles Daily News* (October 20, 1948); Joseph Loftus, "Prosperity Is Seen as Ballot Factor," *New York Times* (October 30, 1948).

3. Douglas Dales, "Dewey to Invade Midwest Monday," *New York Times* (October 6, 1948); Thomas Reynolds, "Dewey Ribs Truman on Pendergast Ties," *New York Star* (October 15, 1948); Jack Steels, "Dewey Assails Missouri Gang," *New York Herald Tribune* (October 15, 1948).

4. George Dixon, "Washington Scene," *New York Mirror* (October 7, 1948); Raymond Brandt, "Dewey Attacks Truman Labor Policy," *St. Louis Post-Dispatch* (October 12, 1948); Marquis Childs, "Dewey's Campaign," *Washington Post* (October 15, 1948); Philip Geyelin, "Dewey Is Running Out of Topics for Talks; Turns to Weather, Children, GOP Goodness," *Wall Street Journal* (October 15, 1948); James Reston, "President and Dewey Spar with Well-Padded Cliches," *New York Times* (October 19, 1948).

5. *Life* (November 1, 1948); "What Dewey Will Do," *Kiplinger's Magazine* (November 1948); Samuel Grafton, "Man of the Times," *Chicago Sun* (October 22, 1948).

6. "Mishap Hits Dewey Train in Illinois," *Washington Post* (October 14, 1948); "Don't Worry About Me," *Time* (October 25, 1948); Brightman Oral History, pp. 27–29, HST.

7. Speeches from *Public Papers of the President,* op. cit.; Anthony Leviero, "President Likens Dewey to Hitler as Fascists' Tool," *New York Times* (October 26, 1948); James Reston, "Truman Strategy Centered on Racial and Religious Plea," *New York Times* (October 26, 1948); Richard Strout Oral History, pp. 35–36, HST; "President Truman's Campaign Trip to Chicago et al.," SRC, Folder 12, HST.

8. "Truman: Trying Hard" and "Dewey: Coasting," *Newsweek* (November 1, 1948); "The Pot Boils," *Time* (November 1, 1948).

9. "The Gallup Poll," *Washington Post* (October 6, 1948); "Crossley Poll Shows Slight Truman Gain," *St. Louis Post-Dispatch* (October 12, 1948);

Joseph Short, "Truman Seen Gaining, But Far from Victory," *Baltimore Sun* (October 13, 1948); "The Campaign: Box Score," *Time* (October 18, 1948); "The Political Picture in the 48 States: A Pre-Election Survey," *New York Times* (October 31, 1948); Richard Norton Smith, *Thomas E. Dewey,* pp. 523–534; letters of Edward Hutton, September 30 and October 25, Series 2, Box 27, TDP.

10. Edward Folliard, "Truman's Defeat by Wide Margin Seen; 51-Million Vote Expected," *Washington Post* (November 2, 1948); Edwin Leahy, "No Matter Who Wins, President Will Be Choice of 1 Out of 4," *Kansas City Star* (November 2, 1948).

11. "Repudiating the Splinters," *Newsweek* (November 8, 1948).

12. The story of Dewey may well be apocryphal. It is taken from James Loeb Oral History, pp. 72–73, HST.

CHAPTER TWENTY-ONE: The Aftermath

1. Statistics taken from *New York Times* (November 7, 1948); *Newsweek* (November 8, 1948); W.H. Lawrence, "An Analysis of the Final Election Figures," *New York Times* (December 12, 1948); Federal Election Commission, in *The World Almanac, 1997* (World Almanac Books, 1996), pp. 77–105.

2. "Damn the Torpedoes!" *The New Republic* (November 15, 1948); Arthur Krock, "President Can Claim Big National Triumph," *New York Times* (November 7, 1948).

3. "The Missed Election," *Life* (November 15, 1948).

4. Funk quoted in Abels, *Out of the Jaws of Victory,* p. 275.

5. This argument was made early on by Samuel Lubell in his *Future of American Politics* (Harper & Row, 1952).

The 1948 Presidential Vote

STATE	TRUMAN, Democrat	DEWEY, Republican	THURMOND, States' Rights	WALLACE, Progressive
Alabama	—	40,930	171,443	1,522
Arizona	95,251	77,597	—	3,310
Arkansas	149,659	50,959	40,068	751
California	1,913,134	1,895,269	1,228	190,381
Colorado	267,288	239,714	—	6,115
Connecticut	423,297	437,754	—	13,713
Delaware	67,813	69,588	—	1,050
Florida	281,988	194,280	89,755	11,620
Georgia	254,646	76,691	85,055	1,636
Idaho	107,370	101,514	—	4,972
Illinois	1,994,715	1,961,103	—	—
Indiana	807,833	821,079	—	9,649
Iowa	522,380	494,018	—	12,125
Kansas	351,902	423,039	—	4,603
Kentucky	466,756	341,210	10,411	1,567
Louisiana	136,344	72,657	204,290	3,035
Maine	111,916	150,234	—	1,884
Maryland	286,521	294,814	2,476	9,983
Massachusetts	1,151,788	909,370	—	38,157
Michigan	1,003,448	1,038,595	—	46,515
Minnesota	692,966	483,617	—	27,886
Mississippi	19,384	5,043	167,538	225
Missouri	917,315	655,039	—	3,998
Montana	119,071	96,770	—	7,313
Nebraska	224,165	264,774	—	—
Nevada	31,291	29,357	—	1,469
New Hampshire	107,995	121,299	7	1,970
New Jersey	895,455	981,124	—	42,683

STATE	TRUMAN, Democrat	DEWEY, Republican	THURMOND, States' Rights	WALLACE, Progressive
New Mexico	105,464	80,303	—	1,037
New York*	2,780,204	2,841,163	—	509,559
North Carolina	459,070	258,572	69,652	3,915
North Dakota	95,812	115,139	374	8,391
Ohio	1,452,791	1,445,684	—	37,596
Oklahoma	452,782	268,817	—	—
Oregon	243,147	260,904	—	14,978
Pennsylvania	1,752,426	1,902,197	—	55,161
Rhode Island	188,736	135,787	—	2,619
South Carolina	34,423	5,386	102,607	154
South Dakota	117,653	129,651	—	2,801
Tennessee	270,402	202,914	73,815	1,864
Texas†	750,700	282,240	106,909	3,764
Utah	149,151	124,402	—	2,679
Vermont	45,557	75,926	—	1,279
Virginia	200,786	172,070	43,393	2,047
Washington	476,165	386,315	—	31,692
West Virginia	429,188	316,251	—	3,311
Wisconsin	647,310	590,969	—	25,282
Wyoming	52,354	47,947	—	931
Total	24,105,812	21,970,065	1,169,021	1,157,172
Electoral Votes‡	303	189	39	—

Source: Voter News Service; Federal Election Commission, in *The World Almanac* (1997).

*The Truman vote in New York includes 222,562 Liberal Party votes
†There is some dispute about the Texas vote. According to the Federal Election Commission, Truman received 750,700, Dewey 282,240. However, according to *Congressional Quarterly Presidential Elections* (Washington, D.C., 1995), Truman received 824,235, Dewey 303,467.
‡Thurmond's electoral votes include one vote from Tennessee.

Other totals: Thomas, Socialist: 139,521; Watson, Prohibitionist: 103,343; Teichert, Socialist-Labor: 29,061; Dobbs, Socialist Workers: 13,613. Others and blank votes, 148,971. Total votes: 48,836,579.

Acknowledgments

In writing this book, I benefited from the advice and input of a number of people who pushed me to hone my arguments and polish my prose. The usual disclaimers apply, and while the following should take full credit for any improvements, responsibility for the rest resides with the author. Conversations with Eric Olson, Nicole Alger, Fredrik Logevall, Jonathan Rosenberg, Colby Devitt, James Chace, Gideon Rose, Fareed Zakaria, Susan Freiwald, Martin Lee, Tiffany Devitt, Deena Balboa, Philip Zelikow, Marvin Kalb, Laurel Touby, Thomas Mallon, David Callahan, Amy Gluck Adachi, Alice Mayhew, David King, Richard Norton Smith, Don Fehr, Nancy Palmer, Thomas E. Patterson, Frederick Schauer, Alonzo Hamby, Susan Rabiner, Douglas Brinkley, and Senator Strom Thurmond were both enjoyable and helpful, and they have contributed to this book in more ways than I can easily express.

Others generously agreed to critique pages of the manuscript, and I have done my best to address their concerns and integrate their comments. For their time and their input, I thank Timothy Naftali, Ernest May, Richard Neustadt, Richard Ben Cramer, Sam Tanenhaus, David Karabell, David Denby, and Jonathan Tweedy.

I am grateful for the generous financial assistance of the Truman Library Institute, which awarded me a Scholar's Grant without which completing this project would have been far more difficult. And a fellowship at the Shorenstein Center on the Press, Politics and Public Policy at the Kennedy School of Government in the fall of 1997 gave me the space, literally and figuratively, to mull over the role of television in presidential politics.

I also thank the research staffs at the Truman Library, the Special Collections section of the Clemson University library, the University of Rochester manuscript division, and especially the custodians of the Henry Wallace Papers at the Special Collections department of the University of Iowa library, all of whom helped me navigate through the vast assortment of boxes and folders.

My editor at Knopf, Ash Green, has been a friend and mentor, and I have relished the opportunity to work with him. Sonny Mehta has graced this project with his approval. Leyla Aker and Asya Muchnick shepherded the book to completion. And Sheila O'Shea made sure that it would have a public life.

To my agent, John Hawkins, I owe more than the usual commission. His wry insights, humor, and sympathetic ear have enlivened me. And no acknowledgment would be complete without mentioning Holly Cohen and Moses Cardona, both of John Hawkins and Associates.

Finally, this book had its genesis in a project initiated by Joseph Nye at Harvard's Kennedy School. Seeking to explain why Americans no longer trust government to the degree that they once did, Nye galvanized the faculty of the school to investigate the question. As a researcher on this project, I began to look for answers as well. Many people were inclined to hold television and the shrinking political spectrum at least partly responsible for changing attitudes toward government, and it seemed to me that 1948 was a good place to test that presumption. In addition to being a good story, the 1948 election shows what American politics were like just before several major shifts occurred. In that respect, it is history whose relevance for the present cannot be overstated, but without Nye and the Kennedy School, it is a history I might never have written.

Index